CUT UP
THIS BOOK

CREATIVE PAPER

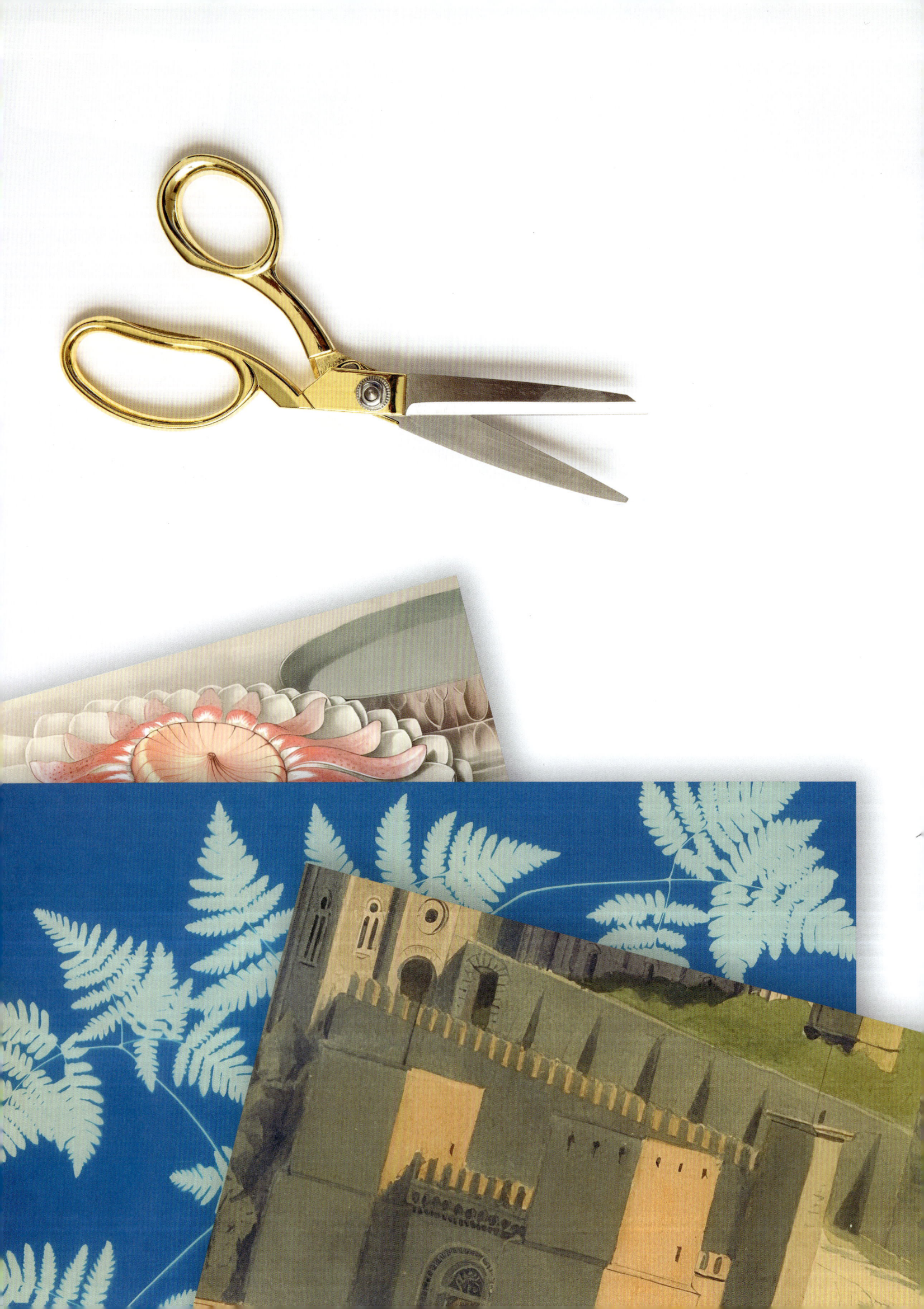

CUT UP THIS BOOK

CREATIVE PAPER

100 Patterns and Backgrounds for Junk Journals, Scrapbooks and Collages

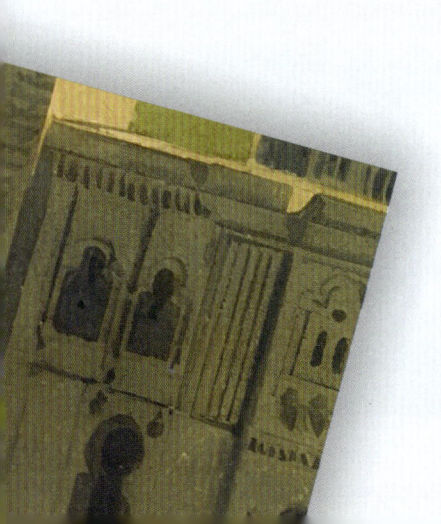

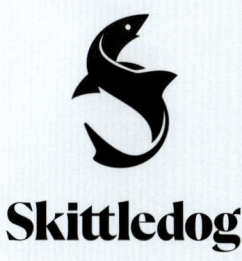

Skittledog

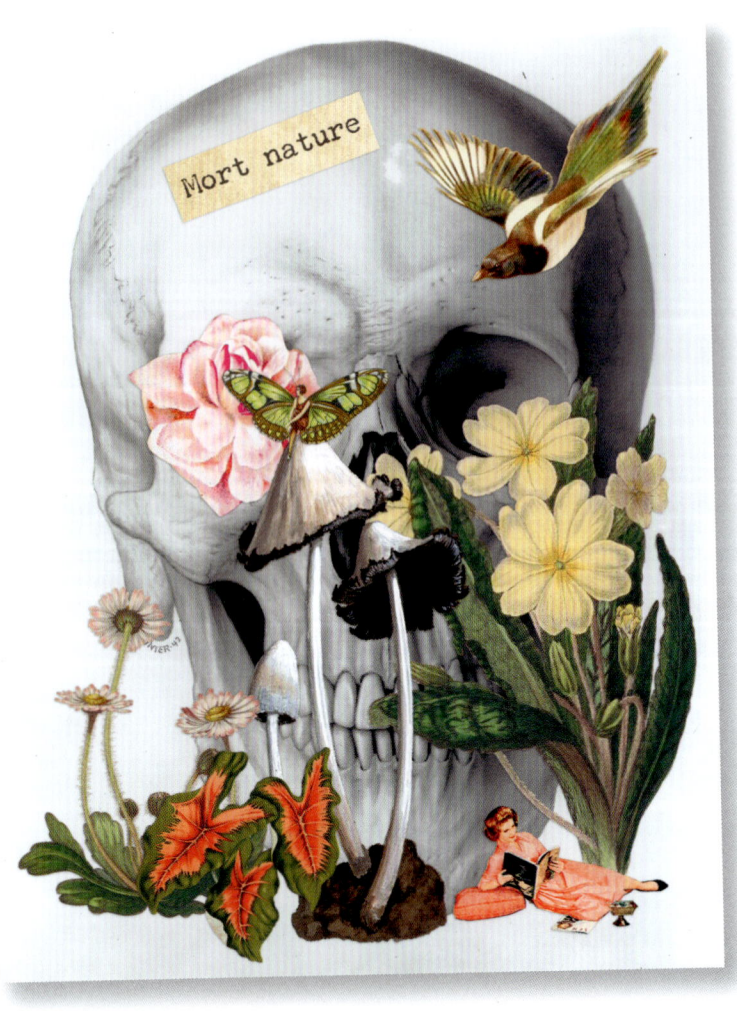

Mort nature

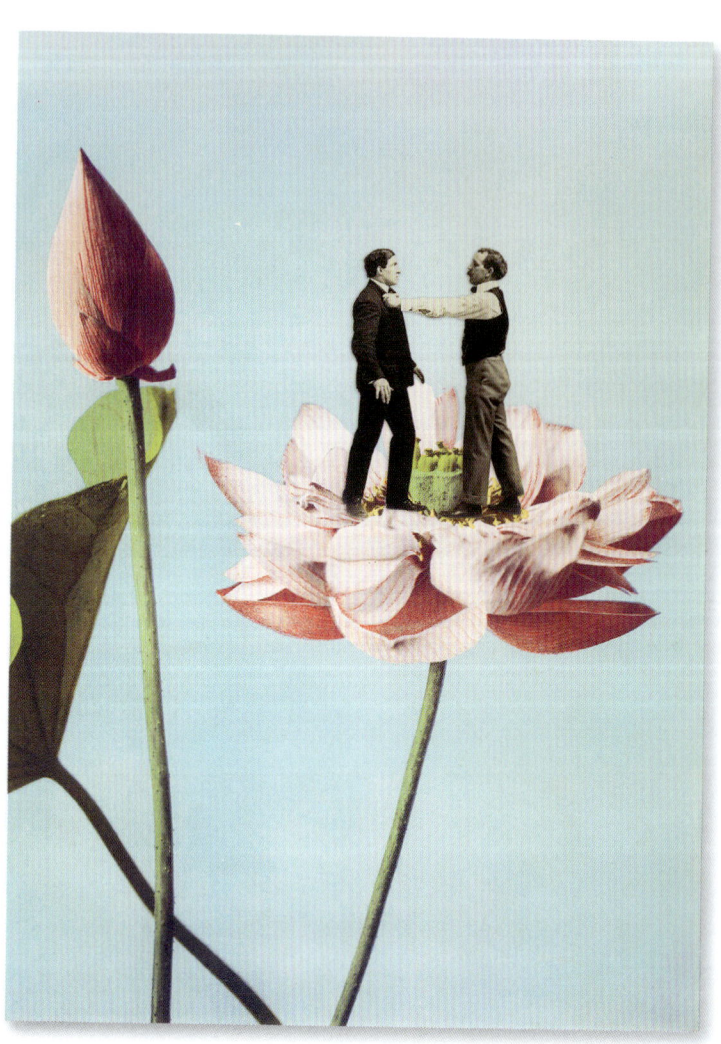

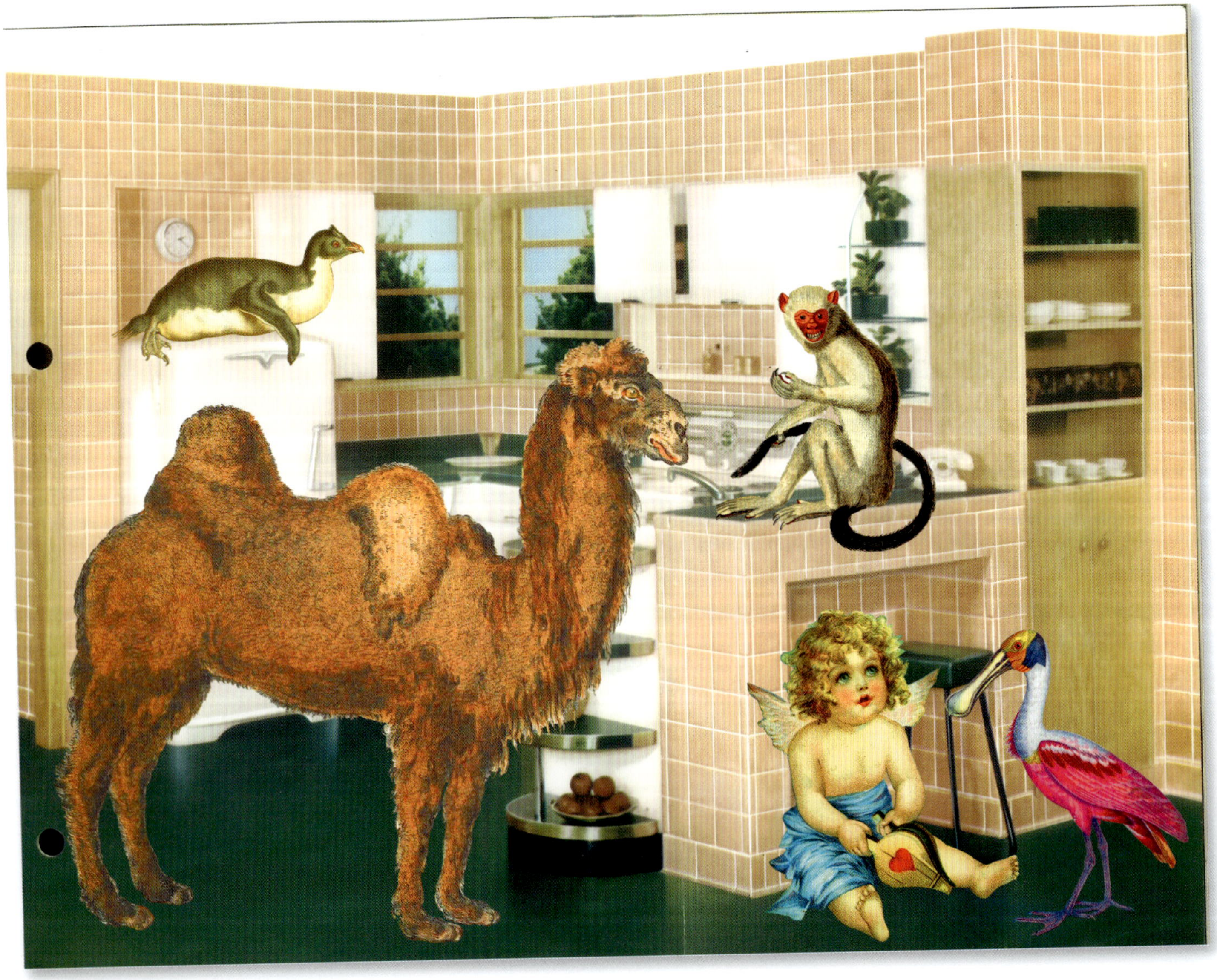

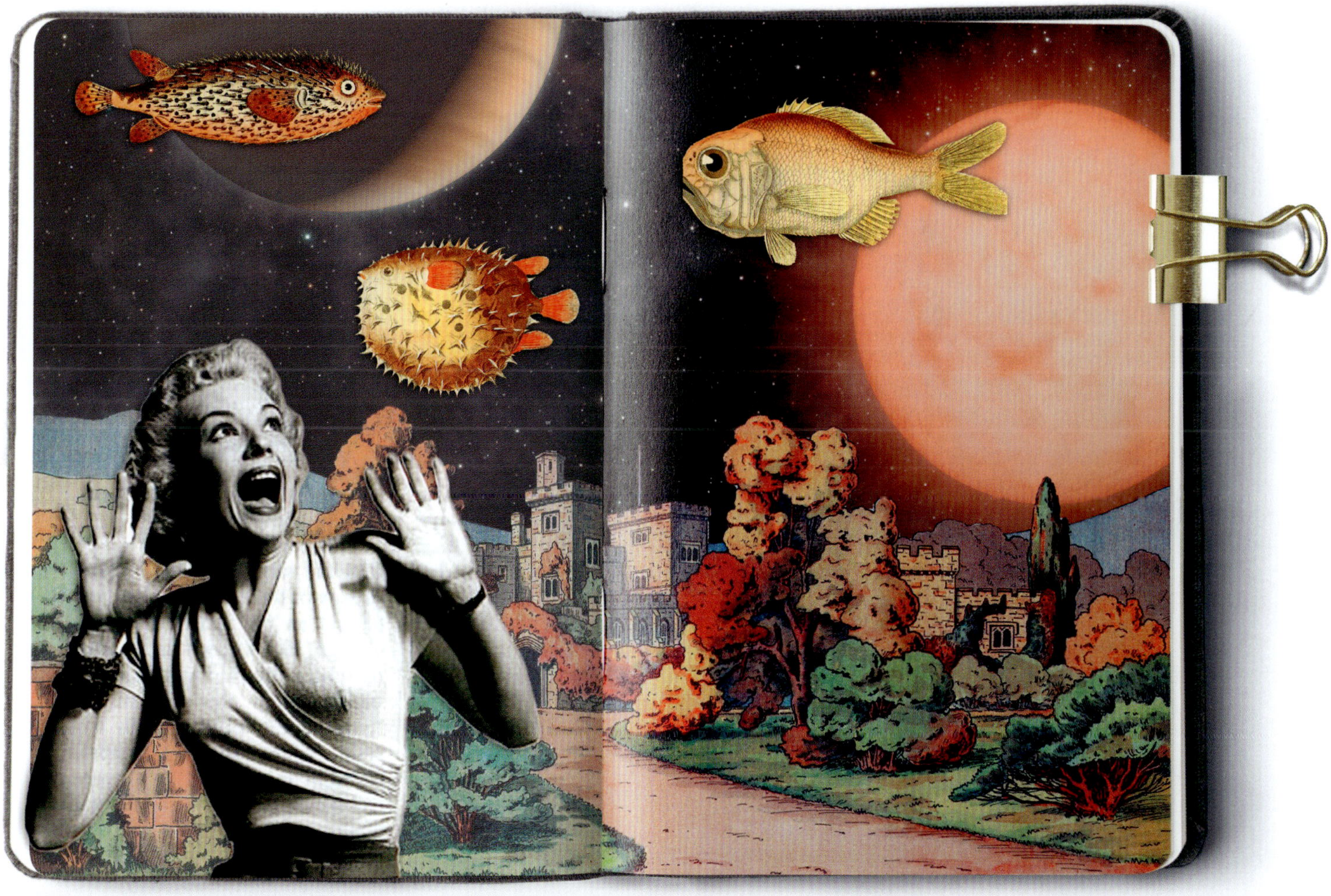

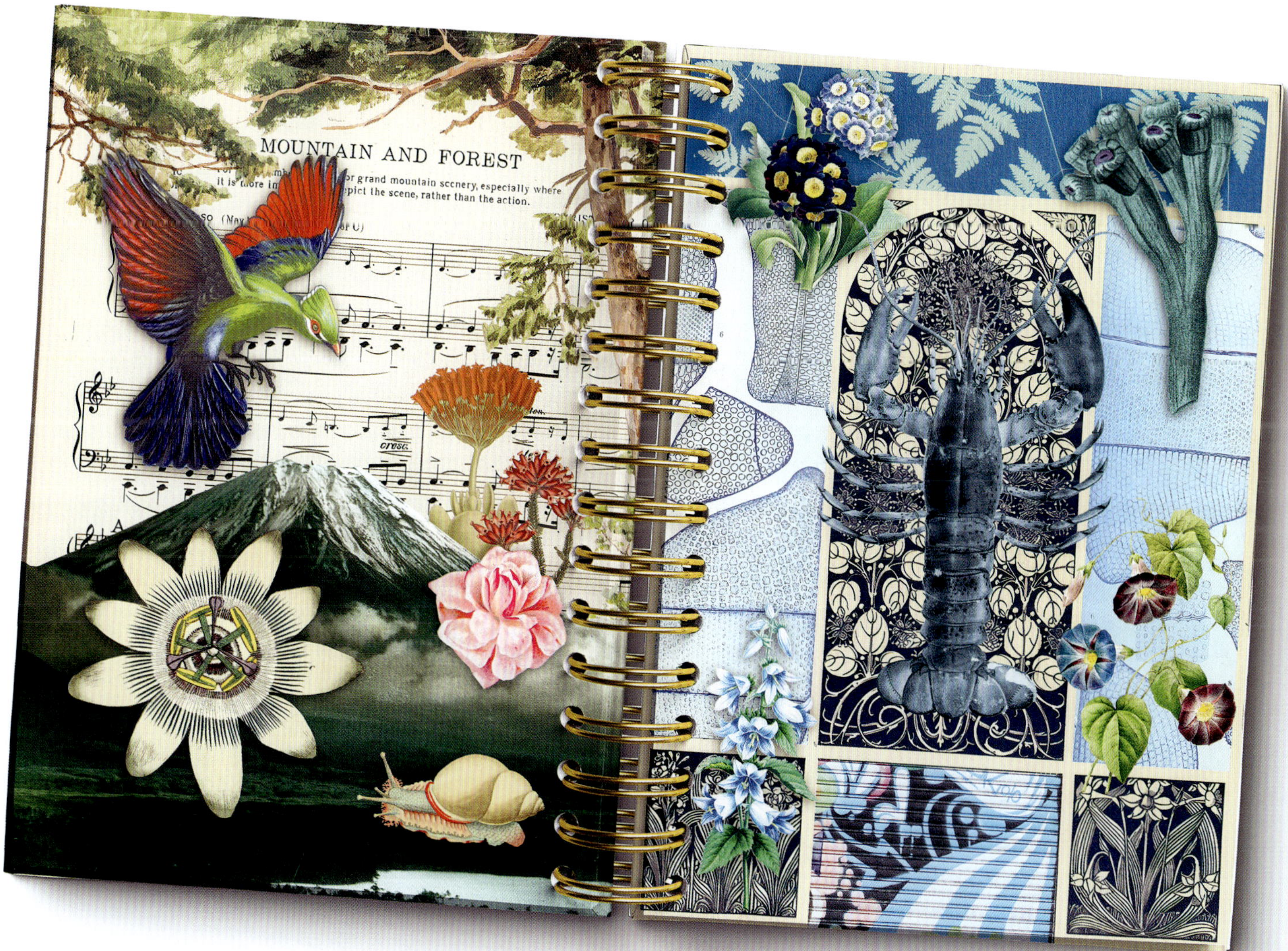

MOUNTAIN AND FOREST

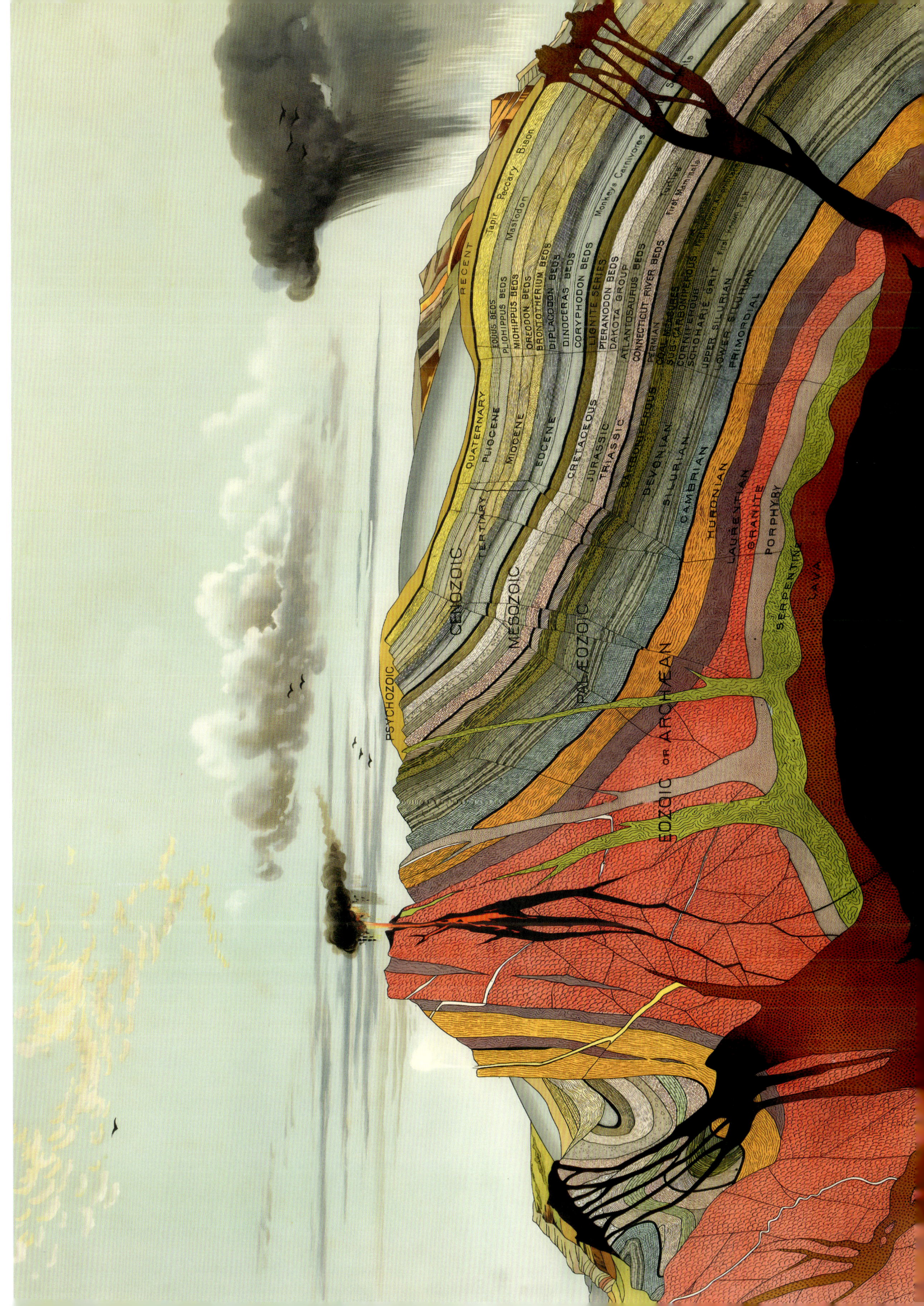

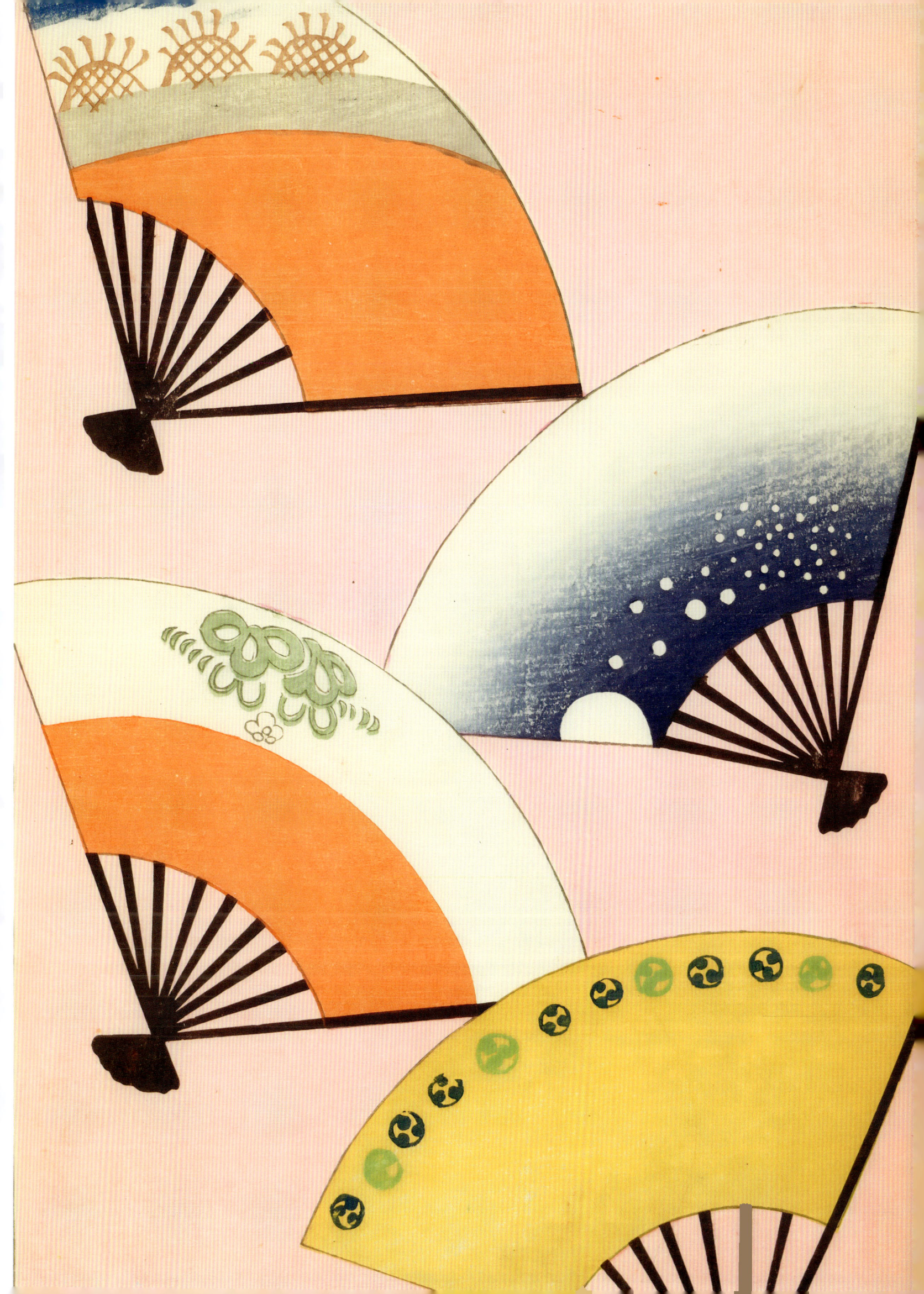

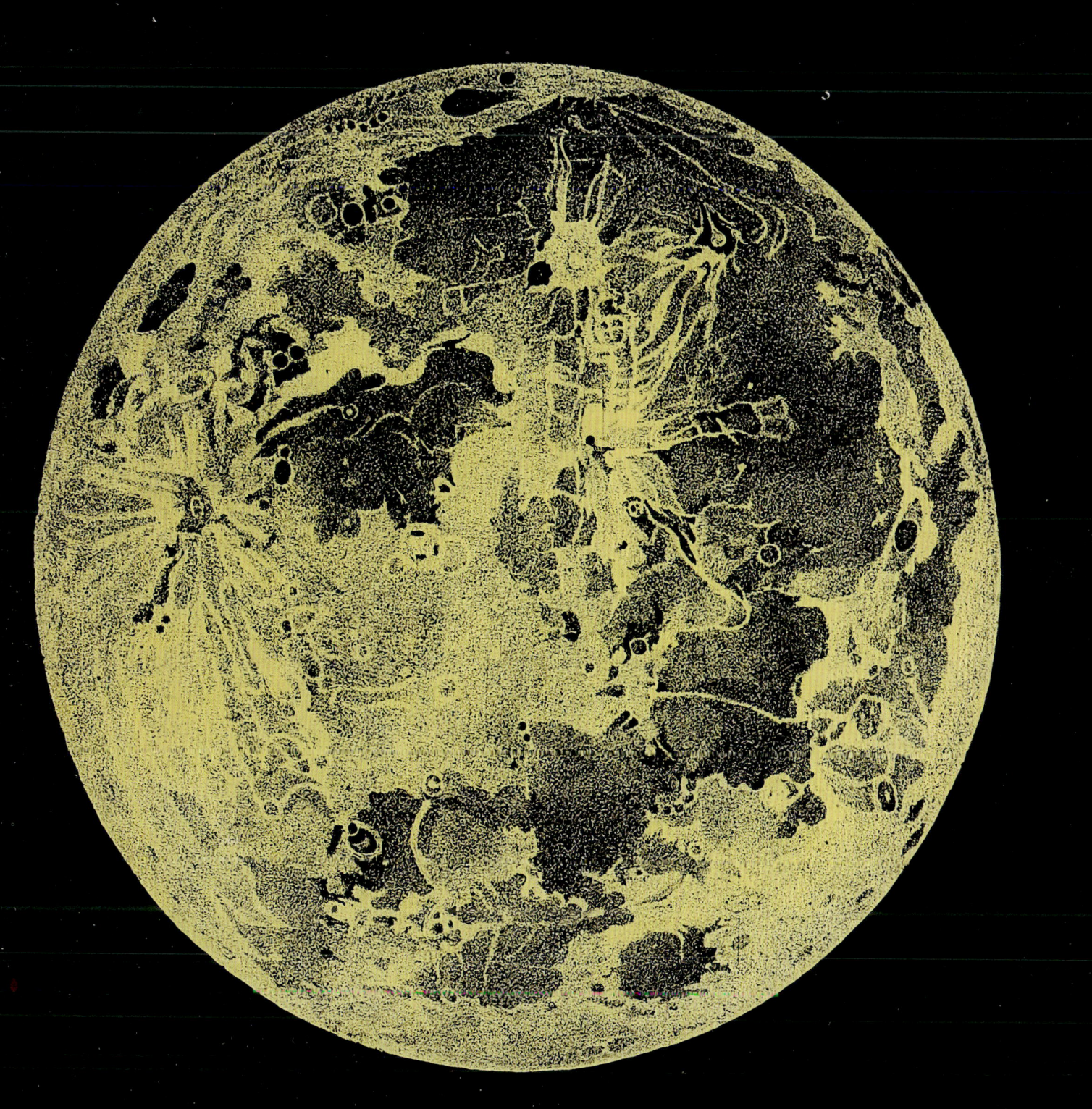

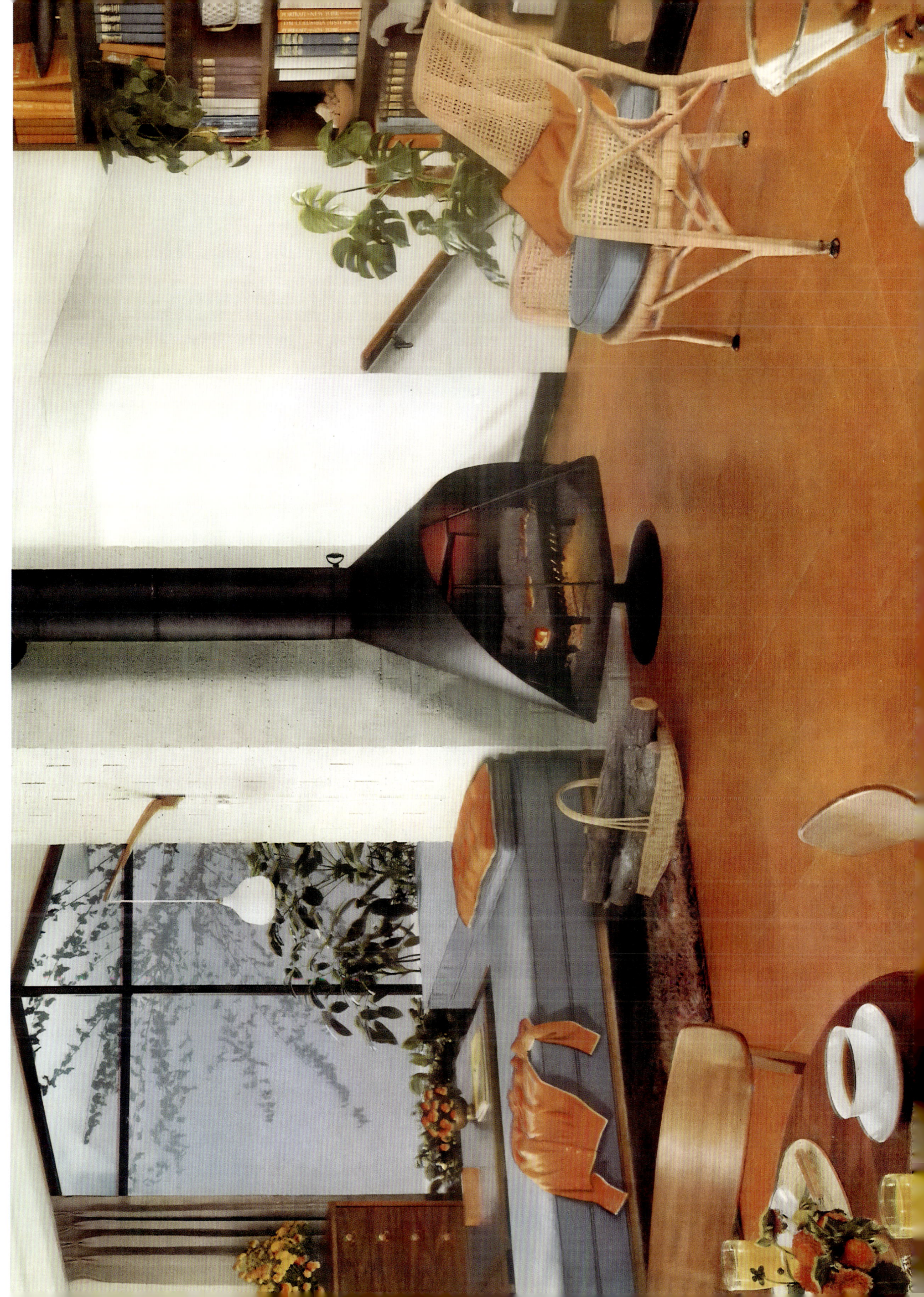

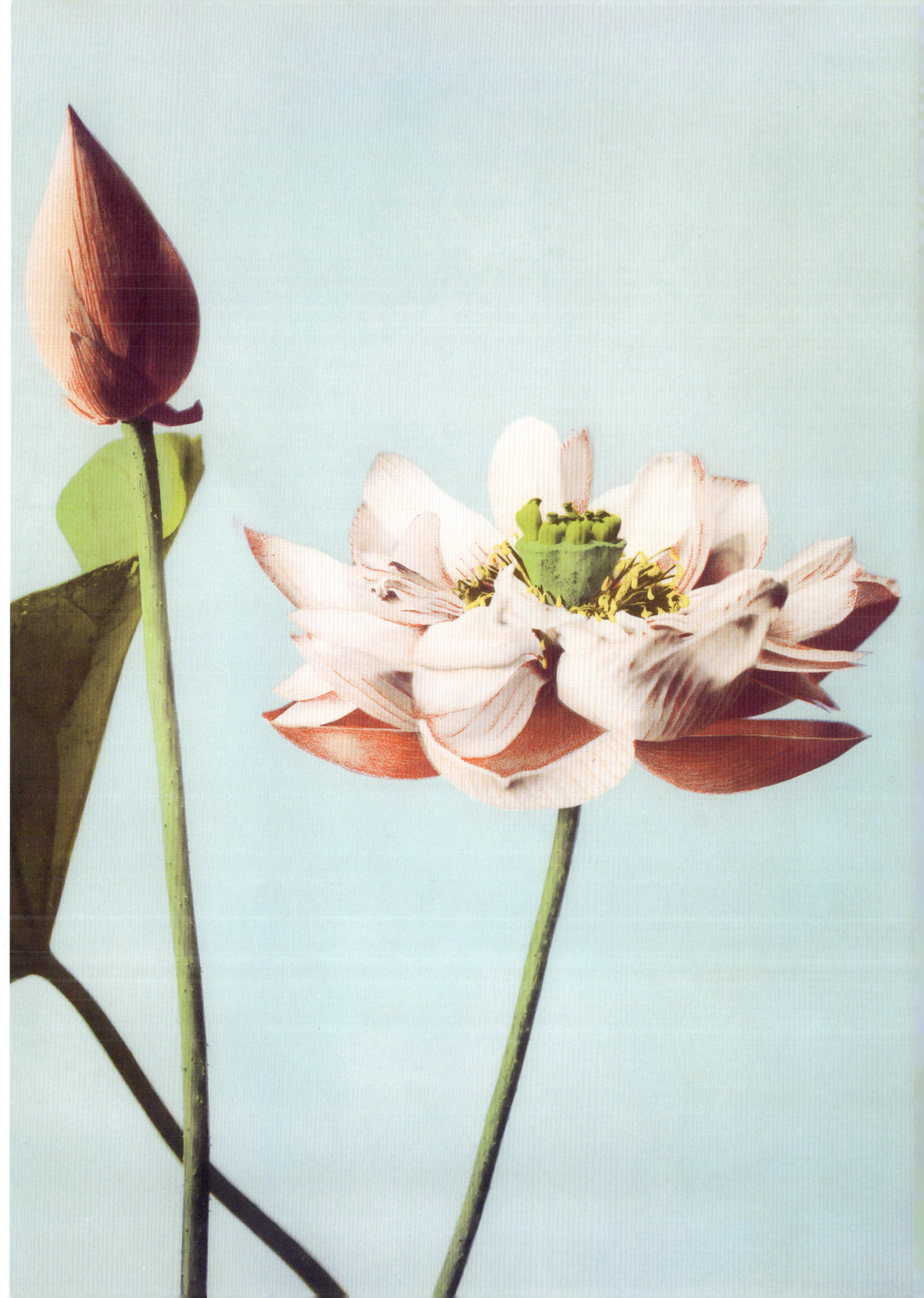

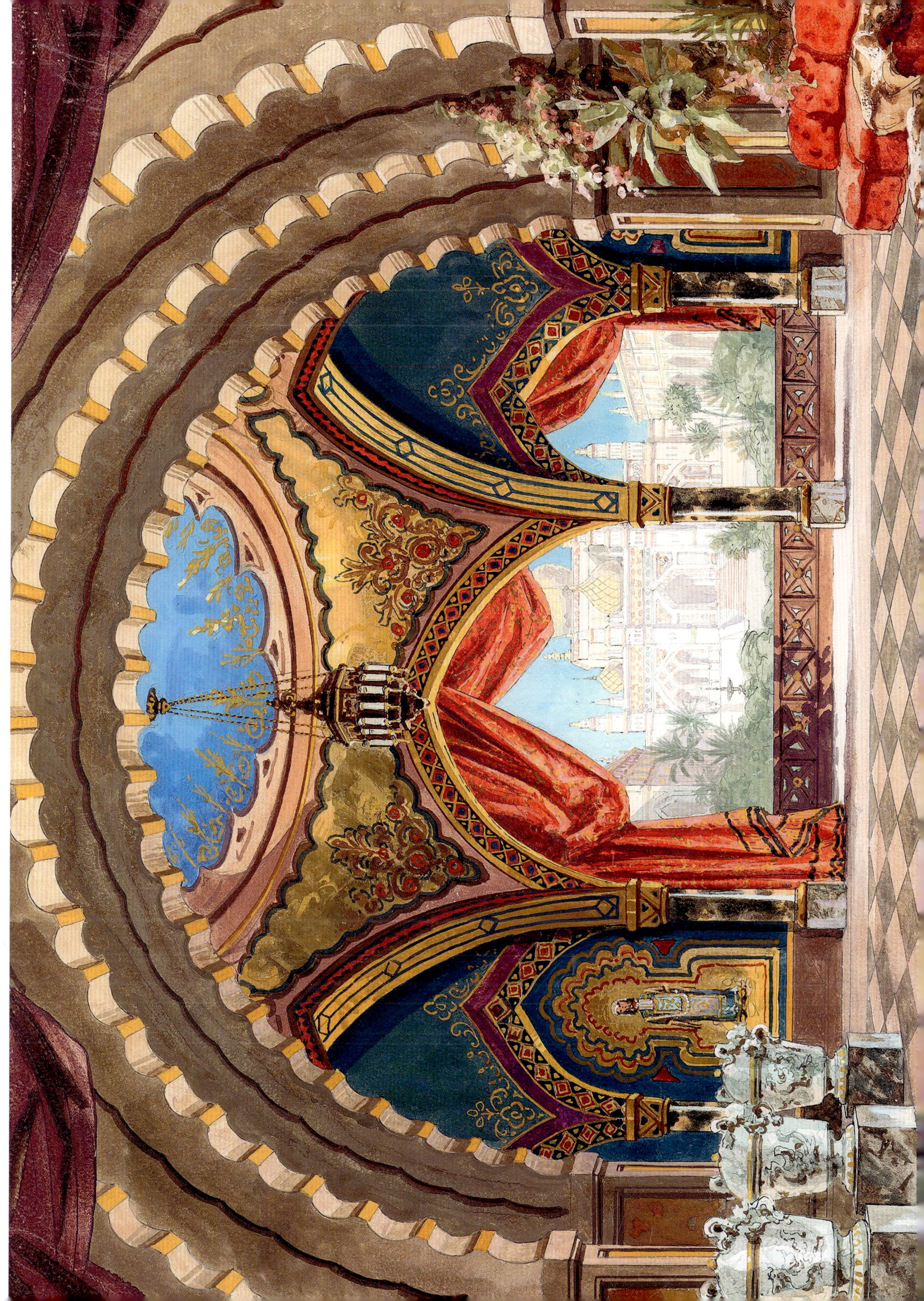

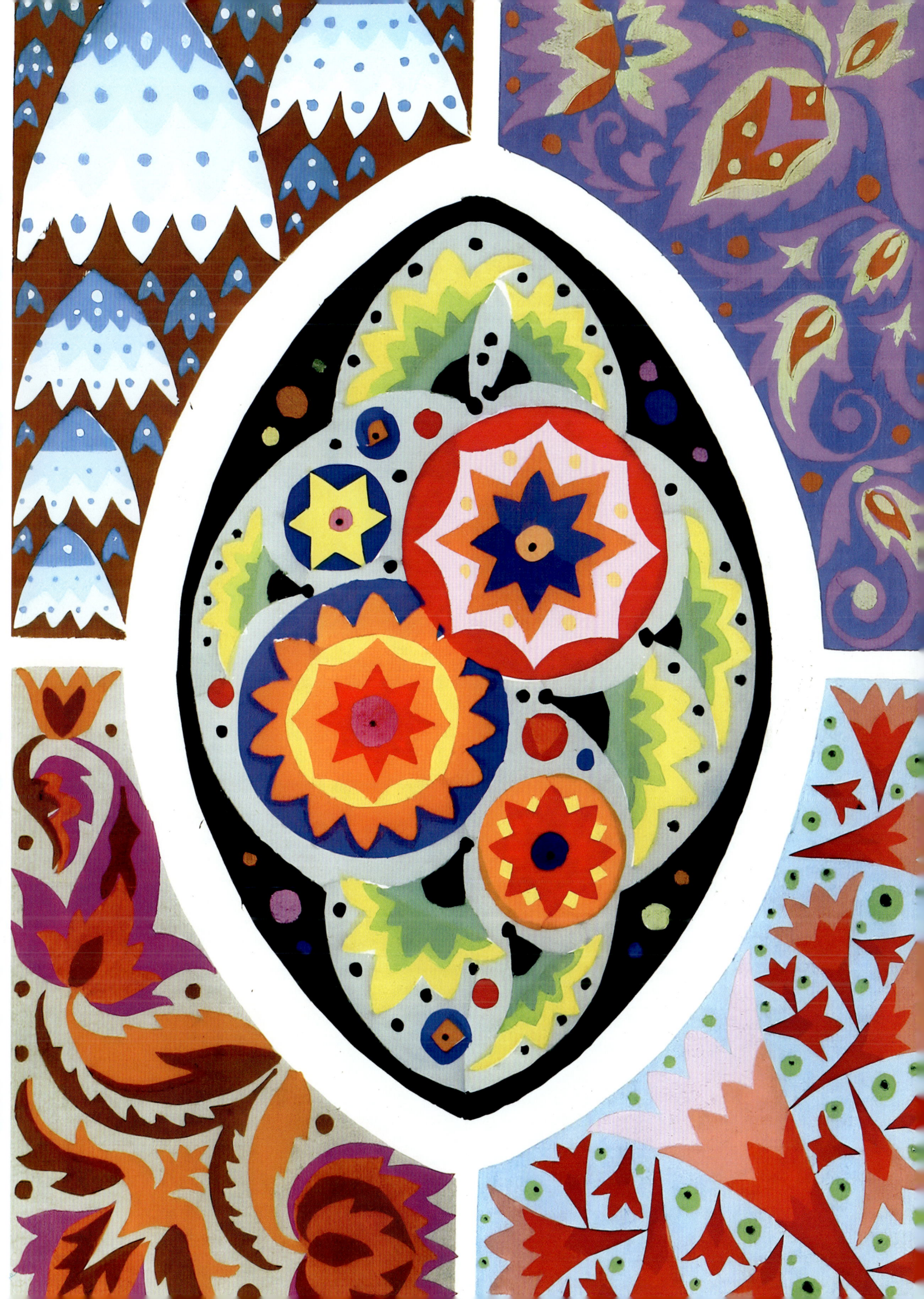

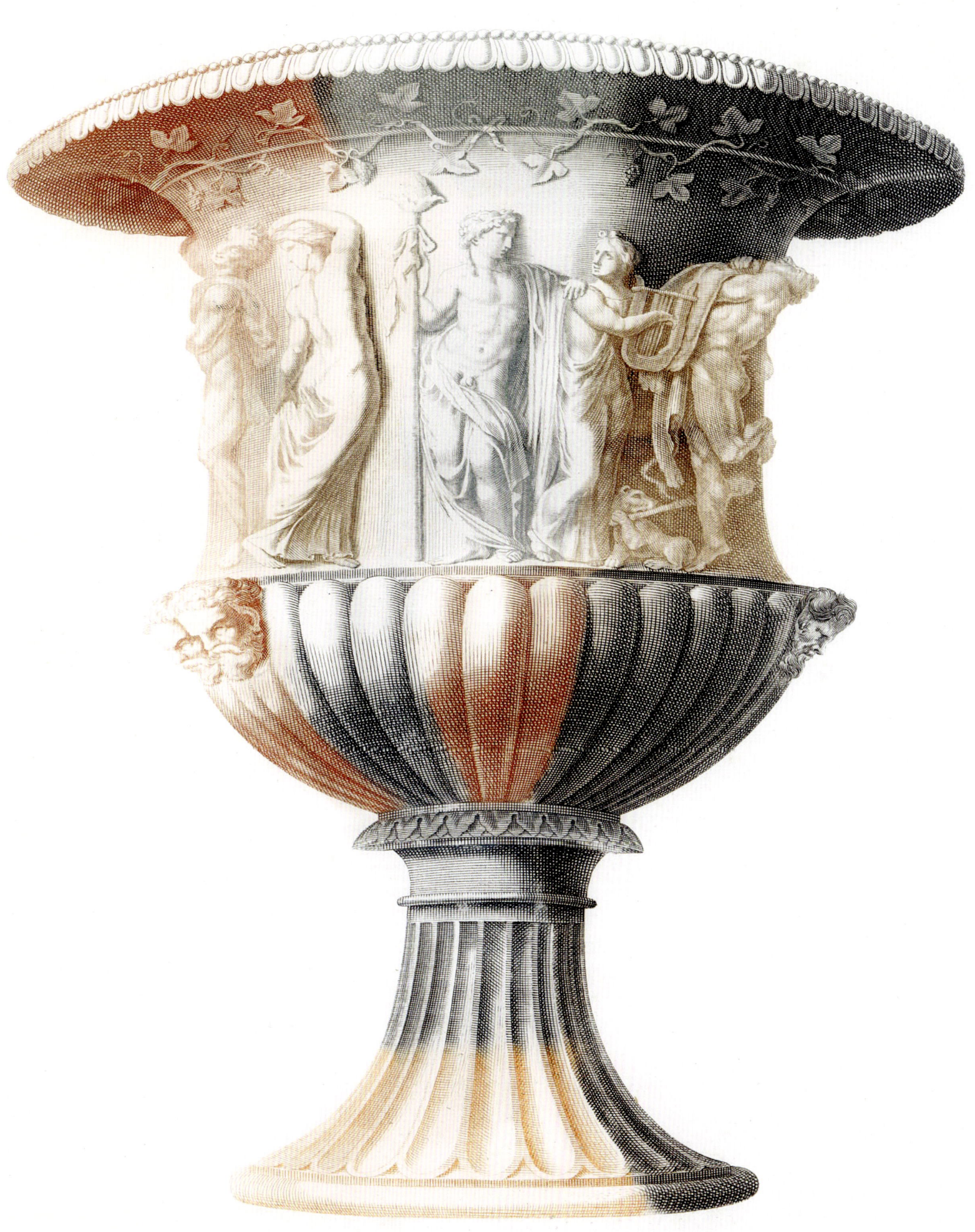

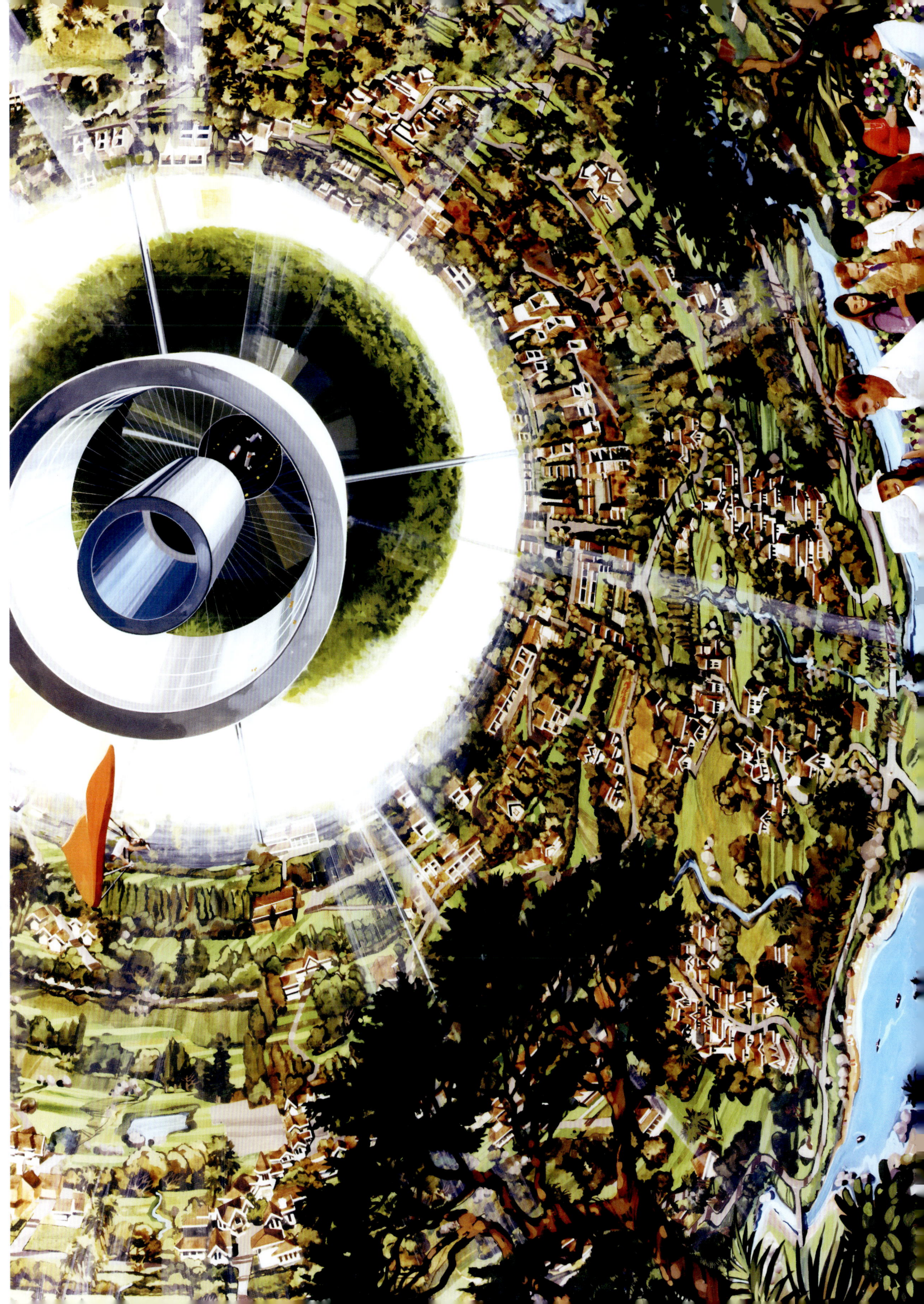

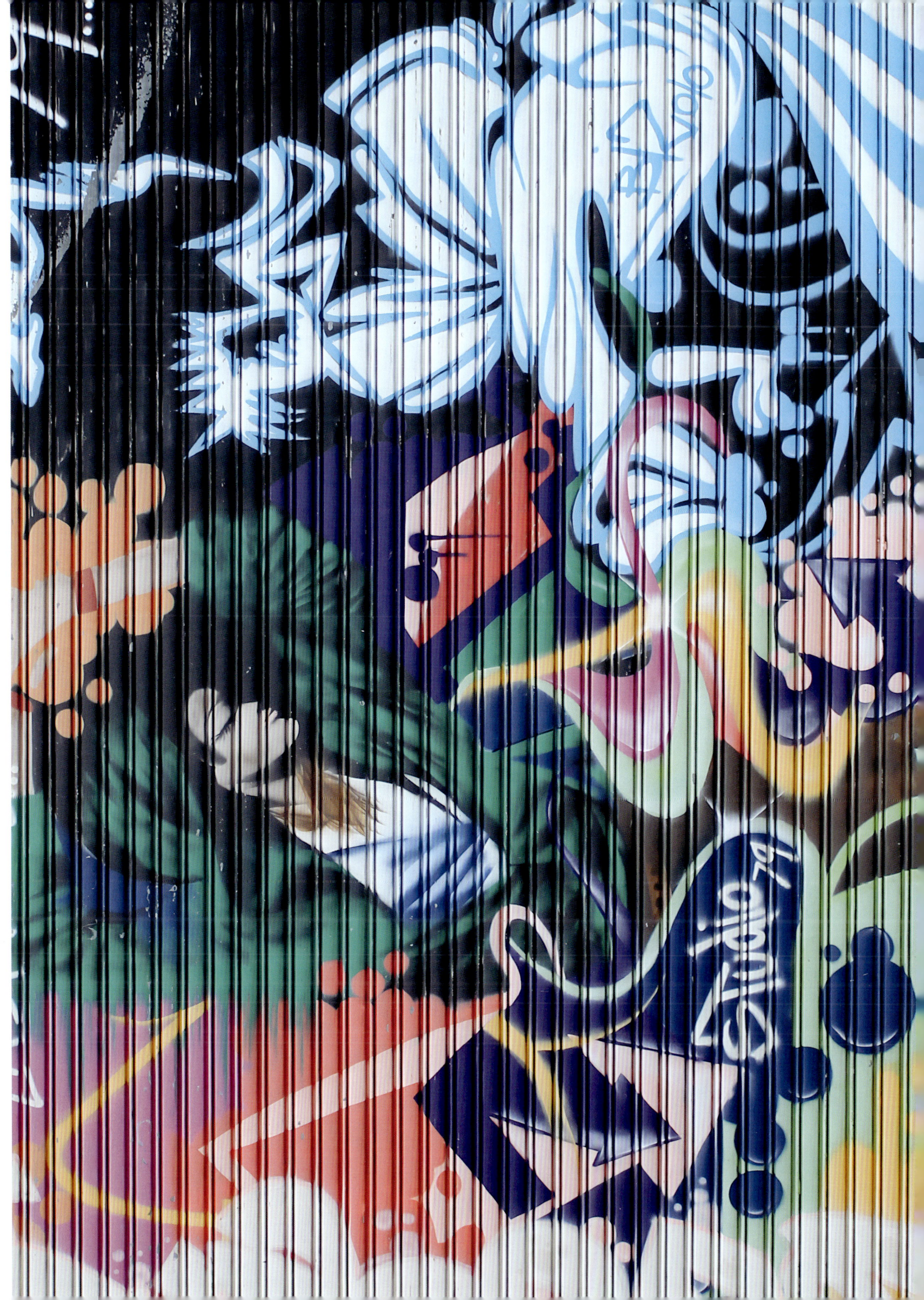

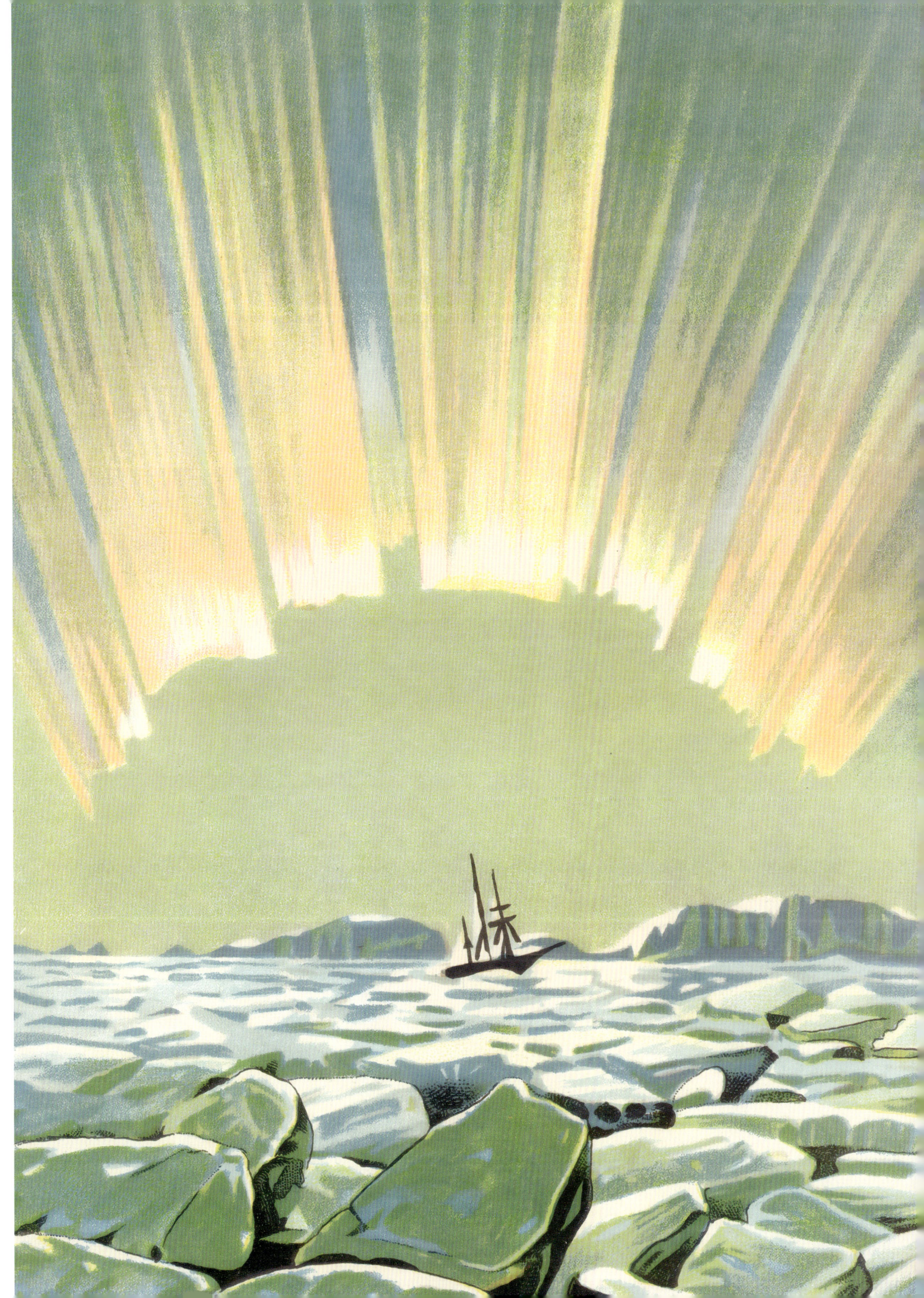

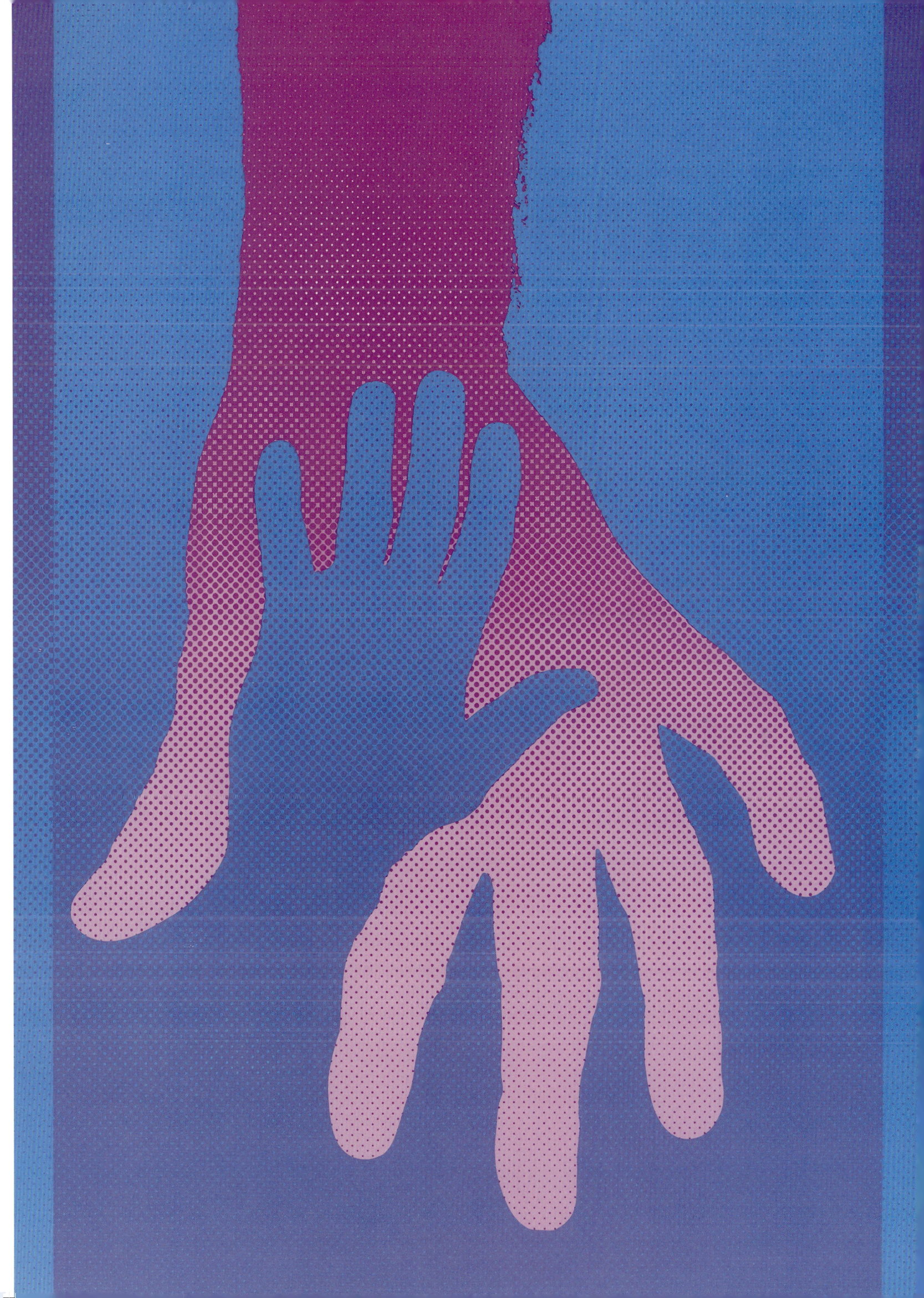

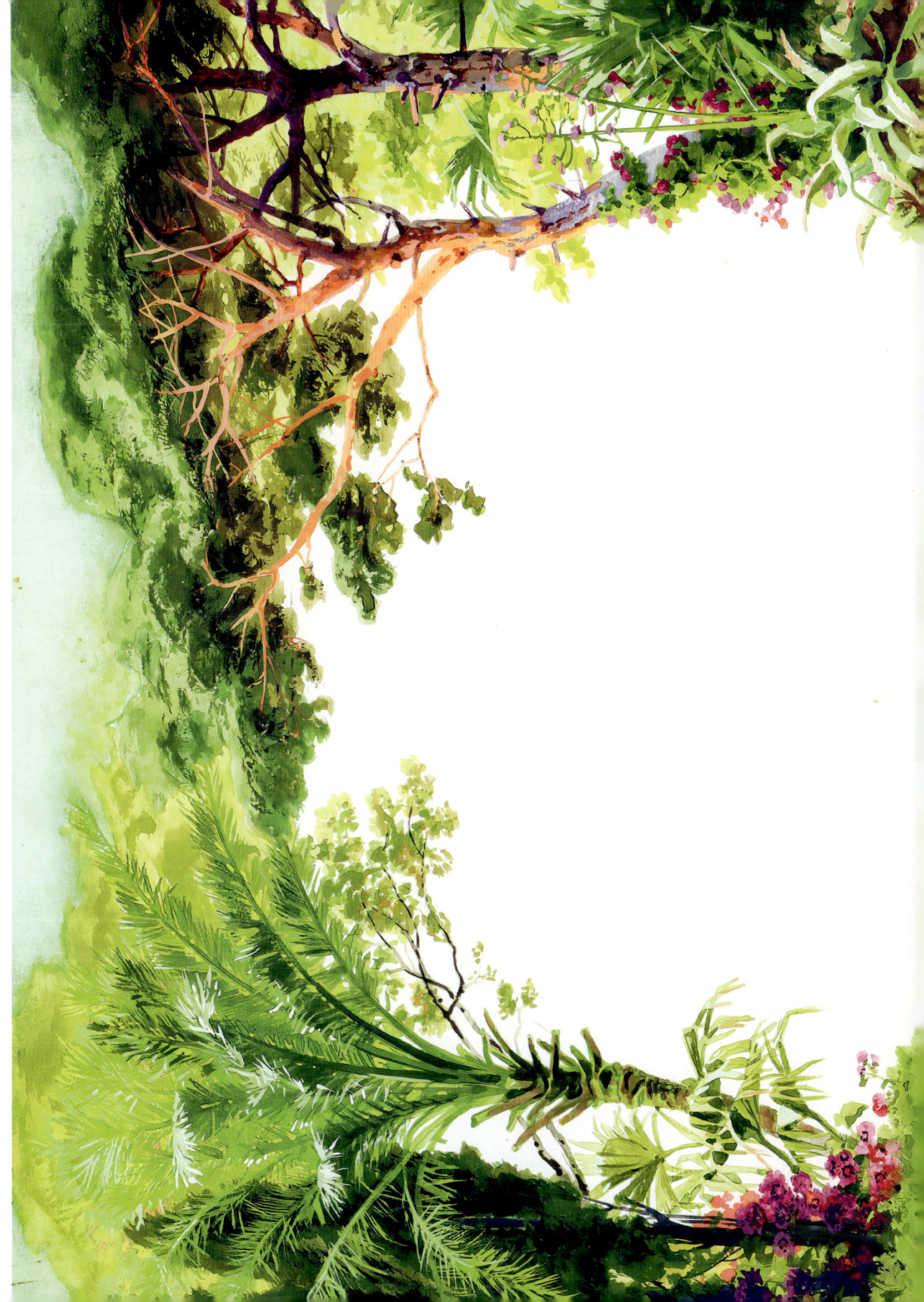

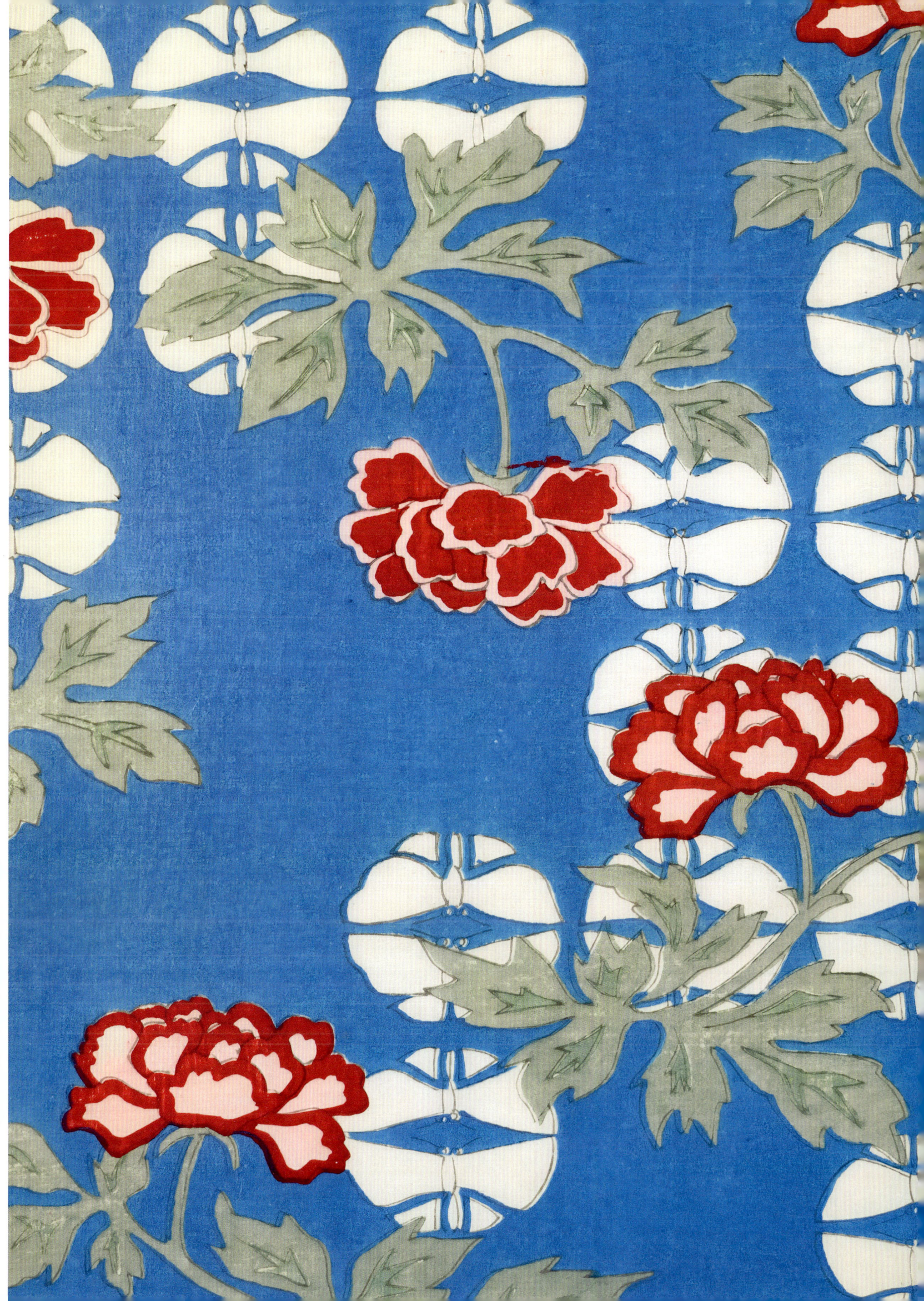

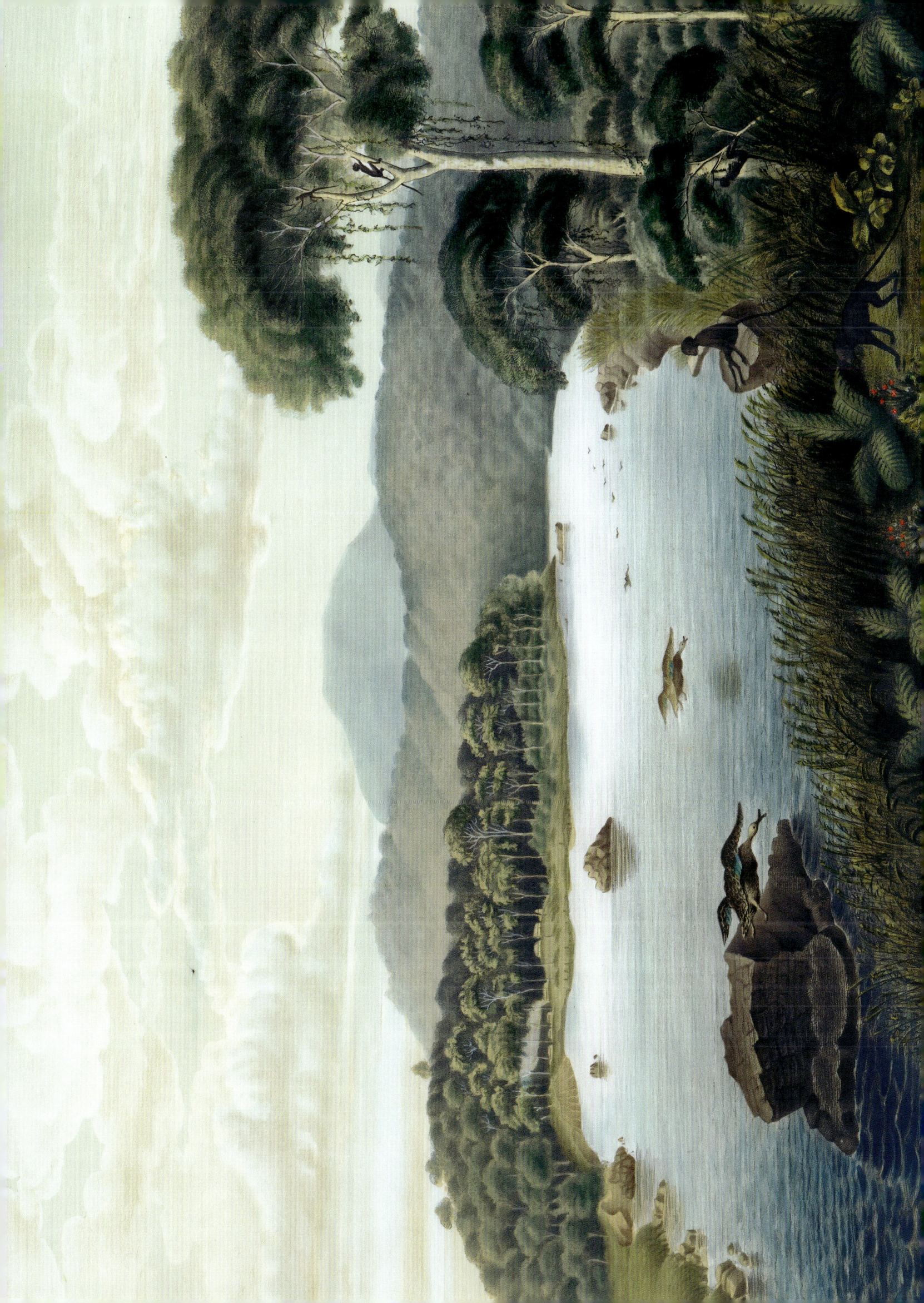

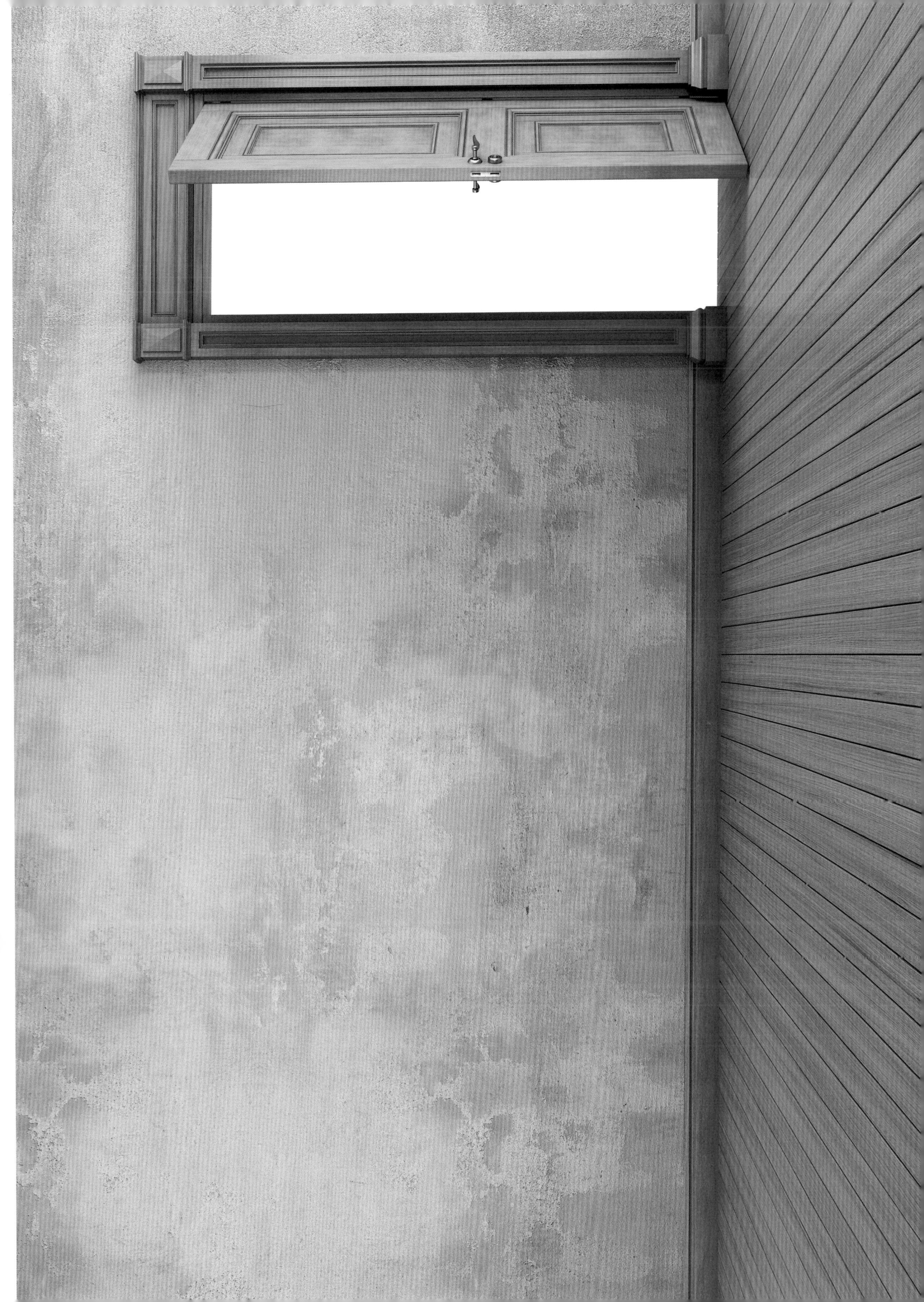

o IN CHRISTMAS PRIZES ❧ THE EVENING WORLD'S PRIZE

—Fair to-night; Wednesday snow.

IGHT EDITION

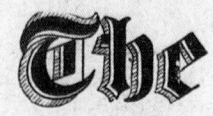

The EVENING EDITION World. EXT

"Circulation Books Open to All." "Circulation Books Open to All."

ONE CENT. NEW YORK, TUESDAY, DECEMBER 8, 1903. PRIC

RDICE HELD ON FORGERY CHARGE

of Young Man Who Was Made Beneficiary of Aged Woman se of Harlem Taken Into Cus- n Accusation of Fraud.

Was Obtained by Assistant Dis- ttorney Krotel, and the Prisoner Taken to the Tombs to Await rival of a Bondsman.

mes S. Alderdice was arrested this afternoon on a war- n with forging the deeds which purported to dispose of the y J. Oliver, the Harlem miser.

was just leaving his office, at No. 304 Broadway, with a hand when he was arrested by Detective Flood, of the y's staff. It was believed that Alderdice was about to

was first taken to the Elizabeth street station, and from tre Street Court for arraignment.

strict-Attorney Krotel, who has had the Oliver investiga- pplied to Magistrate Breen for the warrant.

sked for the warrant in the belief, based upon a handwrit- rt, that the signature to various deeds transferring $100,000 y to Mary S. Alderdice was forged.

ned in court Alderdice, through his counsel, George Simp- of Levy & Unger, entered a plea of not guilty. Assistant Krotel asked that bail be fixed at $5,000, saying that the was tantamount to forgery in the first degree. Mr. Simp- fixed at $2,000, and a compromise was reached at $3,500. noon at 3.30 o'clock was the time set for the examination. ken to the Tombs to wait the arrival of a bondsman.

ce is the daughter of Rev. James Alderdice, who lived next occupied by Mrs. Oliver in Second avenue and acted as her an of affairs. He was found dying in the yard of Mrs. the day she was found dead in her bed.

ere executed before James S. Alderdice, Commissioner of son of Rev. James Alderdice.

Koch, a real estate dealer, of No. 56 Pine street, who figured transfers of Mrs. Oliver, was a caller at the office of the to-day. She was accompanied by her attorney, and told connection with the matter.

evelopments are looked for. District-Attorney Jerome has te report from the Coroner's Physician who examined the ver after death. In case the report should not be satisfac- that the body of Mrs. Oliver, as well as that of the elder exhumed for autopsy purposes.

ternoon Assistant District-Attorney Krotel issued a sub- to-morrow, for Dr. John A. O'Brien, of No. 305 East One teenth street, who was Mrs. Oliver's physician. A rumor t Mr. Krotel was not satisfied with the stories of Mrs. d that Dr. O'Brien will be closely questioned about it to-

ATTACK AMERICAN ONSUL IN ASIA MINOR

Davis, Who Was Stationed at ndretta, Asiatic Turkey, Hauls the Flag Over His Post and o Beirut as the Result of Insult.

TINOPLE, Dec. 8.—The United States flag over the lexandretta, Asiatic Turkey, has been hauled down and Davis has left his post for Beirut in consequence of a ic incident during which Mr. Davis was insulted and as- cal police.

rew out of the arrest of an Armenian, Ohannes Attarian, nerican citizen.

Leen in prison at Aleppo for two months and had just rough the intervention of the American Consular Agent on leaving the country forthwith. Mr. Davis was accompany- board a departing steamer when the police intercepted the and insulted Mr. Davis and, in spite of the resistance of the ttendant guards, rearrested Attarian and took him back to

mediately lowered the flag over the consulate and formally s with the Government.

Consulate in charge of the Vice-Consul. A mob of Moslems casion to make a hostile demonstration against the Con- st the Christians generally.

thorities assert that Mr. Davis struck the police with a ter the rearrest of Attarian the Consular cavasses (military ted to rescue him, and that in the fracas which ensued the he windows of the prison.

ON, Dec. 8.—The State Department has received a brief Consul Davis, at Alexandretta, Asiatic Turkey, saying that ith the local police there and had gone to Beirut in conse- te Department promptly cabled to Minister Leishman, at o make a thorough investigation of the whole affair. It Minister Leishman will call at the Foreign Office to-day to

FAVORITES WIN AT NEW ORLEANS.

BIG BEN BEATEN BY FRANK BELL

"Doc" Street's Horse Was Heavily Played to Win Second Race at Crescent City, but Is Outsprinted by Winner.

IRENE LINDSEY GETS HOME IN FRONT IN FIRST.

Bountiful Graduates from the Maiden Ranks by Taking the Third Event from Symphony and Trossachs.

THE WINNERS.

FIRST RACE — Irene Lindsey (even) 1, Morning Star (5 to 2) 2, Little Jack Horner 3.

SECOND RACE—Frank Bell (3 to 1) 1, Big Ben (2 to 5) 2. Van Ness 3.

THIRD RACE—Bountiful (3 to 1) 1, Symphony (7 to 2) 2. Trossachs 3.

(Special to The Evening World.)

RACE TRACK, NEW ORLEANS, La., Dec. 8.—The track was still soft in spots to-day.

Another good crowd was out and the speculative element kept the bookmakers busy. Jockey Higgins will be here next week. He is now visiting his parents in St. Louis. Gregor K., winner of four straight races and probably the best horse here, has been fired and will not be raced again this winter.

FIRST RACE.

Five furlongs.

Starters, whts., jocks.	St.	Hlf.	Fin.	Betting Str.	Pl.
Irene Lindsey, 134, Gan'n	3	1½	1½	1	2-5
Morn'g Star, 98, Phillips	2	2½	2¼	5-2	7-10
L. J. Horner, 121, Hicks	1	3¹	3⁸	13	4
Alista, 104, Hoffler....	4	5⁸	4⁸	8	2
Mordella, 104, Fisher..	7	8¹	5¼	20	5
Over Again, 124, Conley	8	7¼	6⁸	50	15
Jim Along, 121, Dean..	5	4¹	7⁸	50	15
L'y Contrary, 121, Austin	6	6⁴	8⁸	100	40
Arnold K., 101, Rutter..	10	9⁸	9¹⁰	100	30
Malterferin, 116, Bigley	9	10	10	100	30

Start fair. Won easily. Time—1.02.

Irene Lindsey had the class of the lot which started in the first race. She shouldered 134 pounds, set practically all of her own pace, and won in a common gallop. The time, 1.02 marked a good performance for this track. Little Jack Horner beat the barrier, but was soon caught and outrun by Irene Lindsey.

SECOND RACE.

Six furlongs.

Starters, whts., jocks.	St.	Hlf.	Fin.	Betting Str.	Pl.
Frank Bell, 107, Phillips	1	1ʰ	1ⁿ	7-2	7-10
Big Ben, 110, Hicks....	3	2¹	2²	7-10	1-4
Van Ness, 104, Gannon	4	3¼	3ʰ	15	4
Scorpio, 104, Helg's'n..	2	4⁴	4ʰ	5	11-10
Mynheer, 99, Just......	5	5	5	200	40

Start good. Won driving. Time—1.14 2-5.

Big Ben, one of Dr. Street's favorites, proved a disappointment in the second race. Big Ben looked to be in a soft spot and odds were eagerly accepted against his chances. When it came to running, however, he could never get to the front, Frank Bell holding him safe all the way. Hicks was hard at work on Big Ben all the last quarter, but despite his strong finish he was beaten out half a length by Frank Bell.

MAY INDICT AUNT FOR CHILD MURDER

Chief Justice Gummere Charges the Grand Jury on the Death of Little Mary Canning at Newark.

(Special to The Evening World.)

NEWARK, N. J., Dec. 8.—Chief Justice Gummere in charging the Grand Jury to-day called attention to the recent alleged murder of four-year-old Mary Canning by her aunt, Catherine Ray.

"I think," he said, "you will find that the blows that killed the child were inflicted by Mrs. Ray. If so you must indict for murder without defining the degree and not for manslaughter. The question of degree you must leave to the trial jury."

KAISER GOING SOUTH.

BERLIN, Dec. 8.—Emperor William summoned Capt. von Usedom, who succeeded Admiral Count von Baudissin as commander of the imprial yacht Hohenzollern, to Potsdam, and it is said the yacht will sail for the Mediterranean Dec. 20 and await the Emperor in Italian waters.

The Hohenzollern is now at Kiel, inclosed in temporary covering preventing outside observation; but the Tage-

SPECIAL EXTRA.

LATE SCORES IN CYCLE RACE AT THE GARDEN

Scores of the leaders at 6 o'clock in the bicycle race:

	M.	L.		M.	L.
Leander & Butler.....	783	7	Walthour & Munroe..	783	7
Newkirk & Jacobson..	783	7	Contenet & Breton...	783	7
Bedell Brothers.......	783	7	Galvin & Sardgett....	783	7
Root & Doran..........	783	7	Fl. Krebs & Peterson.	783	7
Bowler & Fisher.......	783	7	Keegan & Moran.....	783	6
Fr. Krebs & Barclay..	783	3	Samson & Vanderst't	783	3
Gougoltz & Rettich...	783	1	Dove & Hedspeth....	774	8

CORBETT MAY AGAIN FIGHT WITH JEFF.

Jim Corbett, according to report, has been offered a purse to fight Jim Jeffries before a club in the Mound City during the world's fair next year. Corbett, who is in Utica, it is said, has accepted the offer. Corbett demands a guaranteed purse.

LATE RESULTS AT NEW ORLEANS.

Fourth Race—Witful 1, Ancke 2, Bondage 3.
Fifth Race—Siddons 1, Adeante 2, Airlight 3.
Sixth Race—Foresight 1, Rainland 2, Inquisitive Girl 3.

FLOOD STOPS WORK IN TUNNEL TO BROOKLYN

Workmen Strike Sand 300 Feet from South Ferry Slip and Water Quickly Drives Them Out.

Work on the rapid-transit tunnel under the East River from the Battery to Brooklyn has been brought to a sudden stop because of a leak at a point three hundred feet from the South Ferry slip.

The workings had been pushed through solid rock, but last night the workmen struck sand and water began to pour in on them in such volume as to compel them to stop work and make for the surface. The men who were on the night shift told widely differing tales of the leak. They had the tunnel flooded anywhere from five to twenty feet deep and finally one more imaginative than the rest told of a great cave-in.

The section of the Battery which is given up to the New York Tunnel Company for its machinery and other appurtenances necessary to the New York entrance to the tunnel is surrounded by a high board fence, and a watchful guard night and day prevents any one except employees or officials of the company from entering the grounds.

Members of the official staff would give no particulars, but said that the stories spread by the men of the night shift were "greatly exaggerated."

At the office of the New York Tunnel Company, No. 40 Wall street, Mr. Brown, one of the officials, said:

"The work will probably be stopped for two or three days. It is nothing unusual nor anything more than we have expected. Up to now we have been tunnelling through rock and had no occasion to use compressed air. We had the machines all ready on our field at the Battery to use air as soon as it became necessary, but until we struck sand there was no reason for it. We knew that sooner or later just what has occurred would come.

"It is nothing more than a part of the usual daily routine, just as the carting up from the tunnel of rock which has been excavated is. Before we can get the air machines to work it is necessary to lay a flooring of sacks filled with gravel to afford resistance. This takes some time."

BOB AMMON OUT OF PRISON FOR A DAY

Brought Here as a Witness in Law Suits—He Has Lost Twenty-Eight Pounds, but His Health Is Good.

Robert A. Ammon came down from Sing Sing to-day under the chaperonage of State Detective Jackson in obedience to a writ of habeas corpus to appear as a witness before Justice Truax in the trials in the Supreme Court of two suits to recover money the plaintiffs said they lost in the get-rich-quick schemes of Alfred Goslin and others.

Col. Ammon appeared in the same suit of black doeskin he wore when he "went away," but he looked in it like Shakespeare's "lean and slippered pantaloon, his youthful hose a world too wide for his shrunk shank."

His hair is now a grizzled gray and cut short, while his mustache is gone.

"But I am feeling fine," said he. "Never felt finer in my life; keep good hours, eat regularly; no high living; sleep like a top. Getting all the bad stuff out of me; lost twenty-eight pounds—all bad stuff; breadbasket all gone; I'm as hard as nails all over."

The cases in which Ammon's testimony is needed will not be reached until to-morrow, and State Detective Jackson said he should take his charge back this afternoon.

No one met Col. Ammon at the sta-

THREE STEDEKERS ARE ALL PAROLED

Raids on Alleged Pool-Rooms Were of Spectacular Order, Detective Butts Holding Up 85 Men with His Gun.

Leon, Sam and Henry Stedeker, who were captured yesterday in pool-room raids at Nos. 96 and 98 Church street and 65 West Broadway, were arraigned to-day before Justice Olmsted in the Court of Special Sessions. On motion of their counsel, Benjamin Steinhart, and with the consent of Assistant District-Attorney Corrigan they were paroled until Dec. 15.

The raids were made by Capt. Burns and twenty policemen. Leon Stedeker is accused of running the Church street place. His brothers are said to be the owners of the pool-room in West Broadway. The raids were of the sensational order. In the West Broadway place eighty-five men, making a rush for the door, were held up by Detective Butts with a gun.

Leon Stedeker conducted the pool-room in Dey street in which Maurice Holahan, then a Tammany office-holder, was captured in a raid a few years ago. Mr. Holahan asserted that he was in the place looking for his wayward son. This was one of the star raids made by William Travers Jerome when he was in the Court of Special Sessions, but Stedeker was never punished.

FIVE IN HOME KILLED BY FIRE

Only One in Entire Family to Escape Flames Was Son Fifteen Years Old, Who Leaped to Safety from Window.

MOTHER, BEWILDERED, WOULD NOT THROW BABY.

While Neighbors Rushed to Find a Ladder the Unfortunate Woman Toppled Back Into the Flames, Holding the Infant.

FREEHOLD, N. J., Dec. 8.—One child, a boy of fifteen, is all of the family of Clayton Fowler, of Carksbury, ten miles from here, who escaped from the flames which destroyed the Fowler home early to-day.

Fowler and his wife and three of their children, one of them an infant six months old, were burned to death, and all that remains of their pretty little home is a smouldering pile of ashes.

The dead are Fowler, who was forty-two years old; Elizabeth, his wife, thirty-six years old; Wilhelmina, thirteen years old; Martha, five years, and Willie, six months old. George, the oldest child, who is fifteen, escaped by jumping from a window of the second floor. He landed safely on the ground below, sustaining only slight injuries.

The Fowlers lived in a two-story frame house in the heart of the village. The entire family was asleep when the house caught fire. Fowler was roused by the smell of smoke and discovered that the chimney had caught fire. Not appreciating the danger, he tried to extinguish the flames, instead of rousing his family and getting them to a place of safety.

Within five minutes the entire lower part of the house was in flames and the family of six were practically imprisoned in the upper part of the house. Clarksbury has no fire department, not even a volunteer one, and although the neighbors turned out and did all they could to save the place their efforts were futile.

Son Leaped to Safety.

With the entire place ablaze, George, the oldest boy, suddenly appeared at a second-story window. Those below shouted for him to jump. His clothing was ablaze and it seemed the only chance. The little fellow didn't hesitate more than a few seconds. Then he took the leap, landing safely on the turf below.

A moment later Mrs. Fowler appeared at the window with her infant child in her arms. The unfortunate woman was frantic with fear and could not understand the advice yelled at her from below. She was told to throw down the child, and a half dozen men stood ready to catch the little fellow.

Meanwhile some one had gone for a ladder, but before it arrived Mrs. Fowler, who only clung the tighter to her little one when advised to throw it down, was seen to fall back into the flames, which had been getting closer all the time. Nothing was seen of Fowler or the other children, but when the building fell down and the fire had practically burned itself out the charred remains of their bodies were found in the ruins.

Business at a Standstill.

In the village the tragedy has had the effect of bringing all business to a standstill to-day. Crowds are gathered around the ruins of the Fowler house. Fowler was one of the best-known residents of the place. He was a member of the Patriotic Sons of America and of other fraternal orders.

His life, the life of his wife and of two of the dead children were insured, and this money will be all that the boy George will have in the world.

The dead children, except the infant, all attended the village school and were among the brightest and prettiest of the pupils there.

MARINES CAMP AT PANAMA.

Detachments from the Dixie Landed at Isthmus for Shore Duty.

COLON, Dec. 8.—A company of marines from the United States auxiliary cruiser Dixie, under Capt. Wirt McCreary, landed at Colon to-day and took a train for Empire, a town on the railroad, near Panama, where a camp will be established, using the Canal Company's buildings.

The purpose of the landing of the marines is to get the men ashore after their long confinement on the Dixie. It is expected that other detachments will be sent ashore this afternoon.

CARNEGIE AT WHITE HOUSE.

WASHINGTON, Dec. 8.—Mr. and Mrs. Andrew Carnegie were guests to-day of the President and Mrs. Roosevelt at luncheon. Mr. Carnegie is in the city on business connected with the Carnegie Institution.

WEATHER FORECAST.

Forecast for the thirty-six hours ending at 8 P. M. Wednesday for New York City and vicinity: Fair and slightly colder to-night; Wednesday cloudy and probably snow; light to fresh westerly winds, shifting to north and northeast.

FEARFUL ST ON BIKE R CALLS FO

Trainers at Garden Grind Looking Bottles as Nig Long Hours of Riding B the Weary Legged Racer

FASTEST SPRINTING OF RACE DURING TH

Moran, After Last Lap, Keep Jump All the Time---Exp to Carry Off First Ho Suffering.

MADISON SQUARE GARDEN, Dec. 8.— into play to-night at the big six-day grind.

The fearful strain on the struggling ride human nature to stand, and the trainers of bo can riders are getting out the queer looking bo important part in races of the past.

Up to the present there has not been any pace has not been fast enough to warrant it, b saddle so long is now beginning to tell, and to- one for every man in the big grind.

BEDELL LOOKS O. K.

Menus Bedell appeared on the track at 3 smiles and his shoulders showing no signs o without pain and rides easily. As soon as he well to the front of the bunch.

Nine teams are now tied, and the present

The colored team loses a lap now and th enthusiasm from riders and spectators.

GOUGOLTZ SPRINTS.

The fastest clip of the day took place a who has been riding steadily, started out for had first place, Gougoltz spurted for two la Leander quickened his speed, however, and Gougoltz then subsided and joined the bunch.

MISS GAST COMES OUT.

At 4.15 all the riders quit the track for with flaxen hair, gave an exhibition of motor- riders quit they struck up a hot two-mile sp endurance of the leaders. As usual, the ca Butler team. Butler had just relieved Lean give Moran a rest. Gougoltz was also there wanted to be included in the reckoning.

RED HOT SPRINTING.

Butler and Keegan let drive with terrific out in a line. Then they all put power in their race of the day was run. Positions changed joined in, and Bobby Walthour helped some. went, and when the scorers summed up result and Dove, were lacking another lap. They have team at losing laps.

LOOKS LIKE LEANDER—BUT

George Leander and his team mate, Nat B winners of the big six-day grind.

Their most dangerous rivals are Moran an to the bad.

Leander is riding in easier fashion than a front or in a safe position he holds his ow When the riders try to steal a march on hi only slows down when the rest drop into the

WINE CAUSES LEA TO SET TER

MADISON SQUARE GARDEN, Dec. 8.—The eccentric string of riders were nodding comfortably on their wheels in the great six-day race at 9.30 this morning, when a stranger, whose sleep has been deferred now since Saturday night, when the race began, appeared at the inner rail which lines the track. Leander, the uncrowned hero of the public, came from his dressing-room at the same time. The stranger had in one hand a bottle of "wine" eager to pop. Leander and the unknown met.

The wine popped. The uncrowned hero drank thereof, mounted his wheel and was off. Into the tired legs of the rider the champagne sizzled, and the awakening excitement of the day proper began.

Leander's "fizzing" legs made Newkirk jealous, and the contest between the two made circles round the track grow fast and furious. Before the

Leander
Gougoltz
Contenet
Samson
Floyd K
Newkirk
Walthou
J. Bedell
Root an
Galvin
Keegan
Bowler
Dove a
Franz K

crowd h life into out anot As Ke

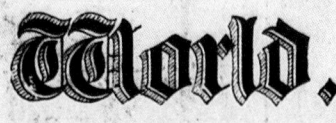

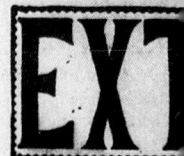

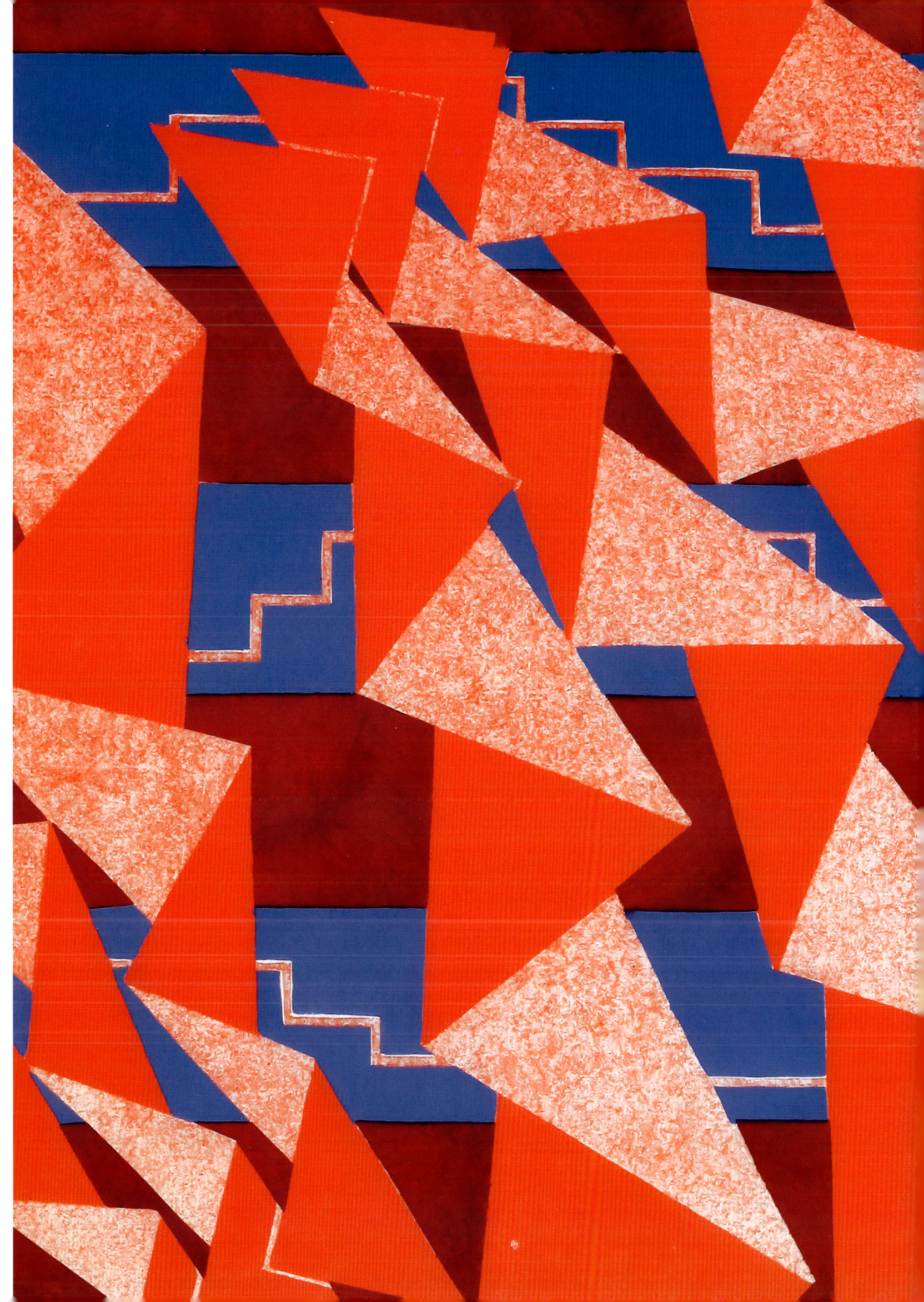

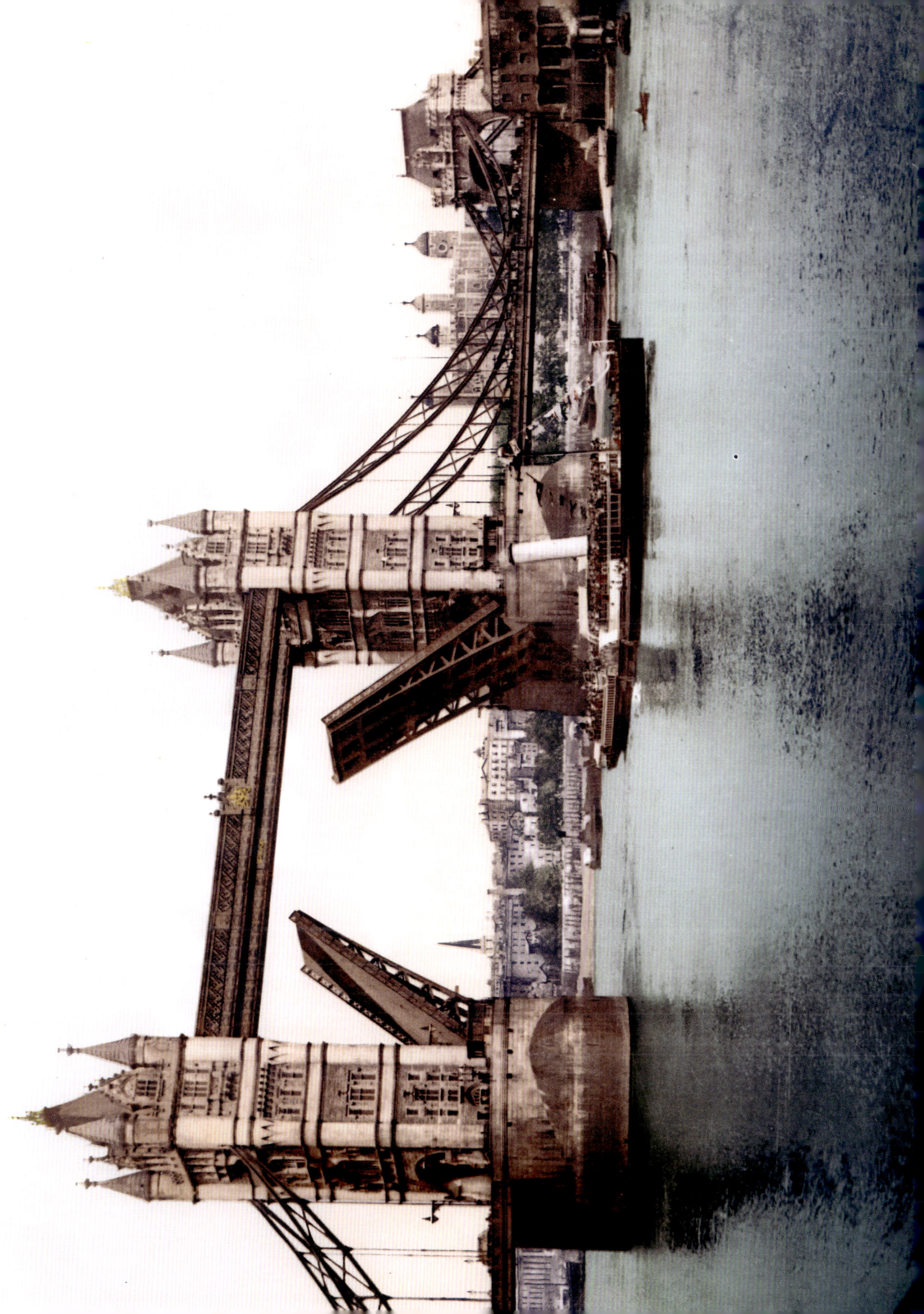

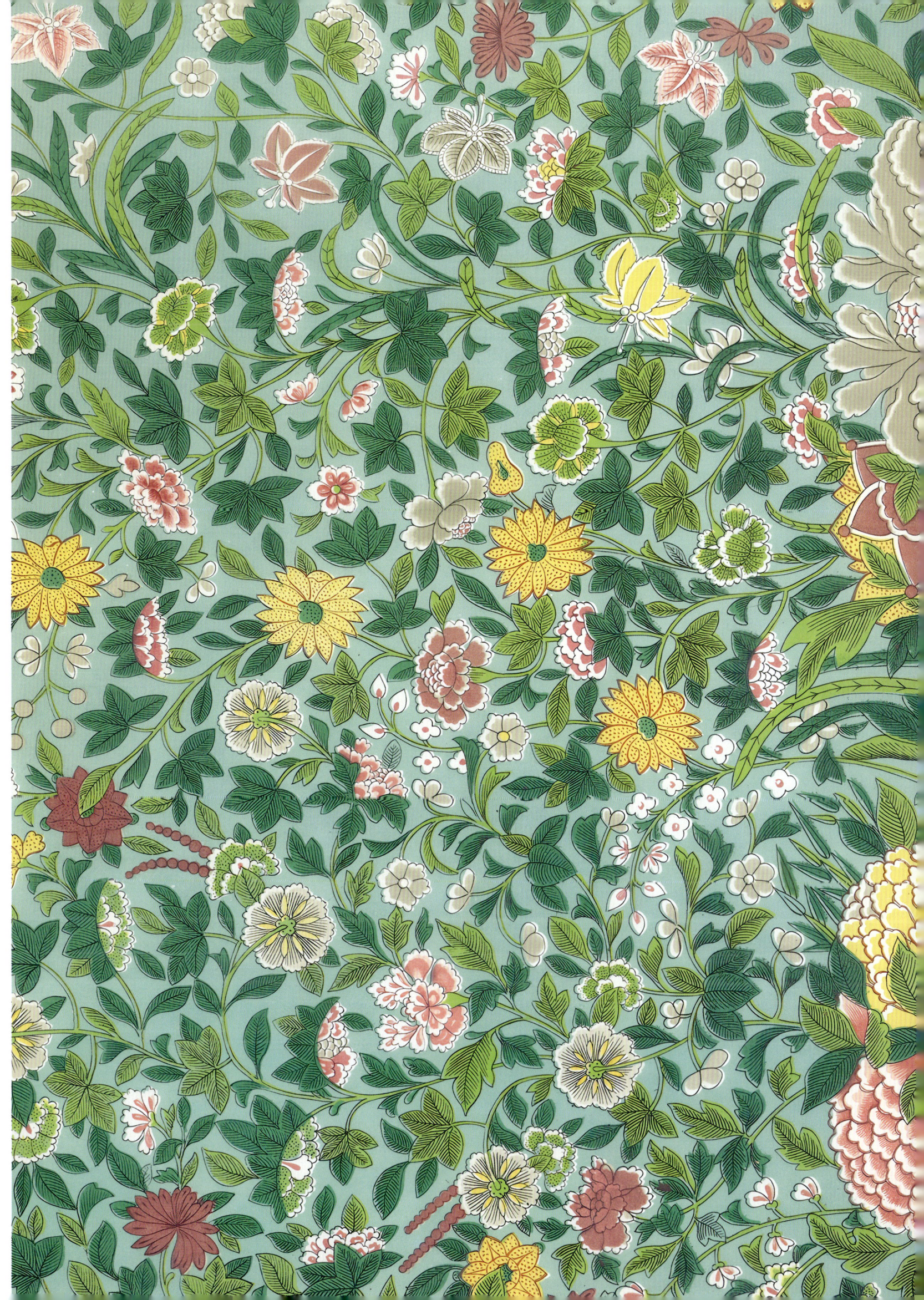

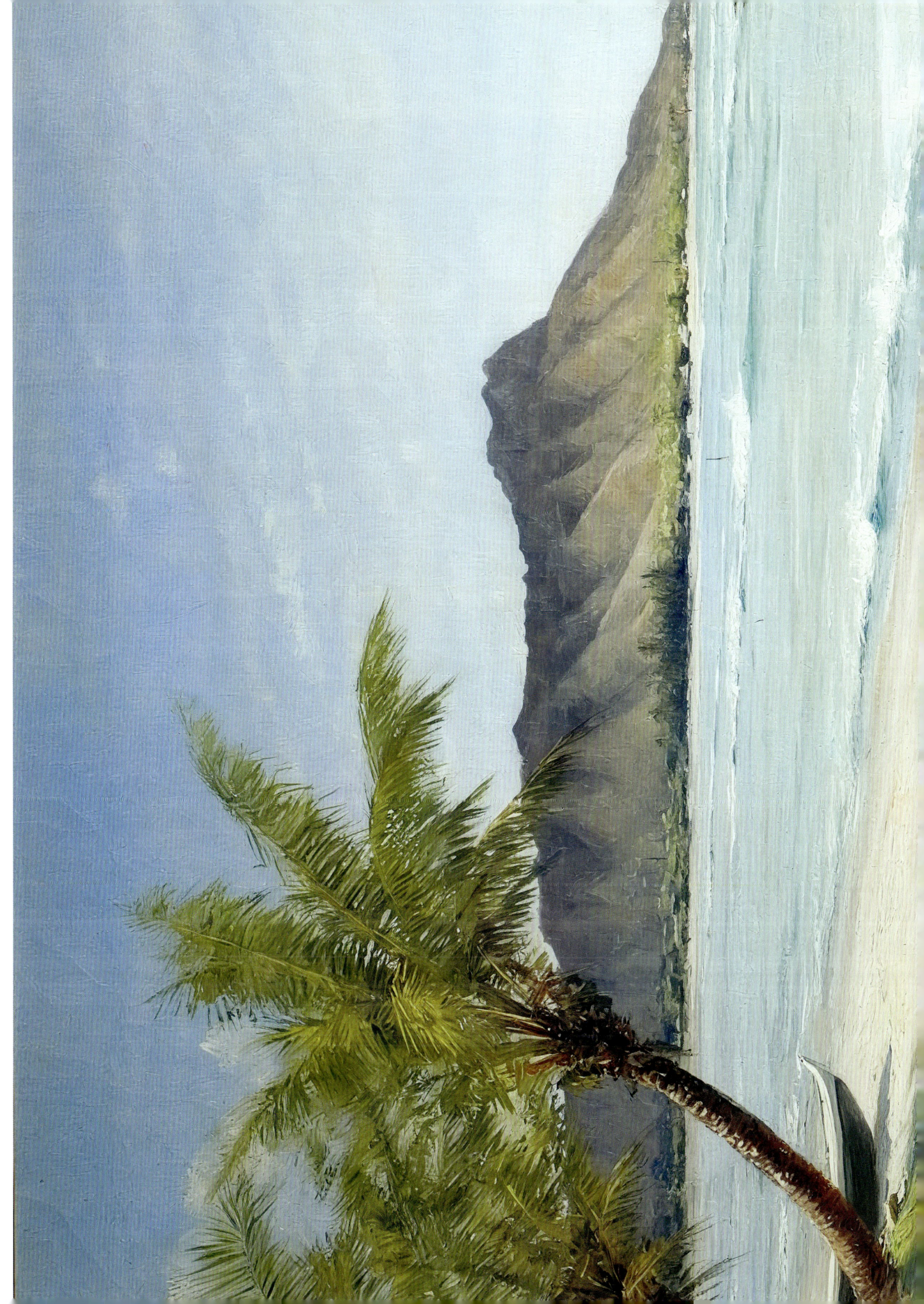

MOUNTAIN AND FOREST

PIANO

Ditson's Music
For the Photoplay
Nº 44

For heavy timbered woods or grand mountain scenery, especially where
it is more important to depict the scene, rather than the action.

CHRISTOPHER O'HARE

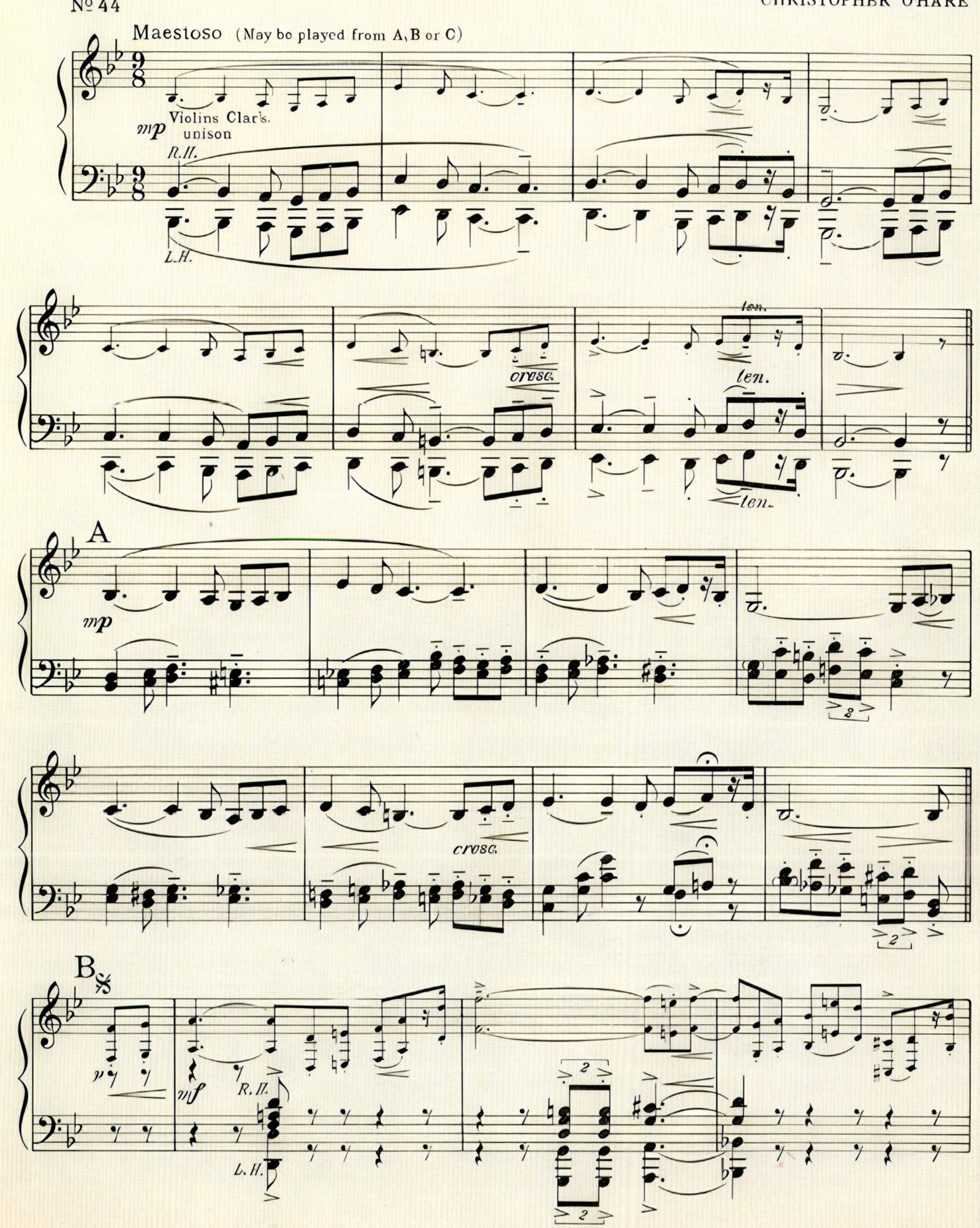

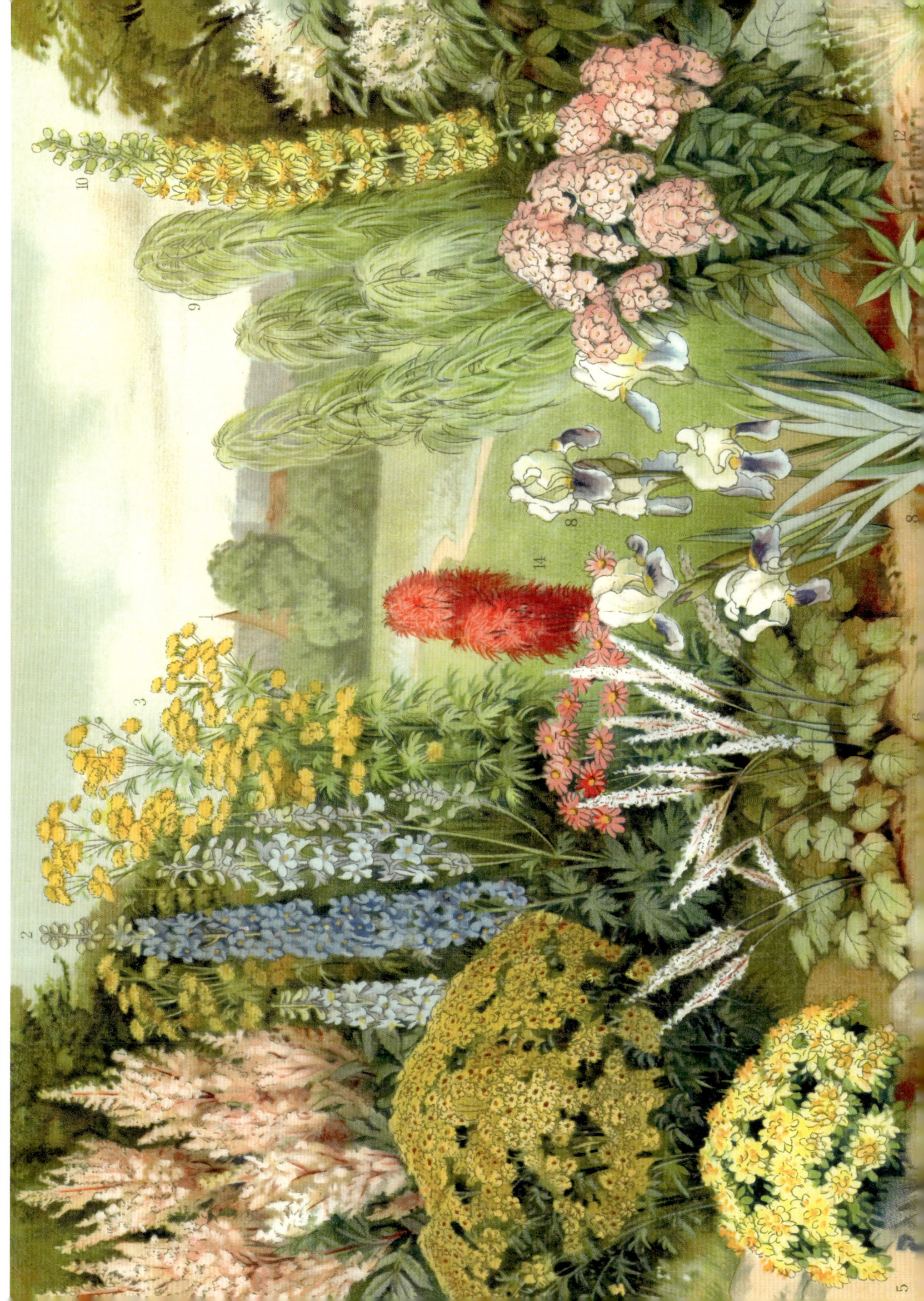

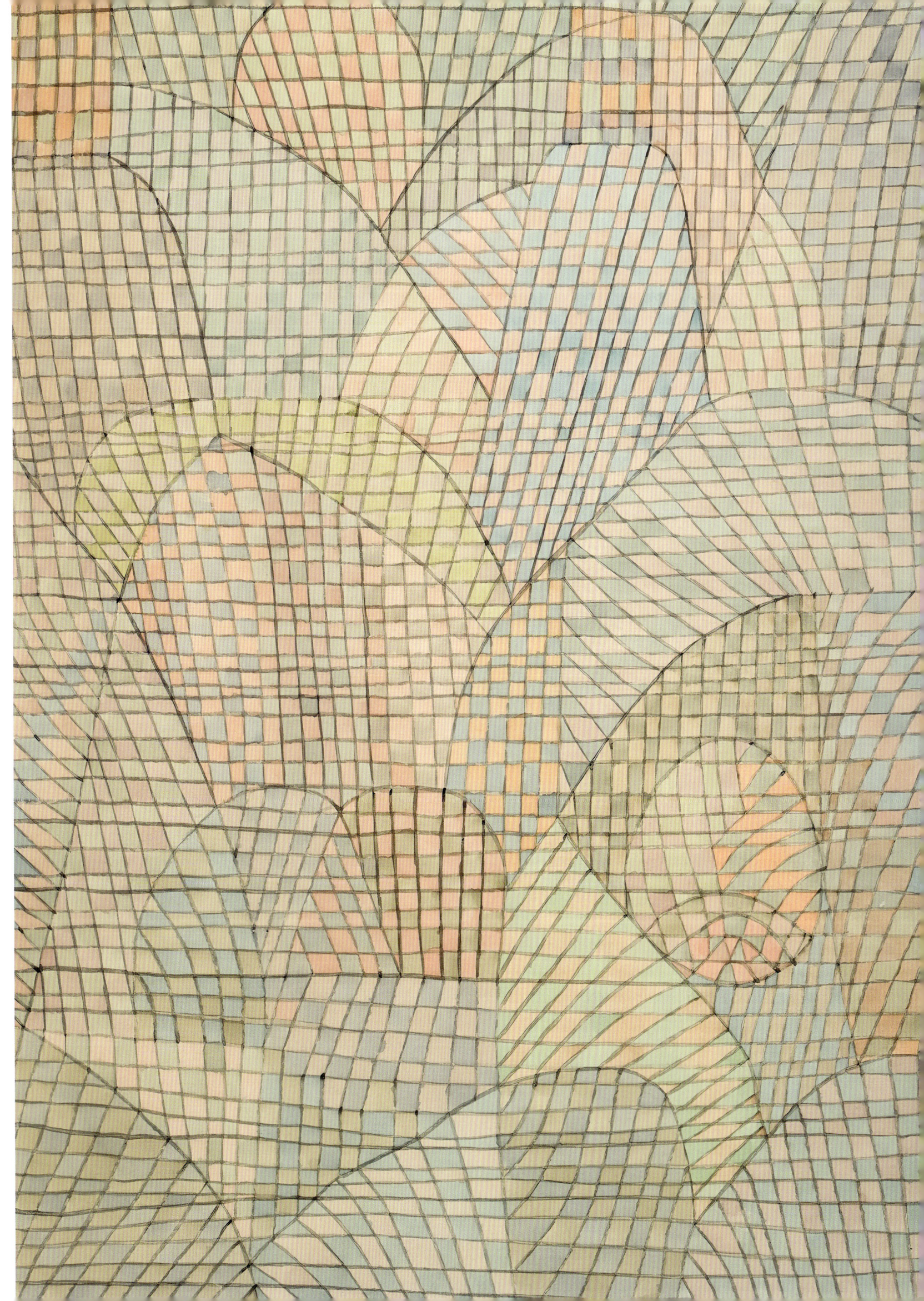

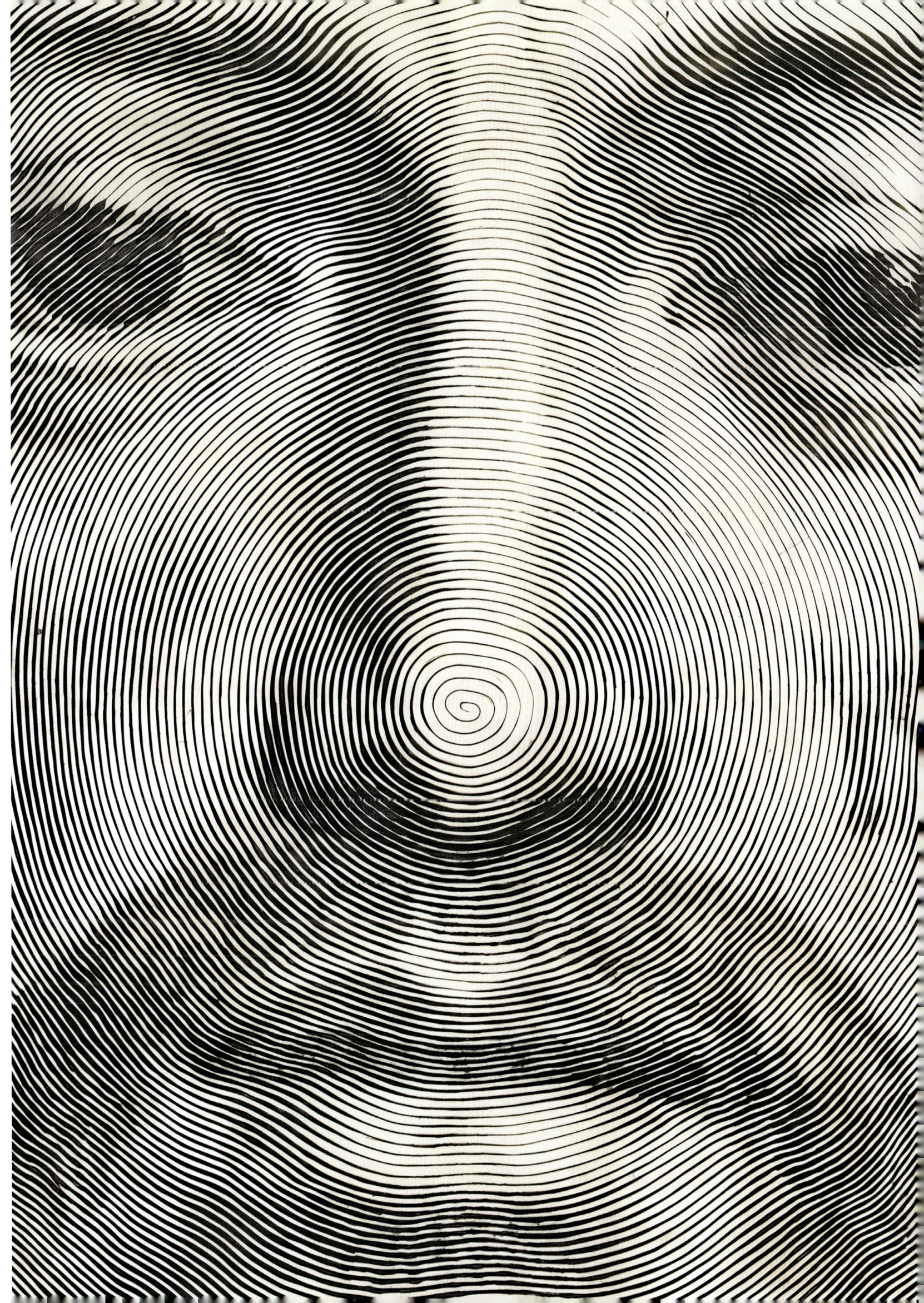

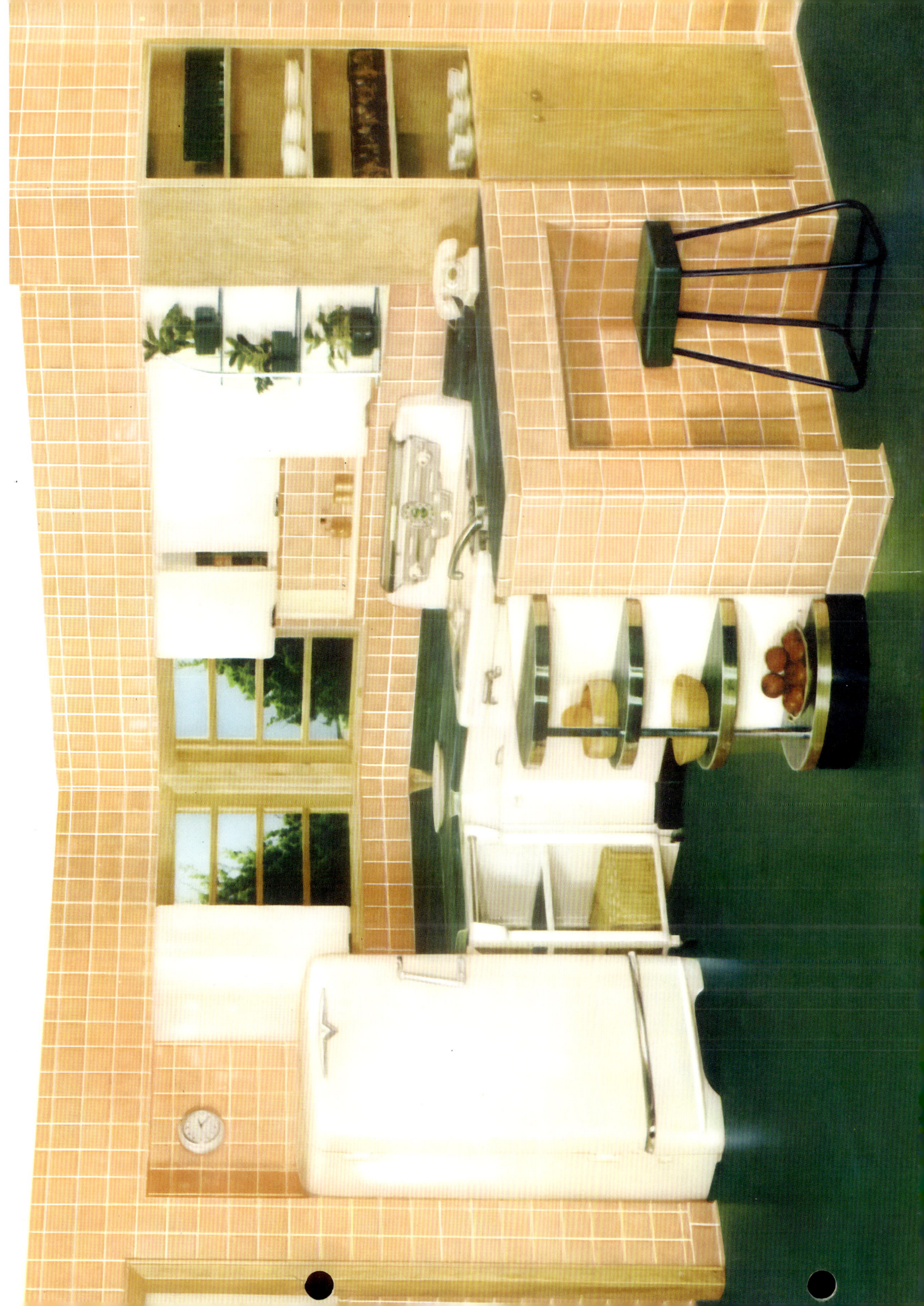

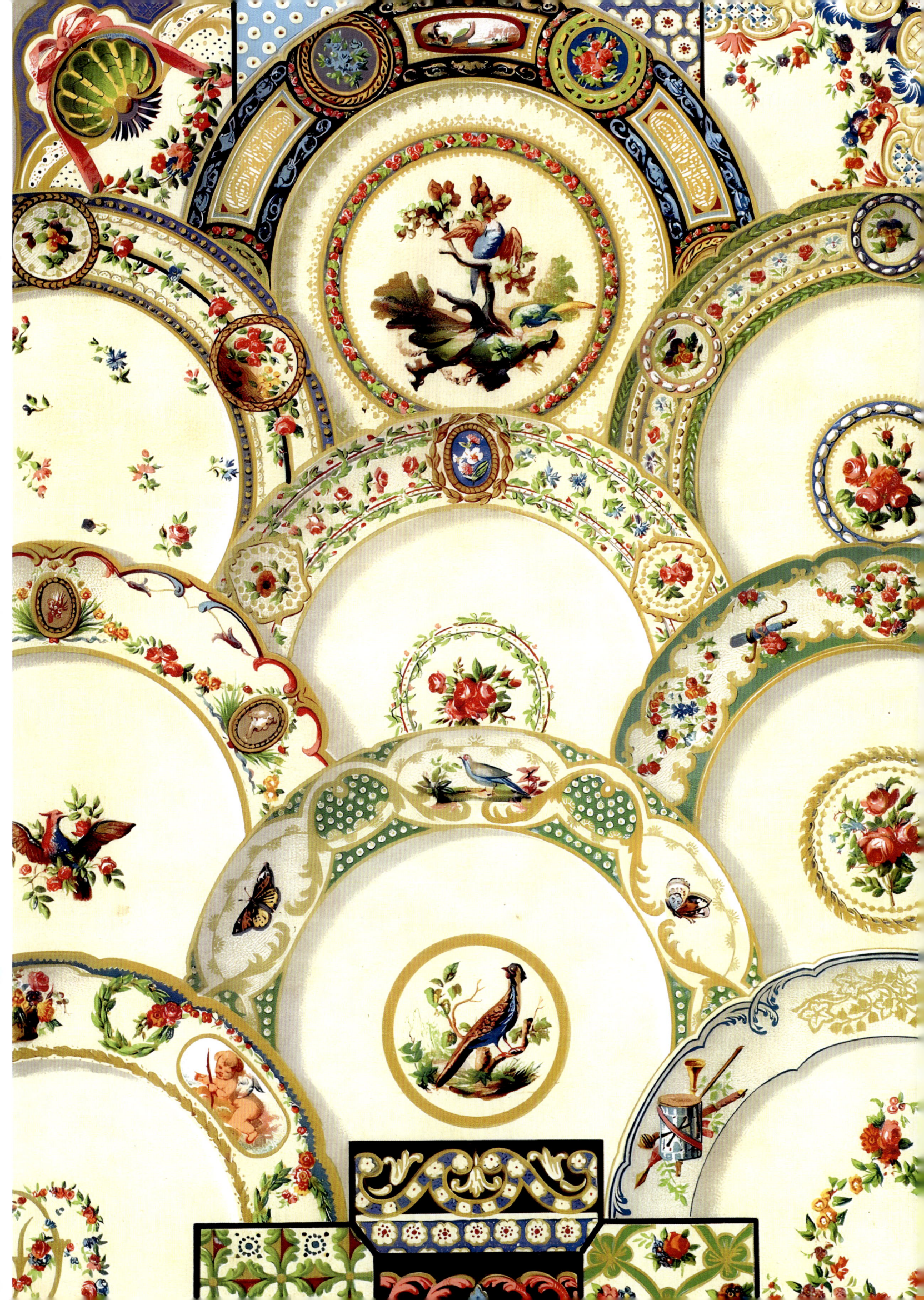

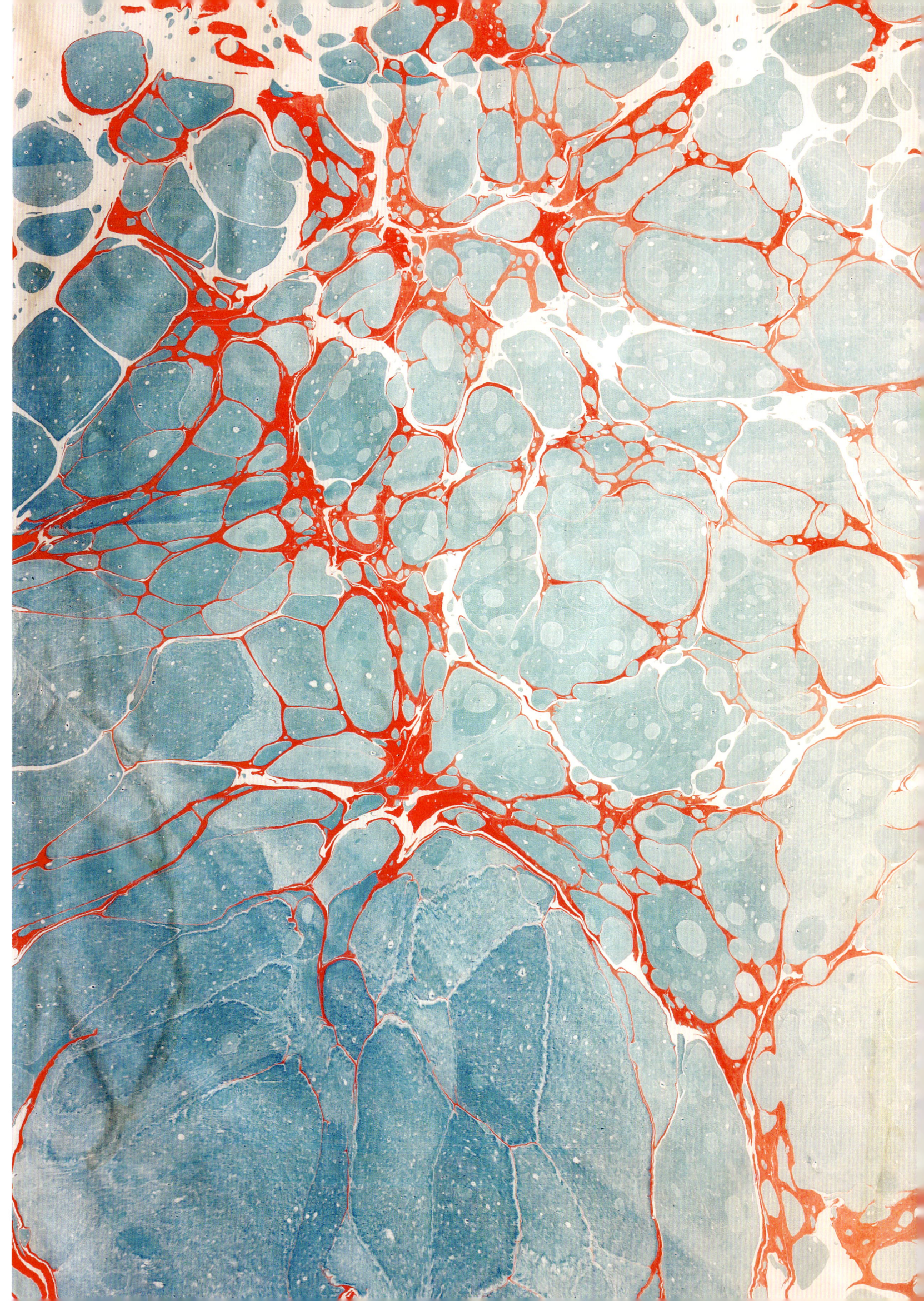

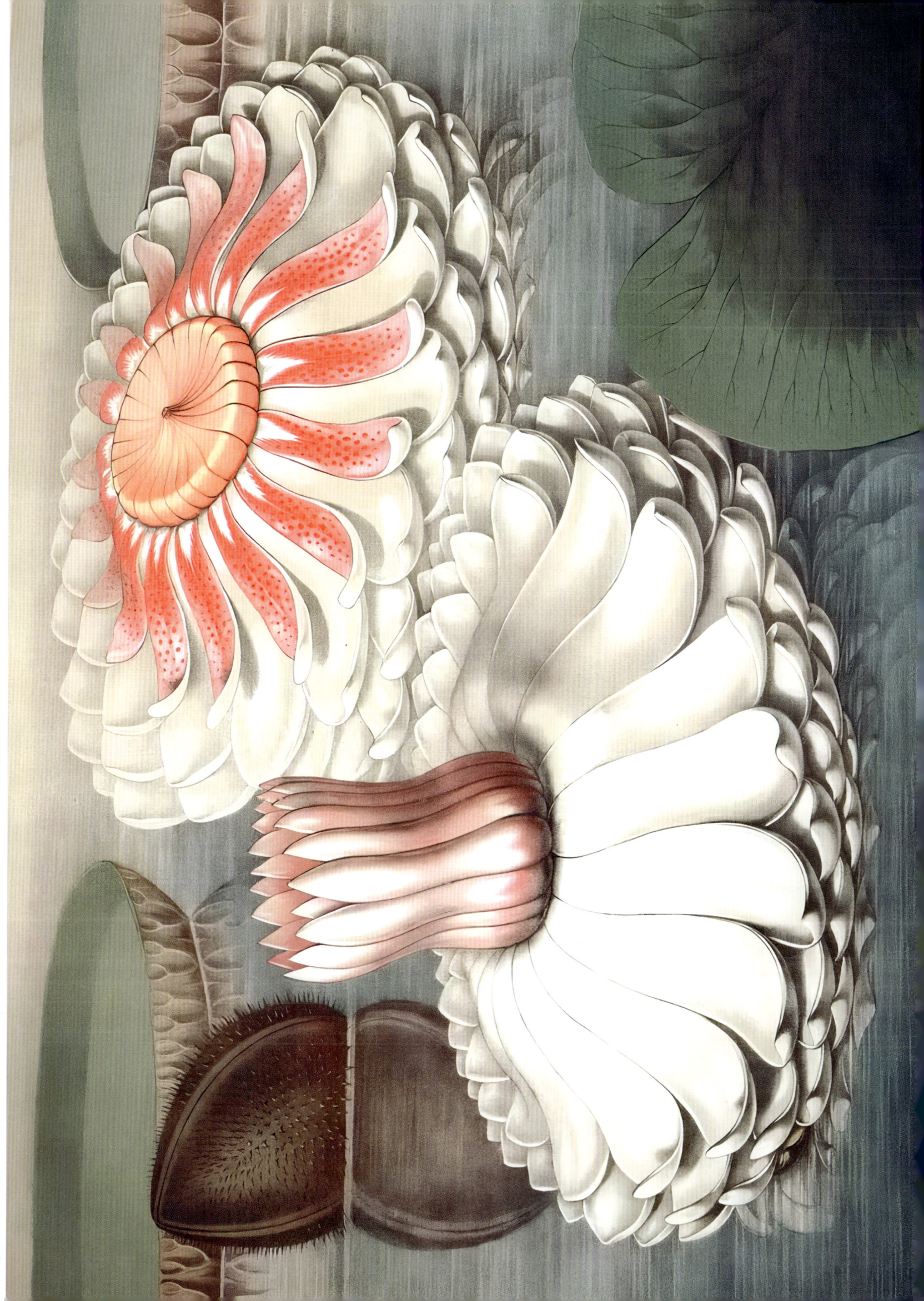

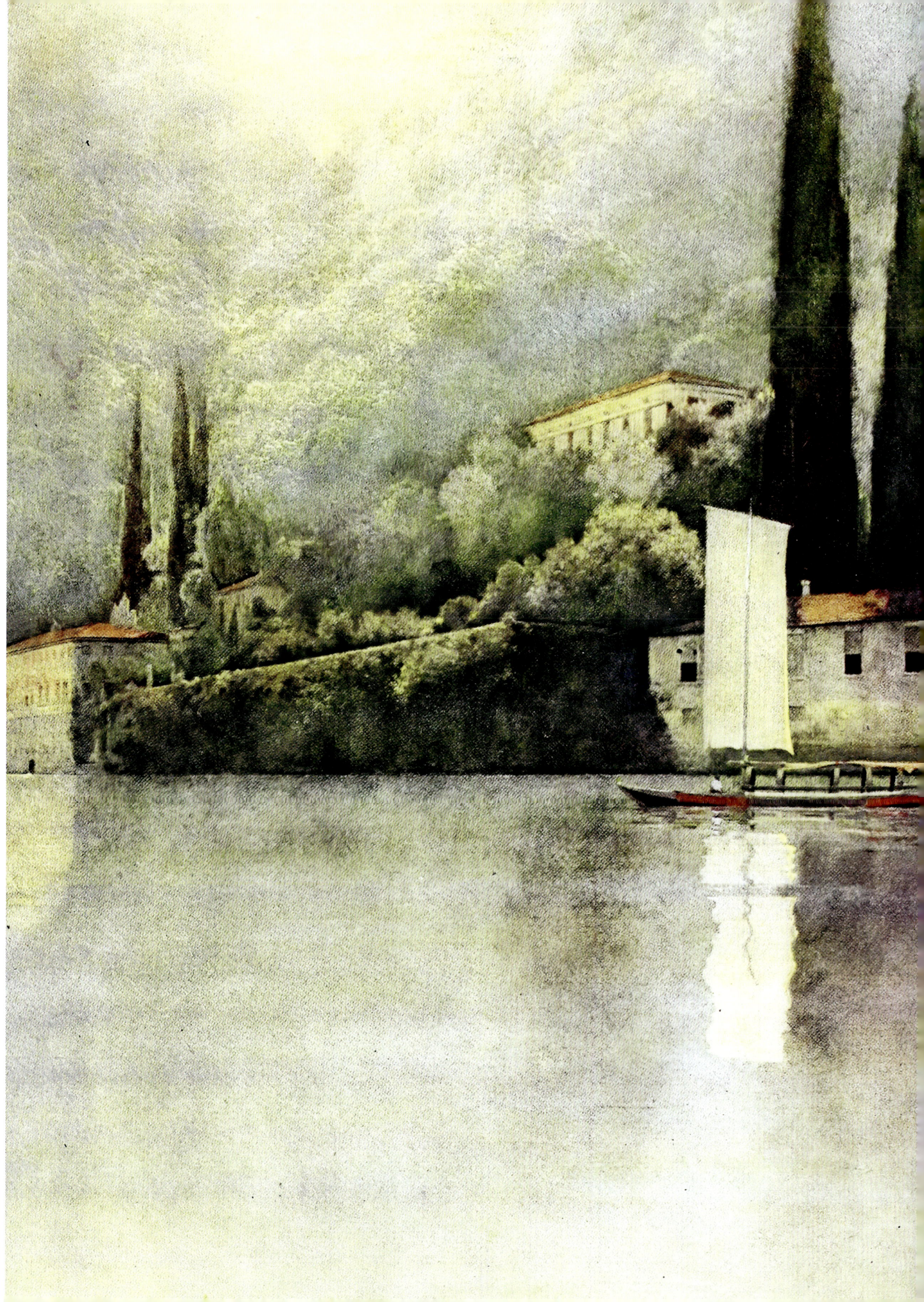

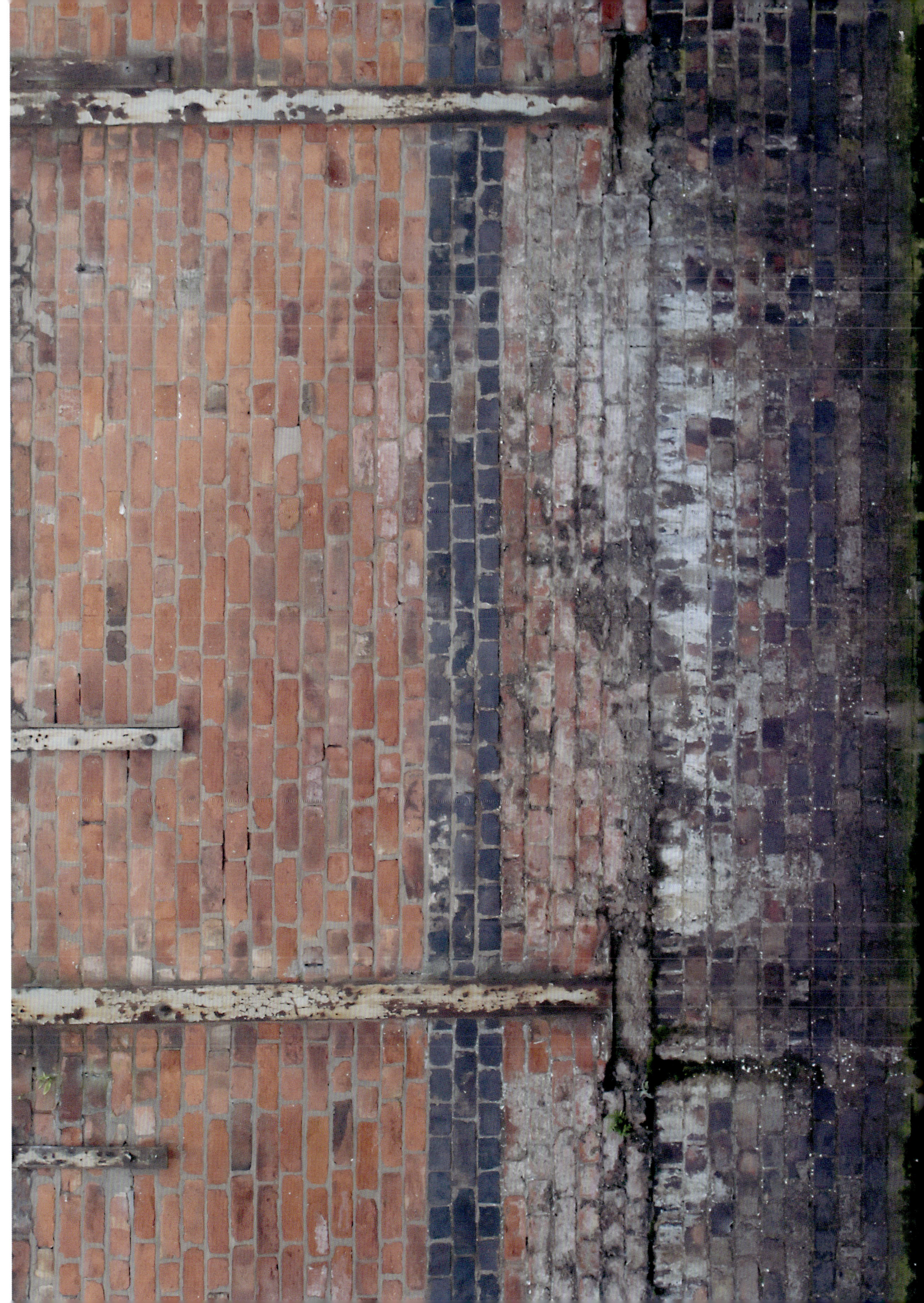

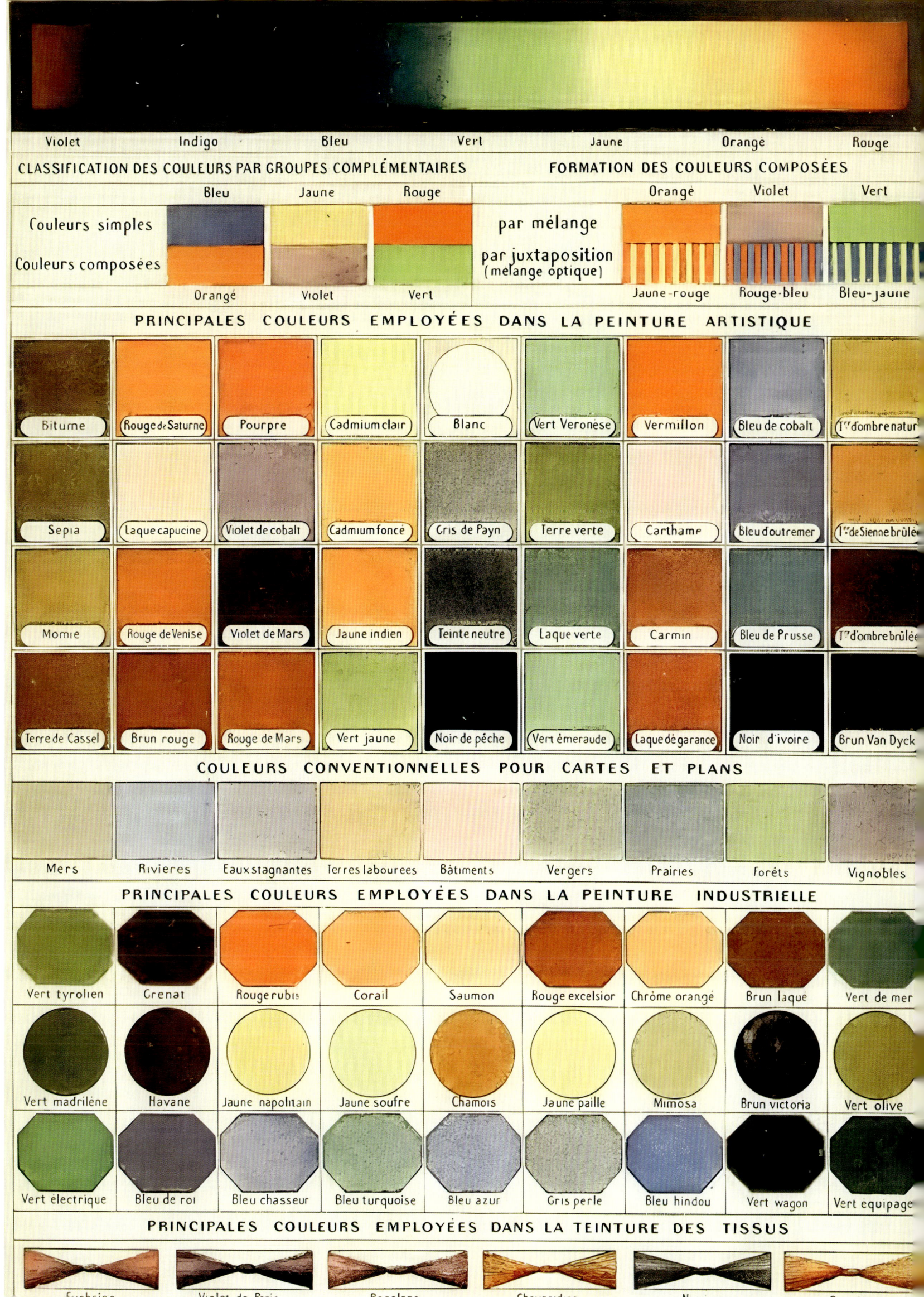

| Violet | Indigo | Bleu | Vert | Jaune | Orangé | Rouge |

CLASSIFICATION DES COULEURS PAR GROUPES COMPLÉMENTAIRES

FORMATION DES COULEURS COMPOSÉES

	Bleu	Jaune	Rouge		Orangé	Violet	Vert
Couleurs simples				par mélange			
Couleurs composées				par juxtaposition (melange optique)			
	Orangé	Violet	Vert		Jaune-rouge	Rouge-bleu	Bleu-jaune

PRINCIPALES COULEURS EMPLOYÉES DANS LA PEINTURE ARTISTIQUE

Bitume	Rouge de Saturne	Pourpre	Cadmium clair	Blanc	Vert Veronèse	Vermillon	Bleu de cobalt	T.re d'ombre natur.le
Sepia	Laque capucine	Violet de cobalt	Cadmium foncé	Gris de Payn	Terre verte	Carthame	Bleu d'outremer	T.re de Sienne brûlée
Momie	Rouge de Venise	Violet de Mars	Jaune indien	Teinte neutre	Laque verte	Carmin	Bleu de Prusse	T.re d'ombre brûlée
Terre de Cassel	Brun rouge	Rouge de Mars	Vert jaune	Noir de pêche	Vert émeraude	Laque de garance	Noir d'ivoire	Brun Van Dyck

COULEURS CONVENTIONNELLES POUR CARTES ET PLANS

| Mers | Rivieres | Eaux stagnantes | Terres labourees | Bâtiments | Vergers | Prairies | Foréts | Vignobles |

PRINCIPALES COULEURS EMPLOYÉES DANS LA PEINTURE INDUSTRIELLE

Vert tyrolien	Grenat	Rouge rubis	Corail	Saumon	Rouge excelsior	Chrôme orangé	Brun laqué	Vert de mer
Vert madrilène	Havane	Jaune napolitain	Jaune soufre	Chamois	Jaune paille	Mimosa	Brun victoria	Vert olive
Vert électrique	Bleu de roi	Bleu chasseur	Bleu turquoise	Bleu azur	Gris perle	Bleu hindou	Vert wagon	Vert equipage

PRINCIPALES COULEURS EMPLOYÉES DANS LA TEINTURE DES TISSUS

| Fuchsine | Violet de Paris | Rosolane | Chrysoïdine | Nigrisine | Coccéine |

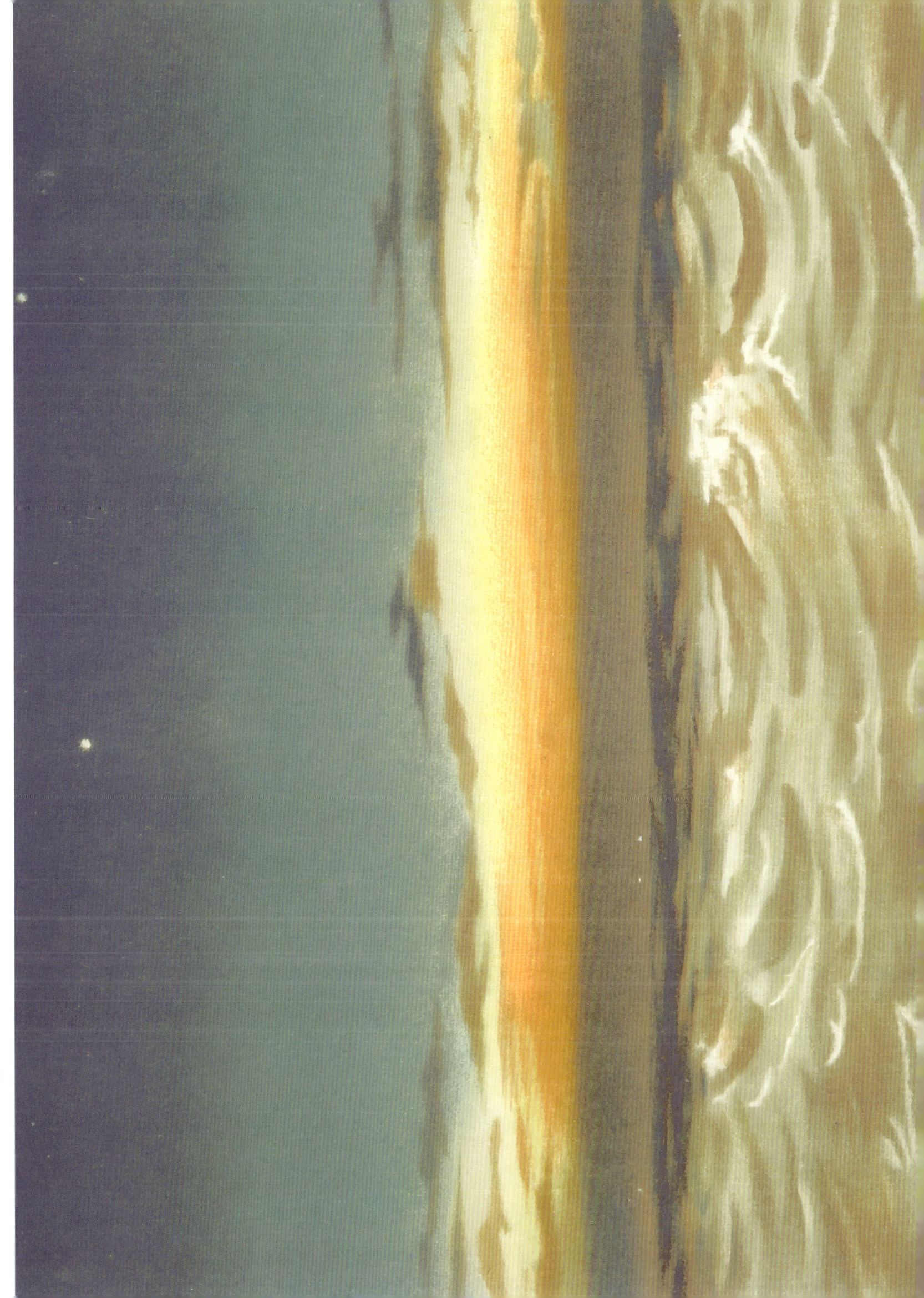

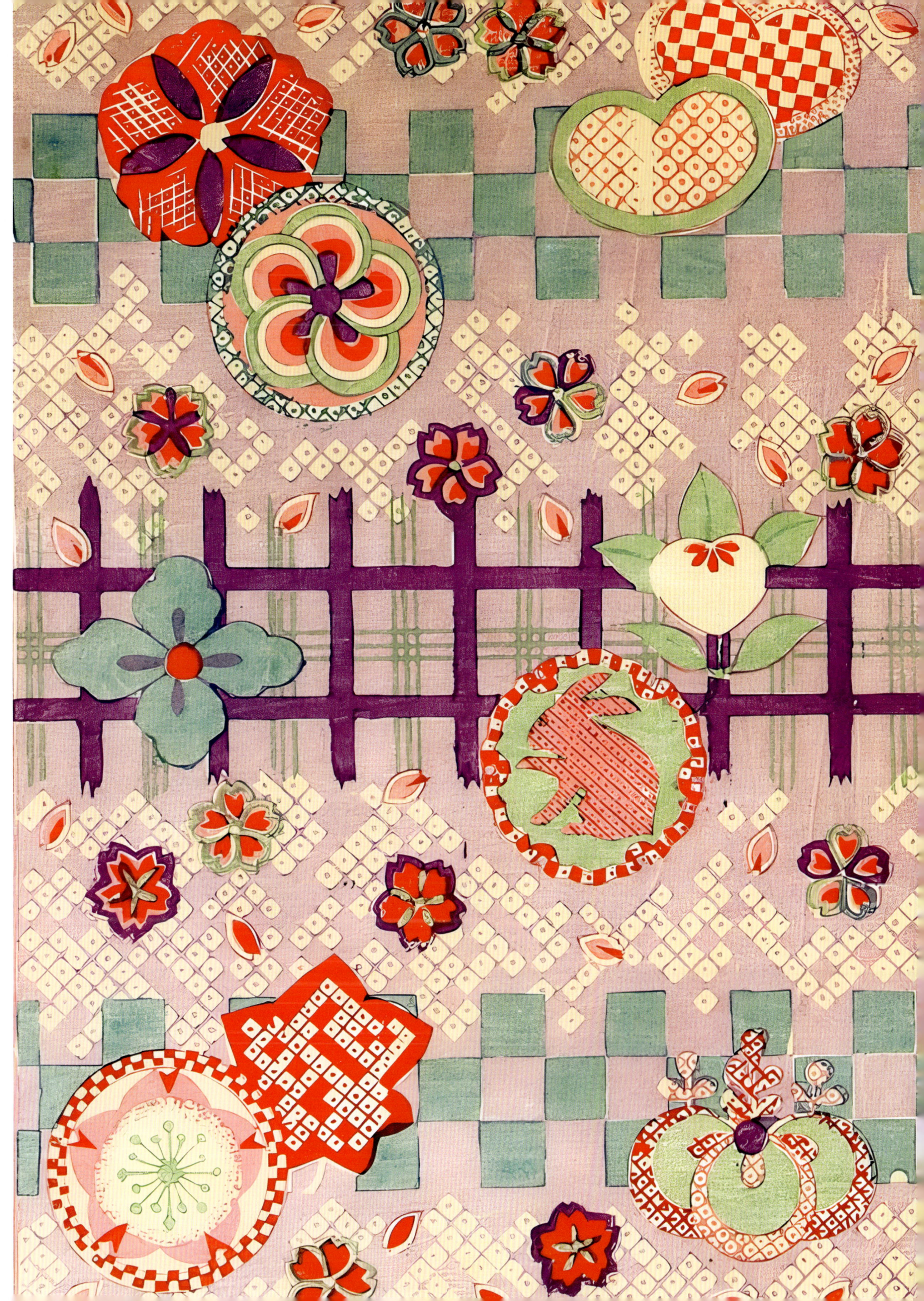

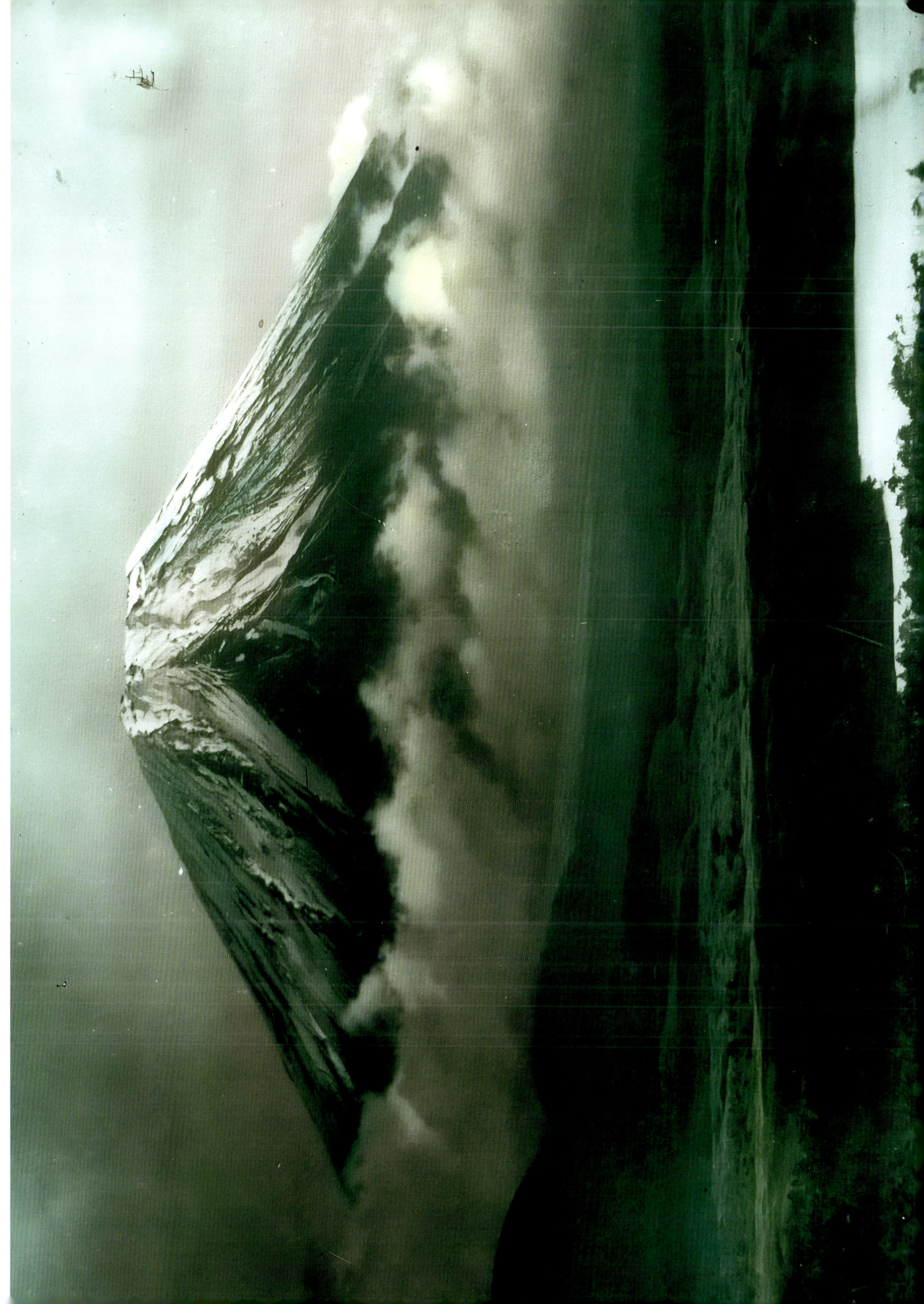

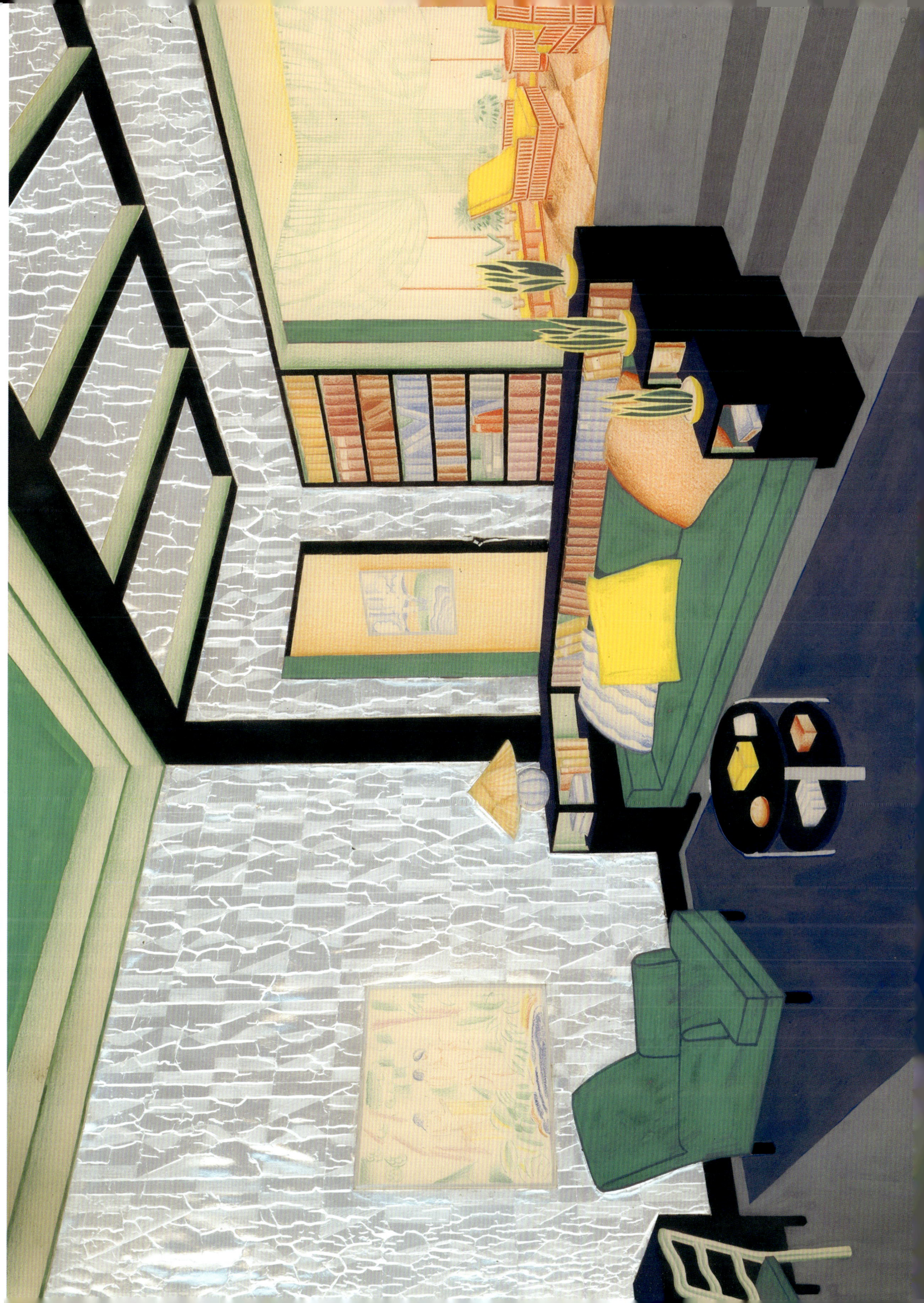

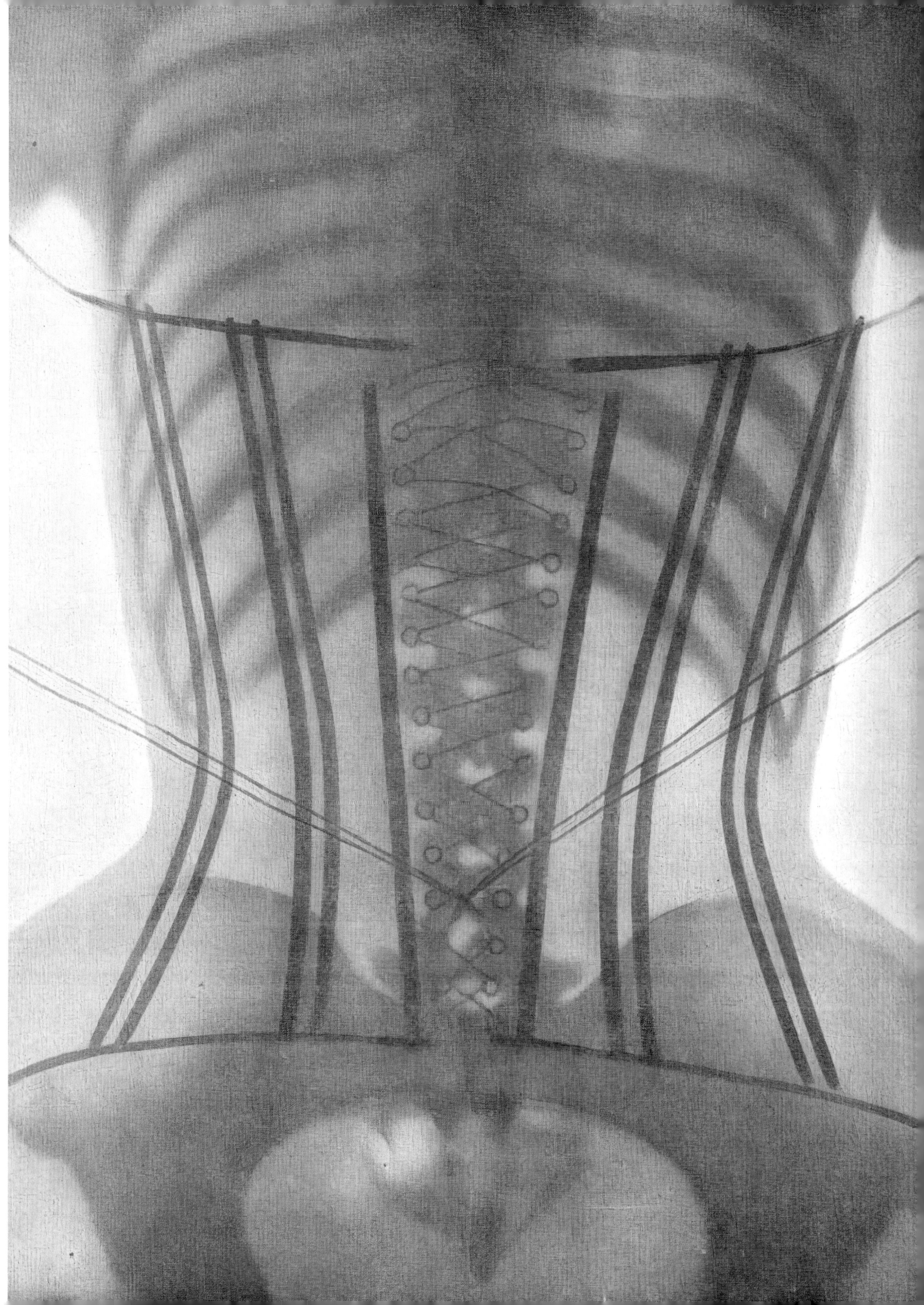

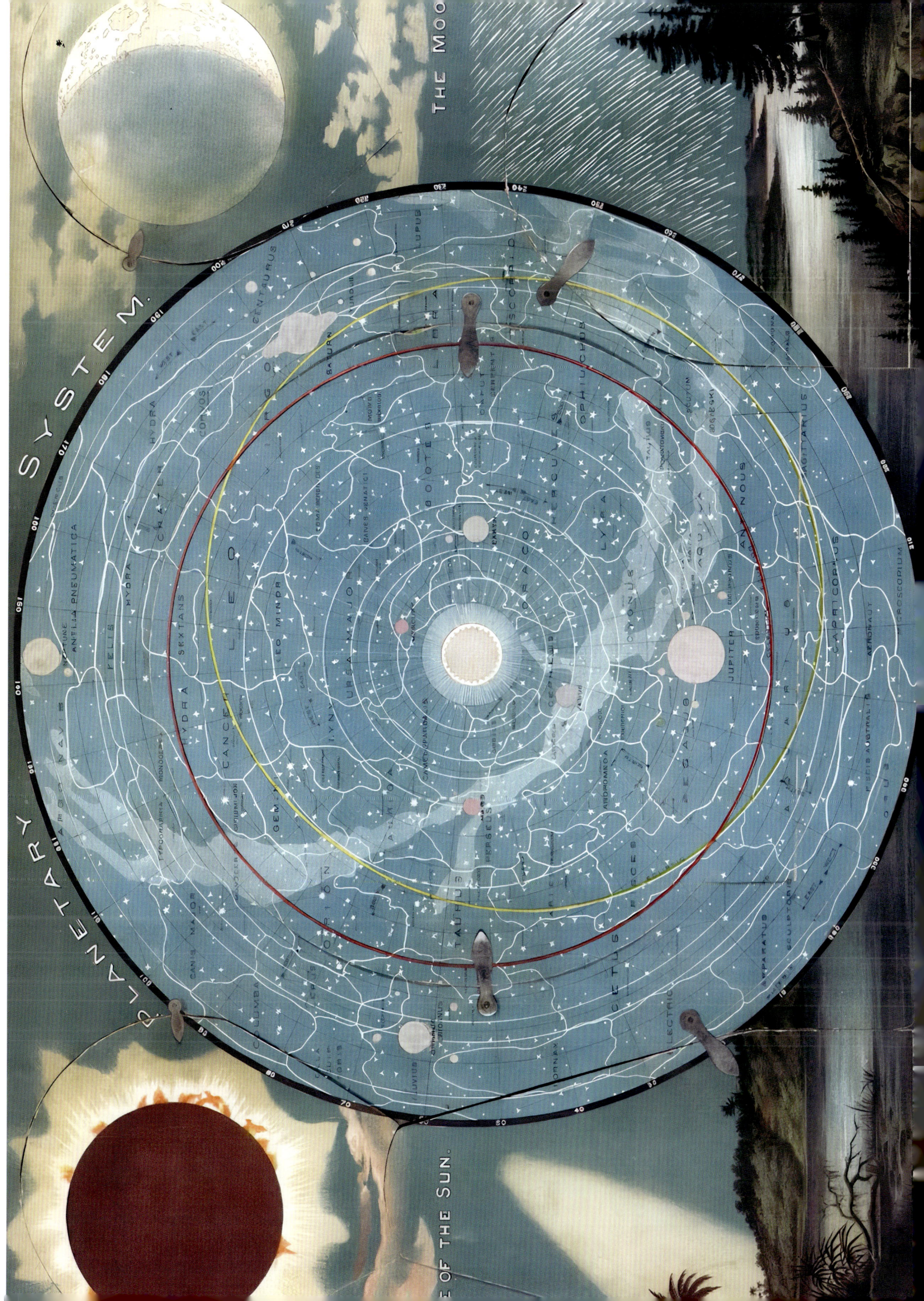

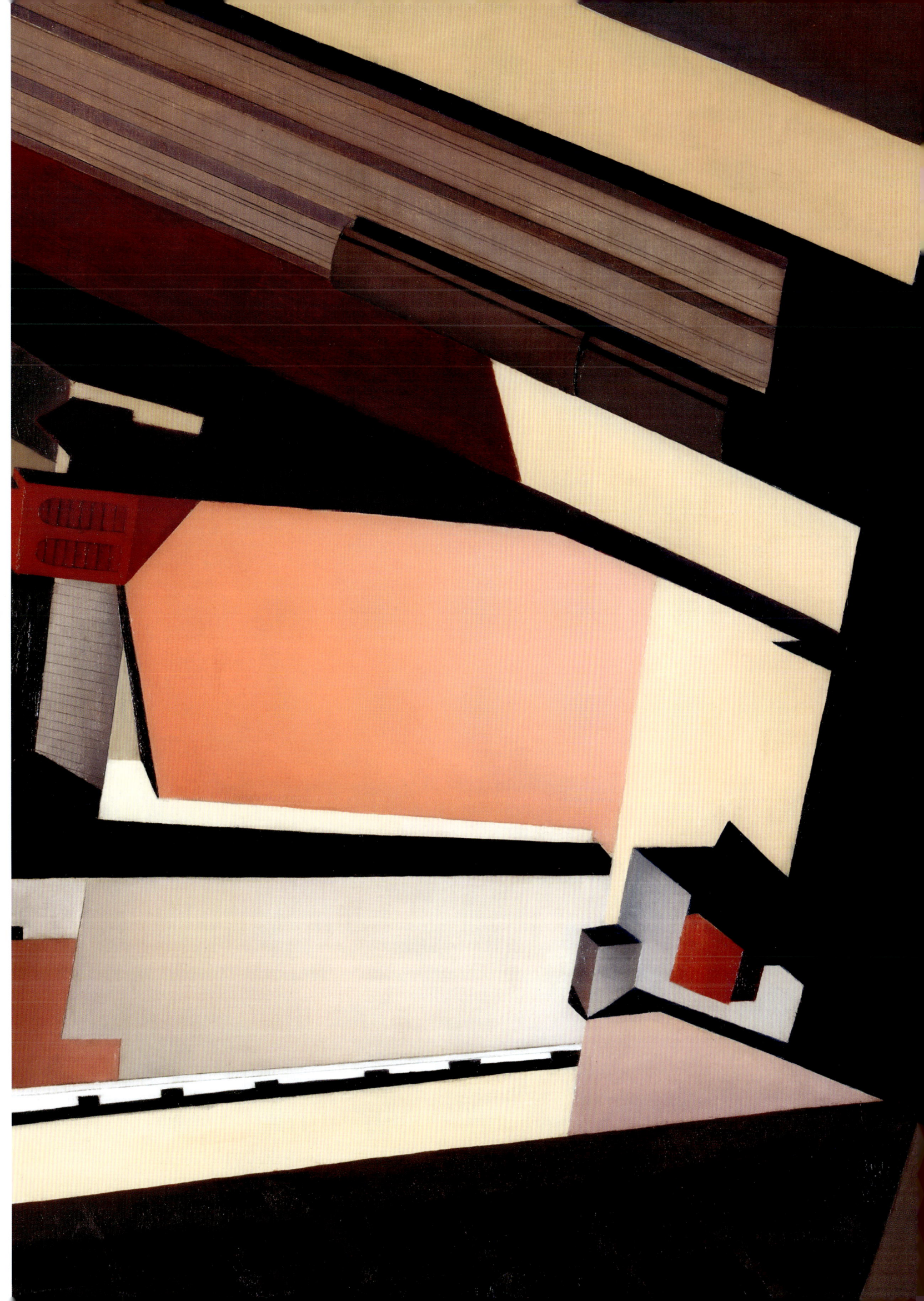

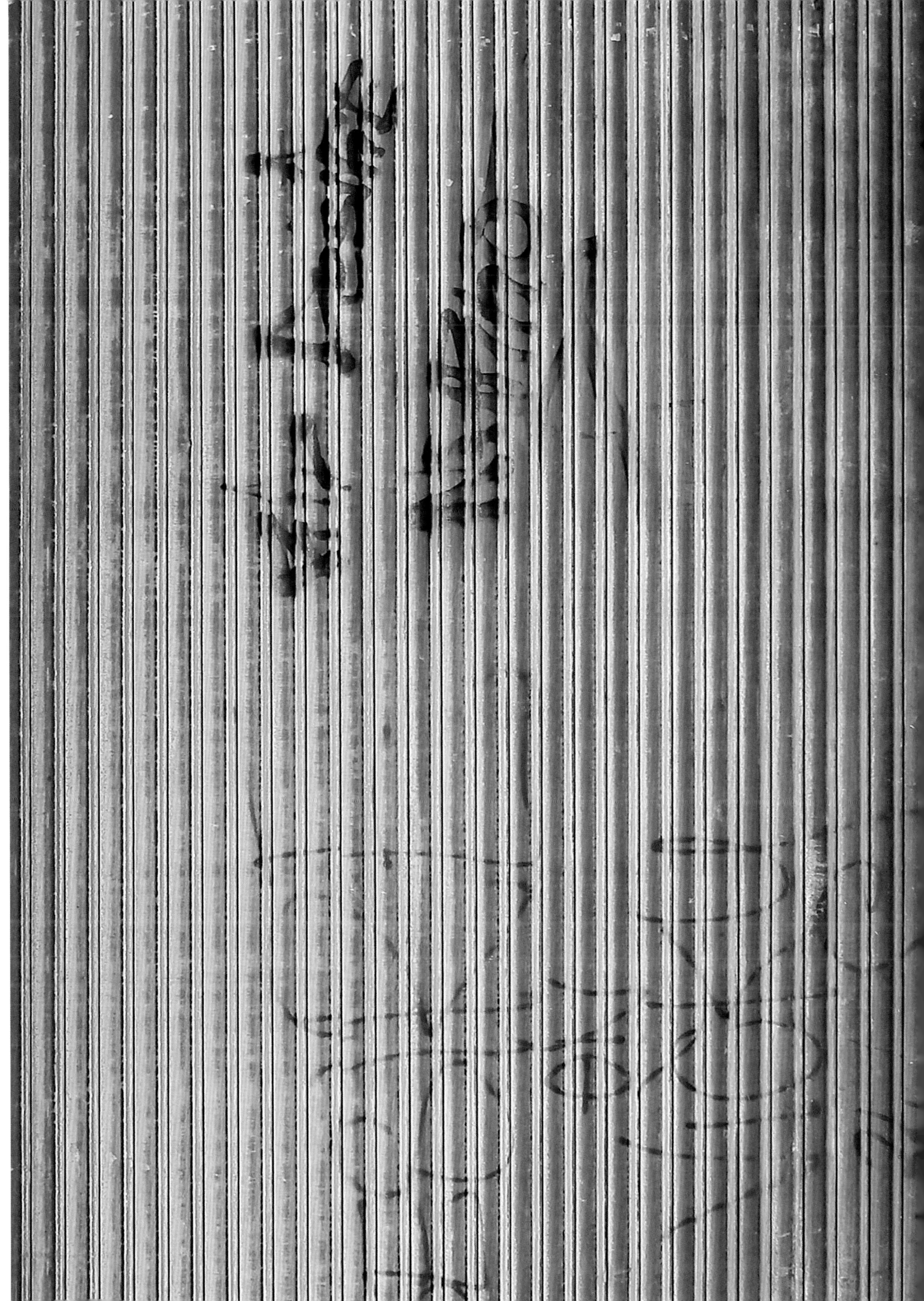

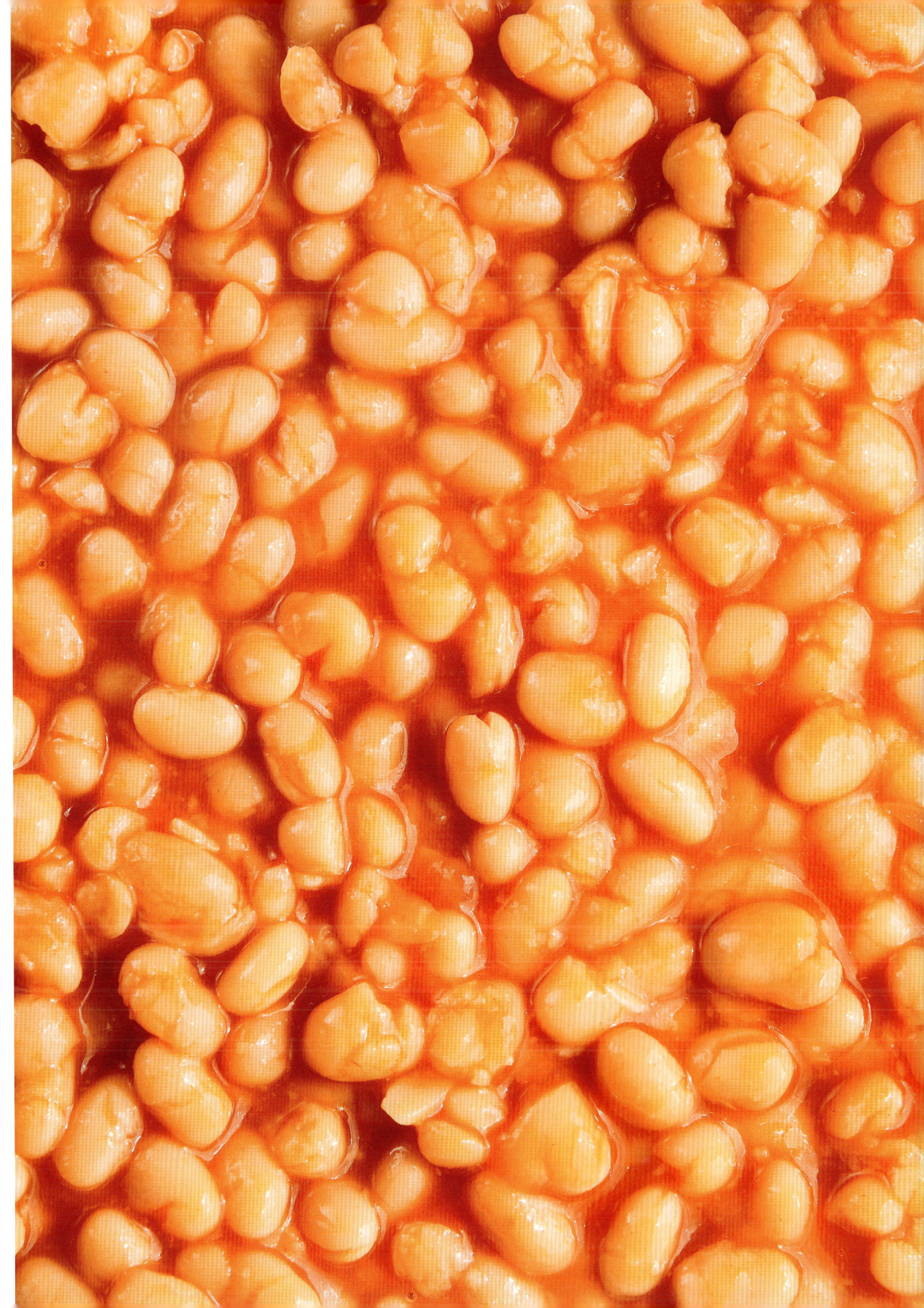

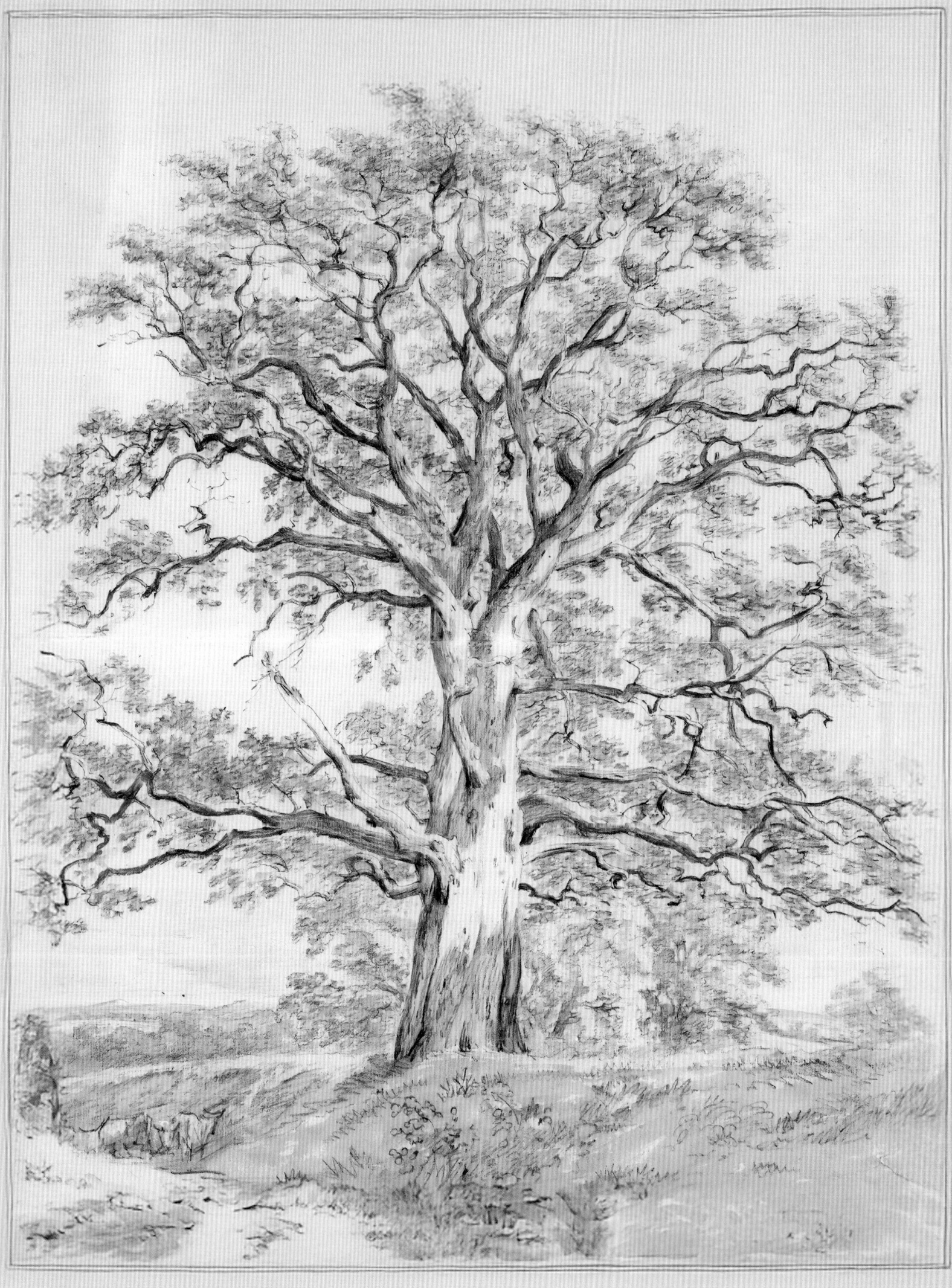

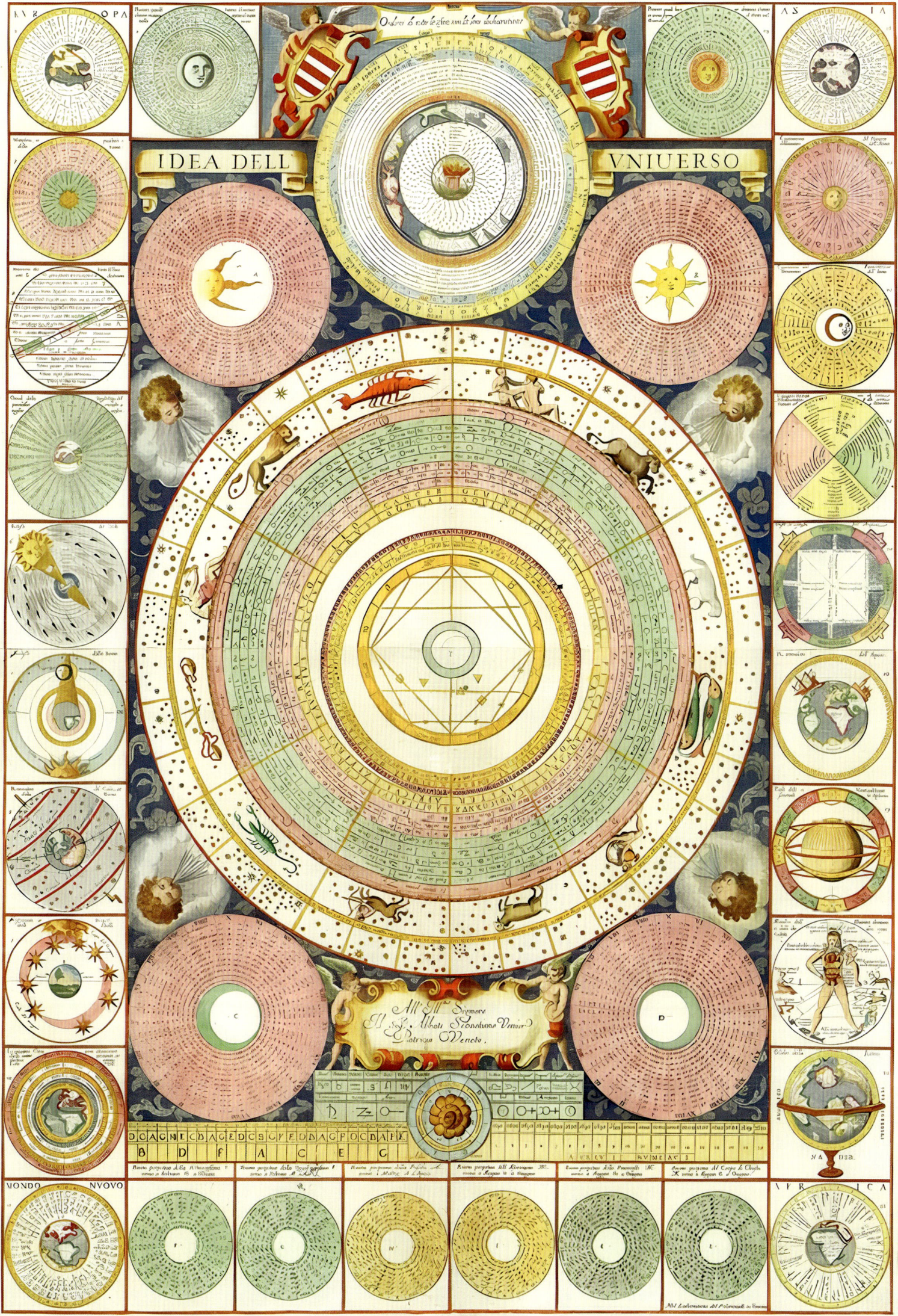

IDEA DELL VNIUERSO

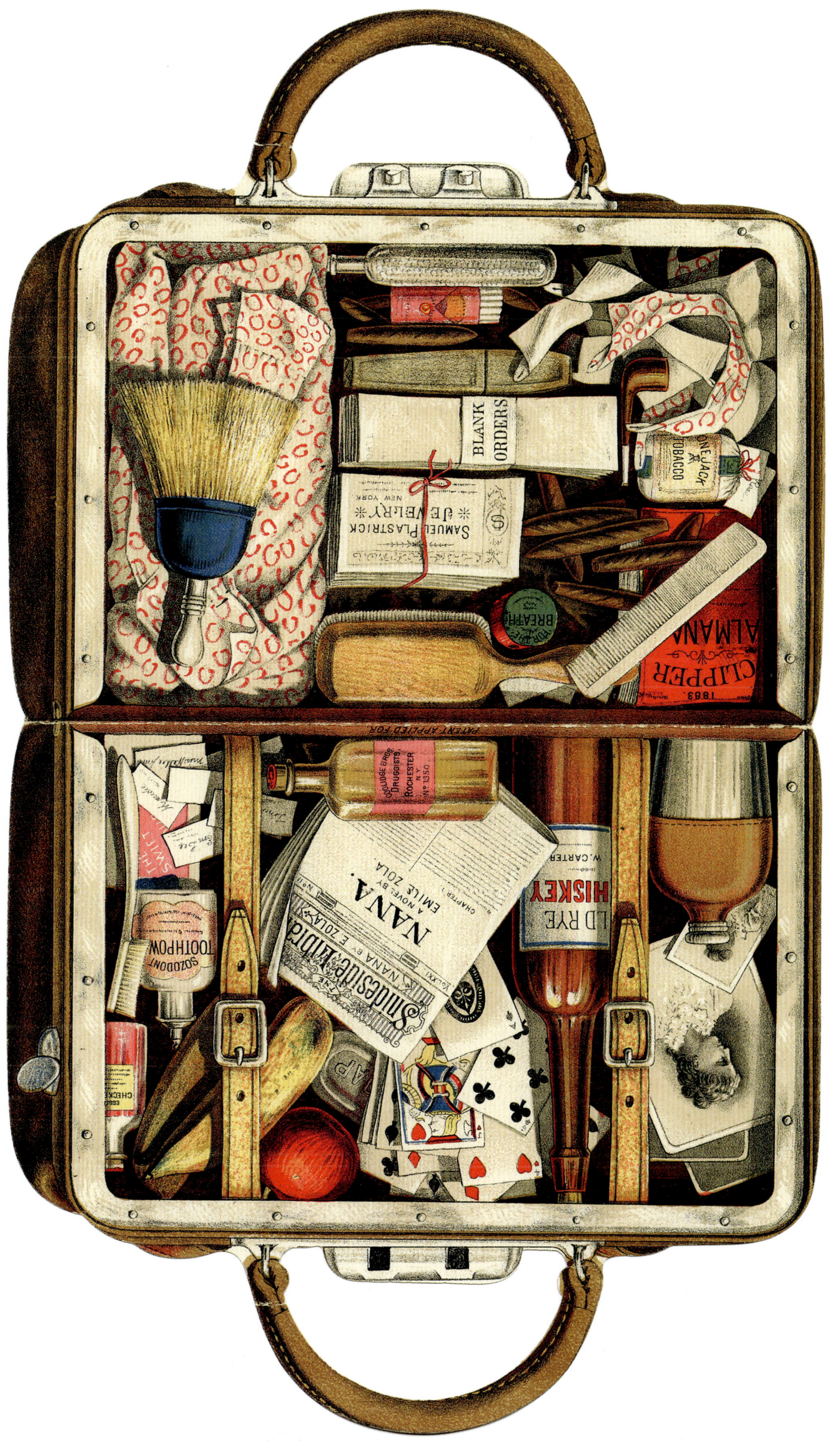

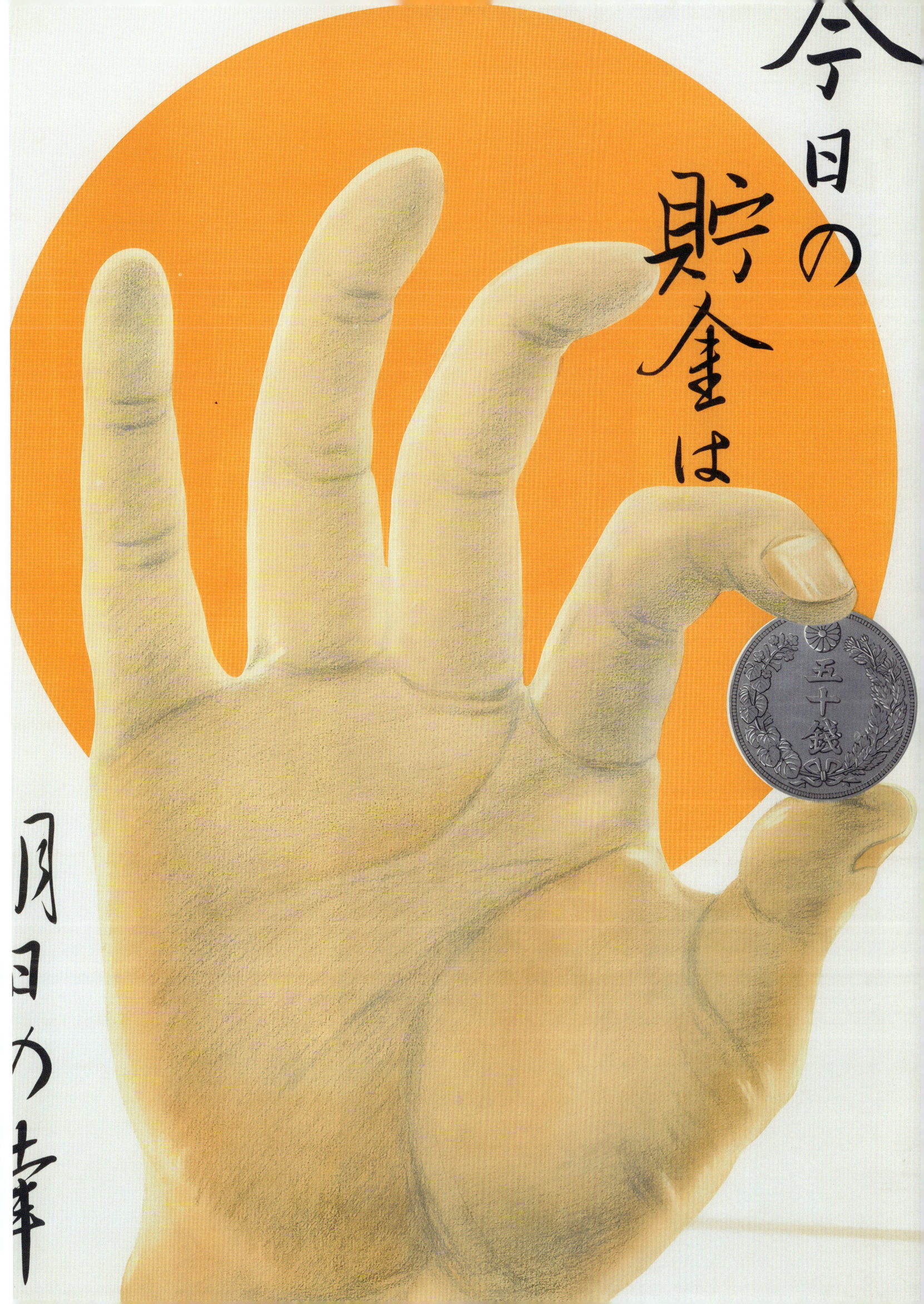

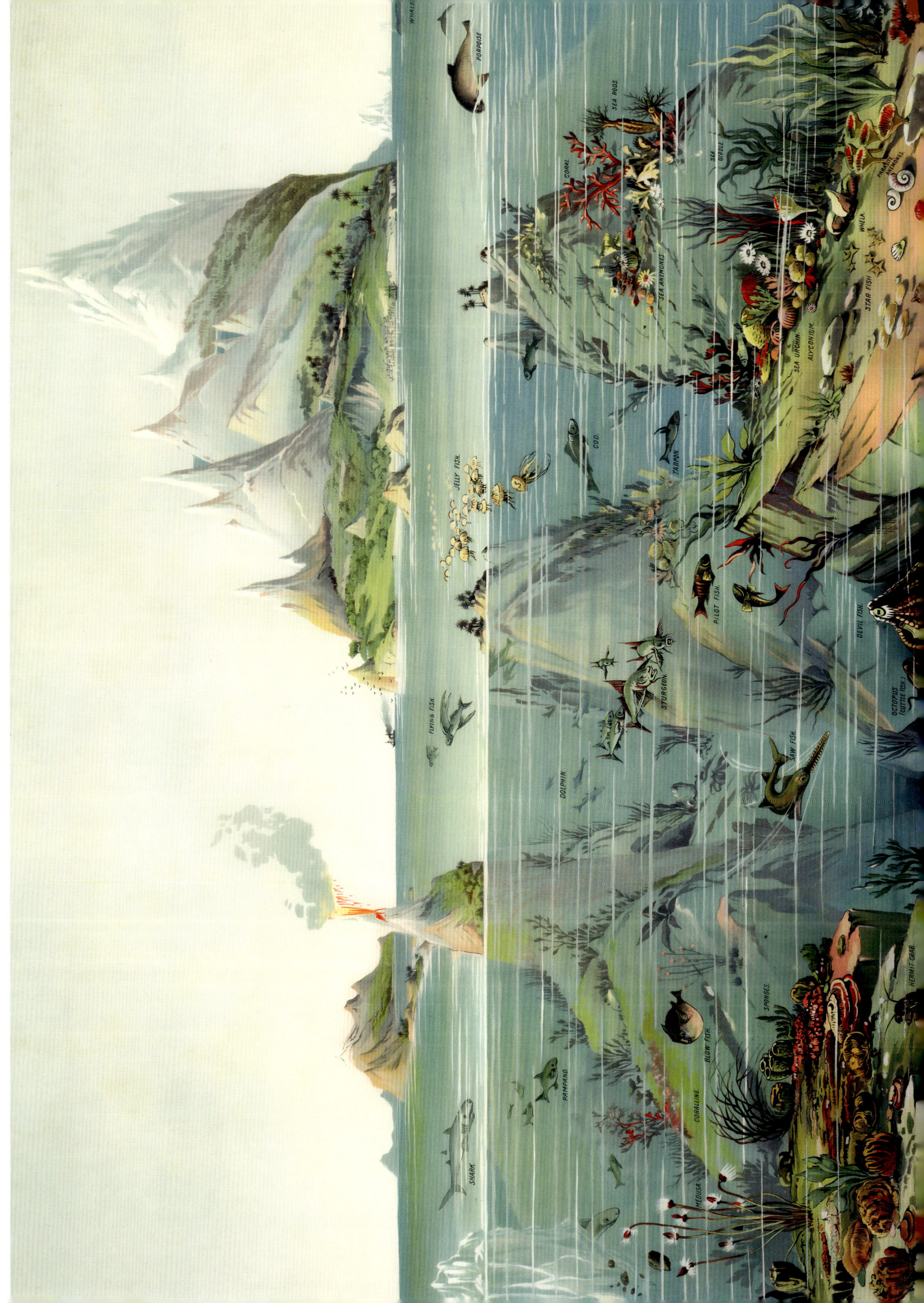

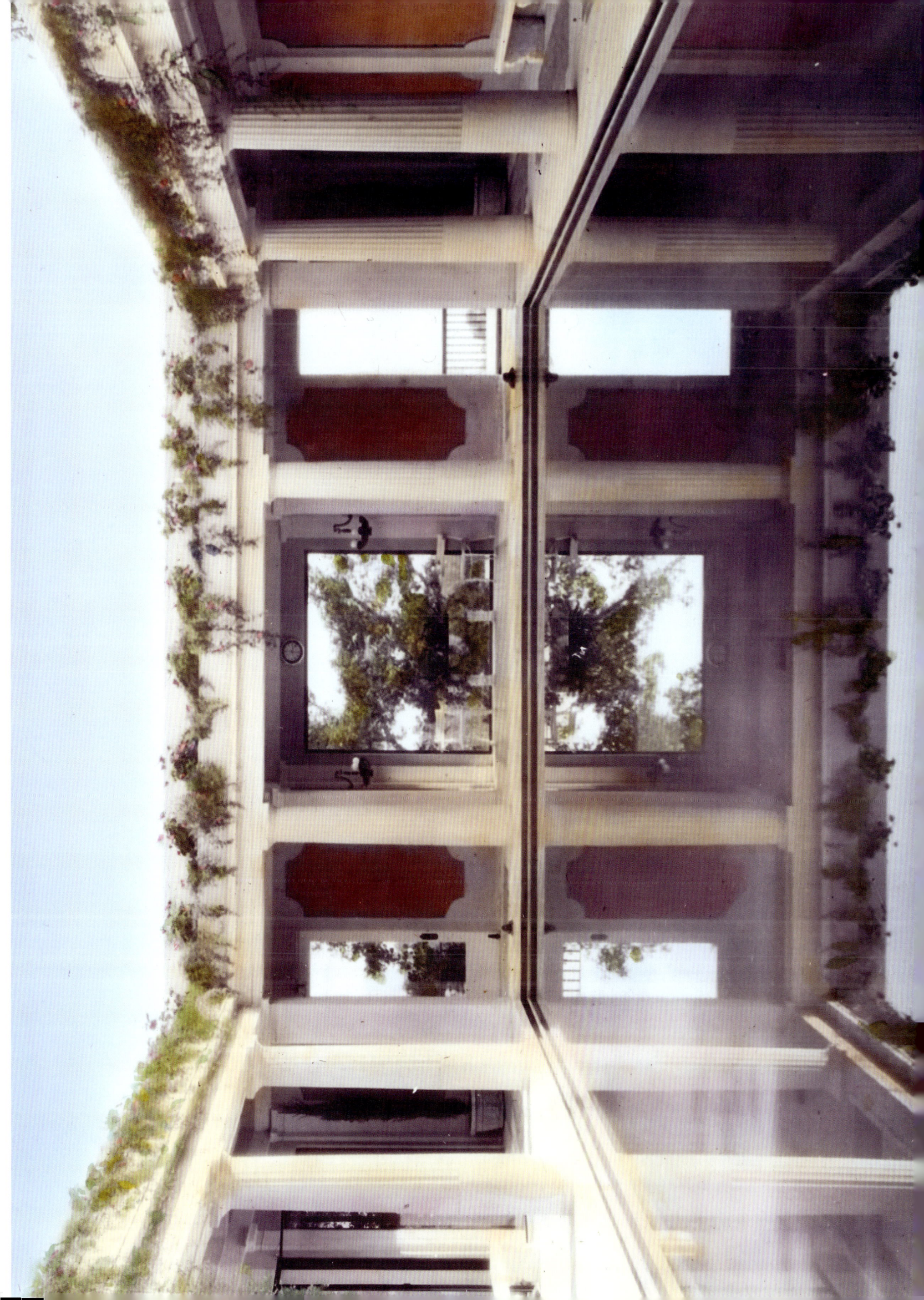

Medulla crescit extendendo se & inte-
gumenta.

Fibræ medullaris extremitas per cor-
ticem protrusa soloiq in Gemmam imbri-
catam ex foliolis nunqm renascituris.
Herbæ spindq gemæ & extenditr in infi-
nit., donec fructificao imponat ultim,
termin, antiquæ vegetaoni.

Fructificao fit, q folia distinguen-
da cohærent ni Calycem, quo rumpit
ramuli apex in floren annuo spatio
praecocius, q fructus ex medullari
substantia nequit novam vitam in-
choare, nisi prius stamin essent,
a Lignea absorpta fuerit ab hamo-
re pistilli. Vide doct. de Gemis.

Nova creao nulla, sed continuata ge-
nerao, q Cortex seminis estat ple radicis medullari.

80. Radix (79) aliment hauriens, herbam
3 (81) q fructificaoni (IV) producens, cpo-
nit, medulla, Ligno, Libro, cortice; estat,
9 e Caudice & radicula.

A. Radicula e ps radicis fibrosa, in
qm terminat Caudex descendens, & qua
radix nutriment hauxrit pro vegeta-
bilis sustentaoni. Wurzelfasernn.

B. Caudex descendens sub terra se
sim subducit, & radiculas (A) profert, a Bota-
nicis ex varia structura variis nnib, distinc-
tus 1. ppendicularis, quo recta descendit.

2. horizontalis, qd sub terra transversim
extendit: iris

3. simplex (fig. 129) qe n subdvidit

4. Ramosa (F. 130) qe in laterales ramos dvidit

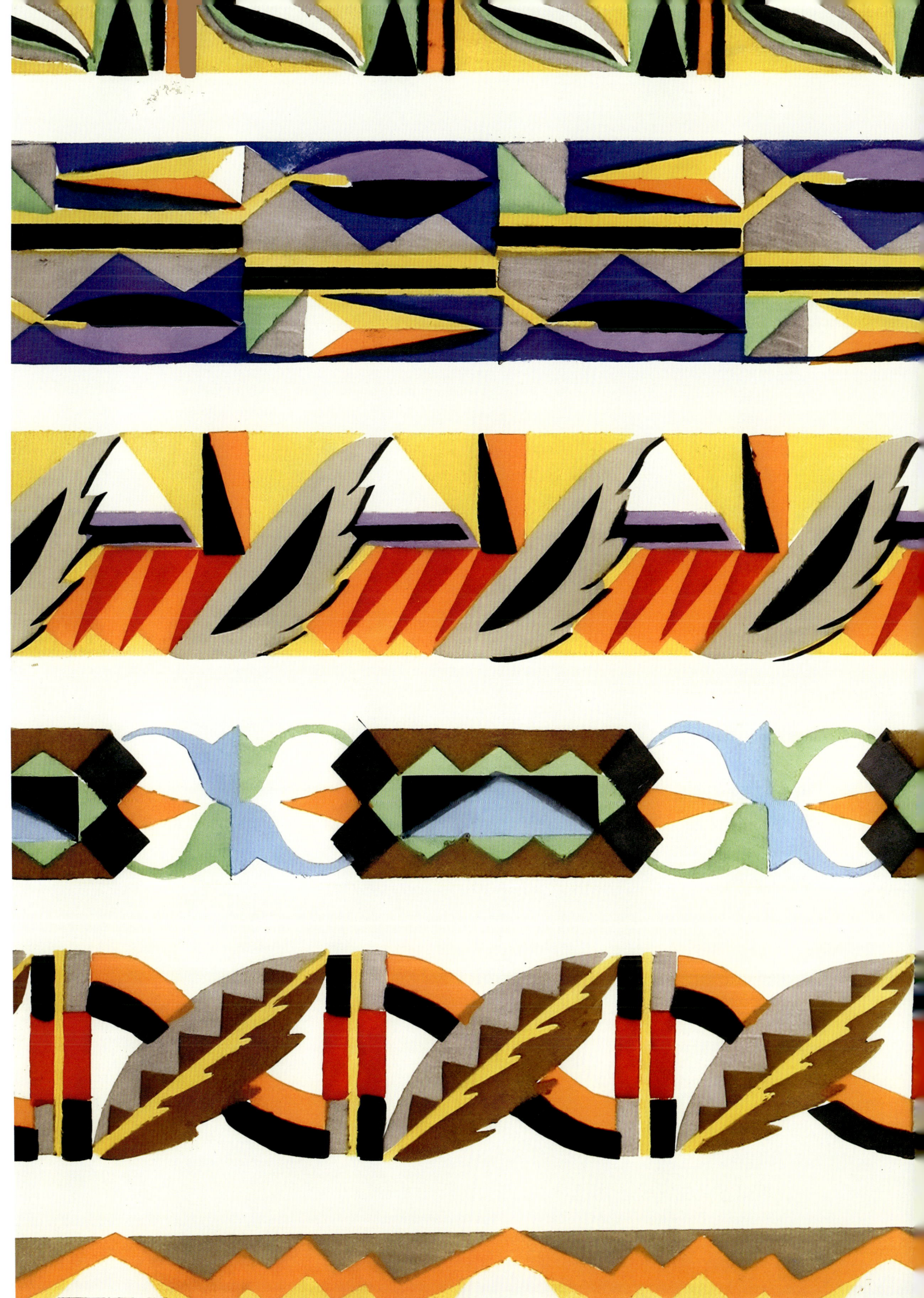

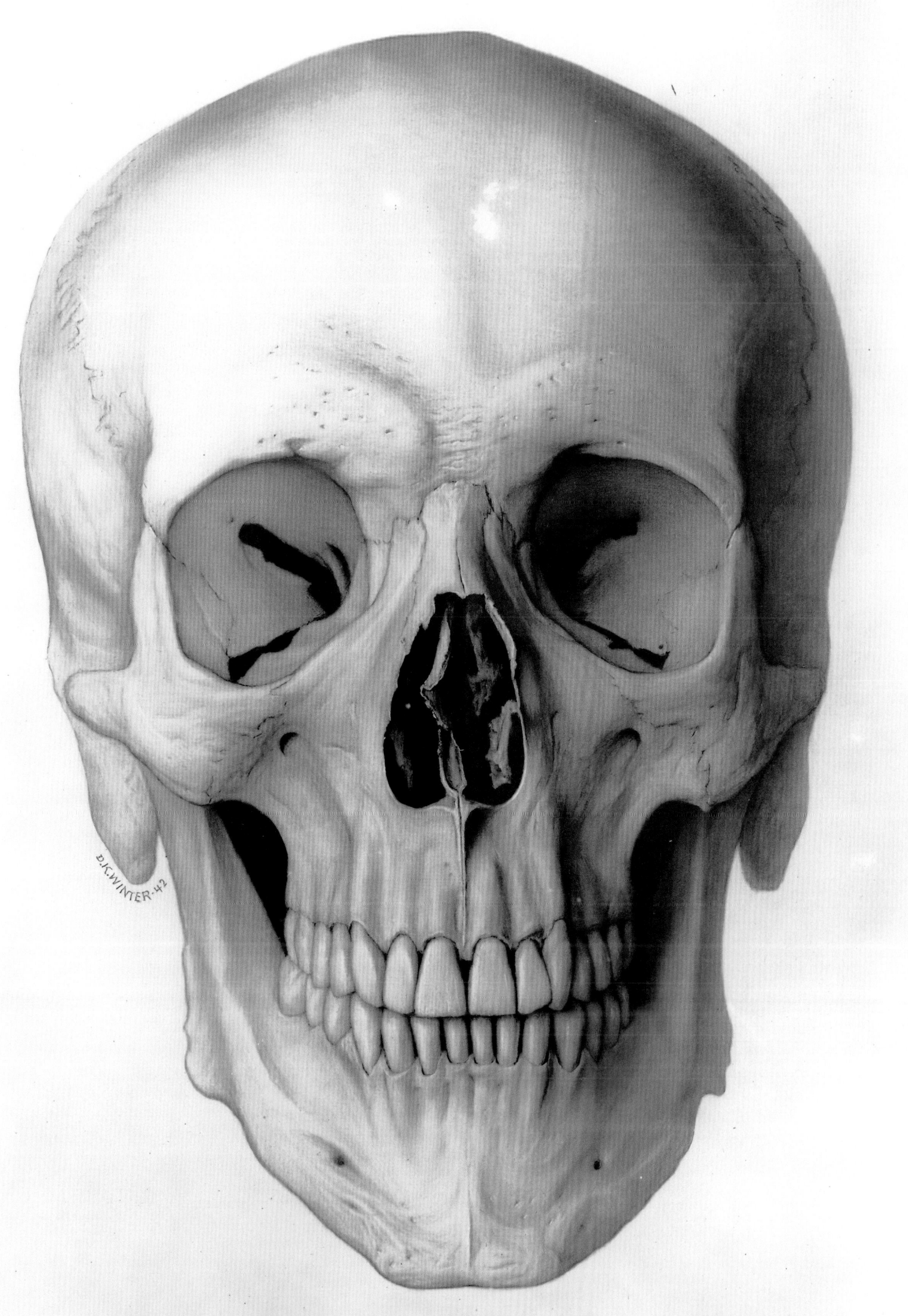

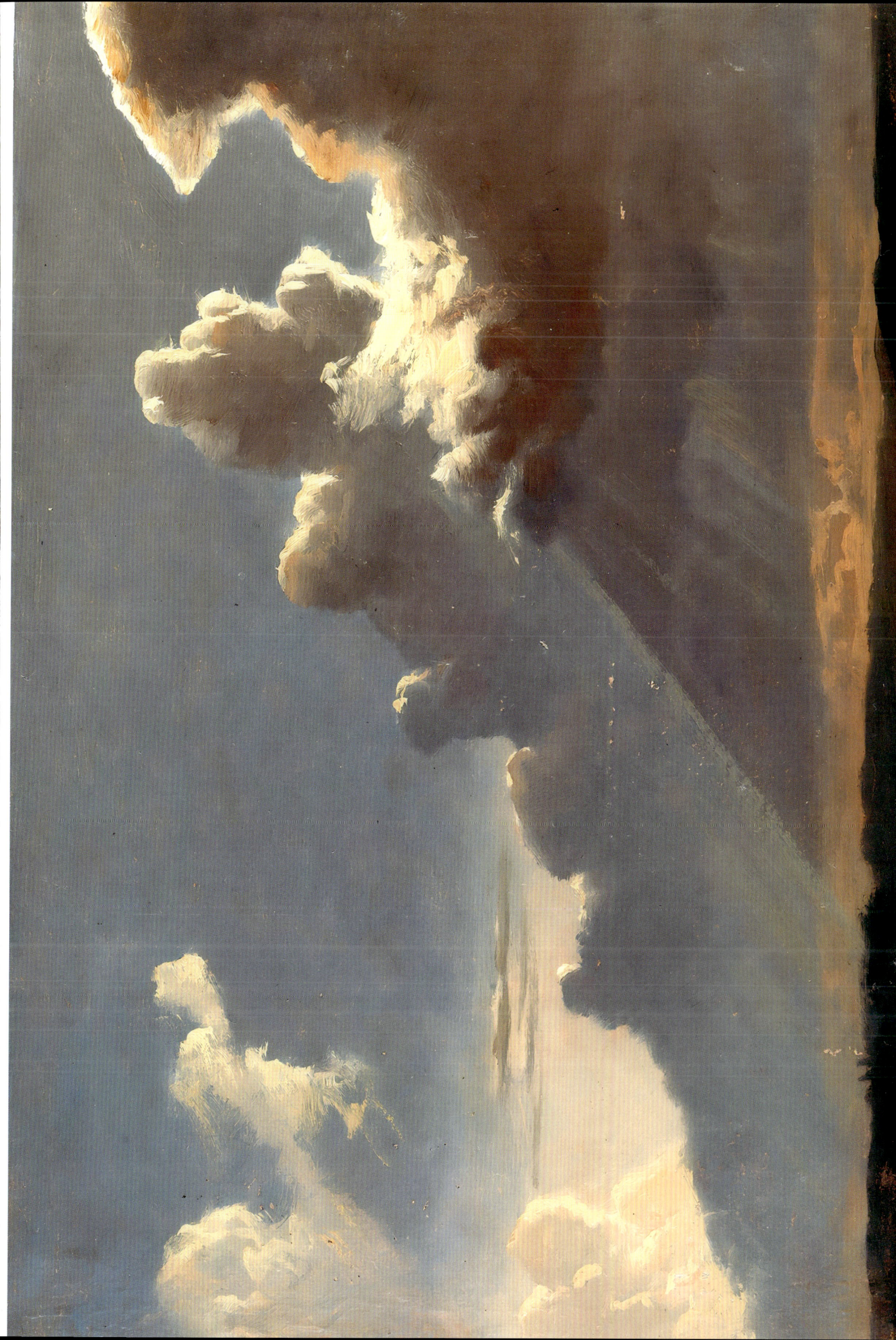

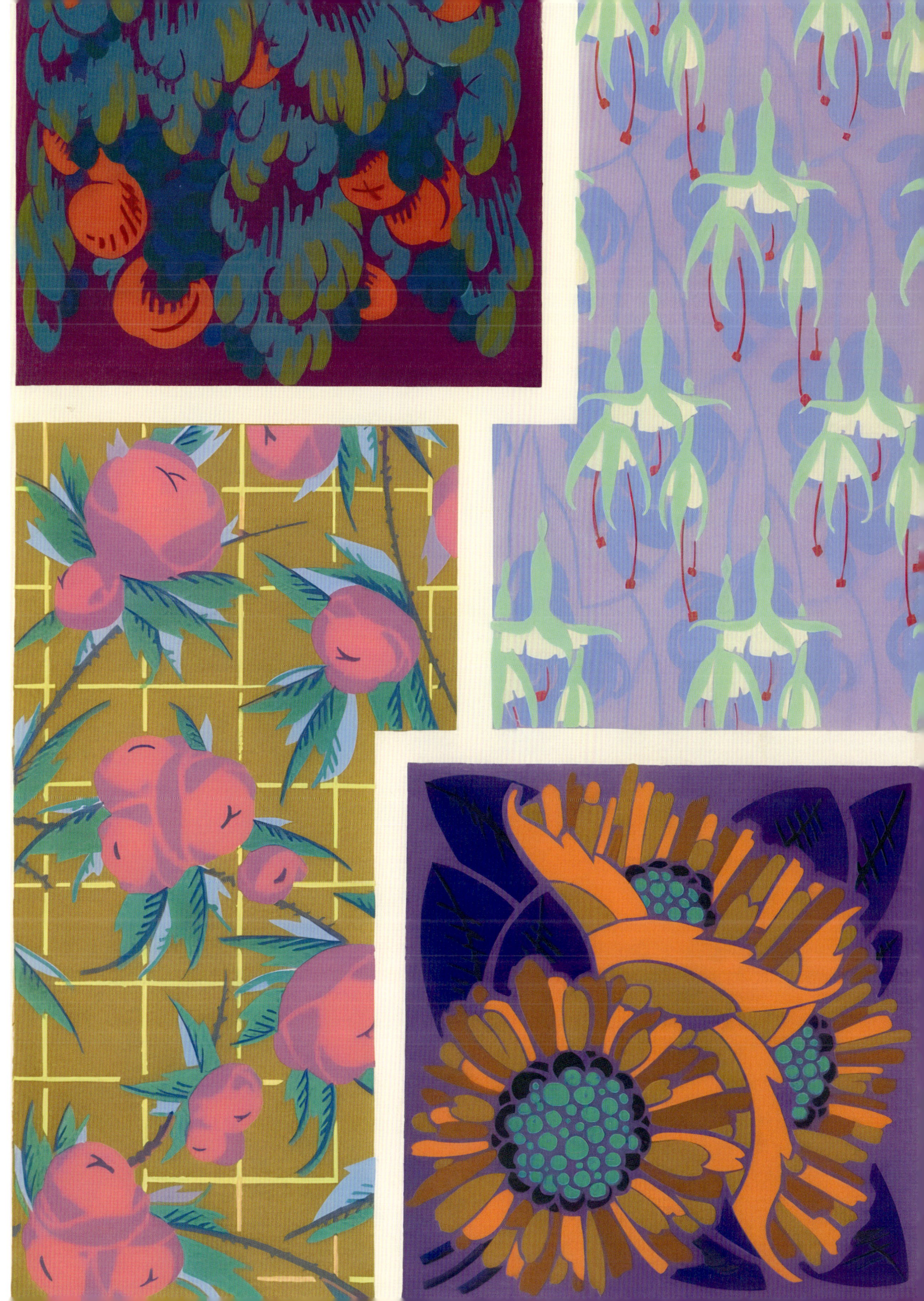

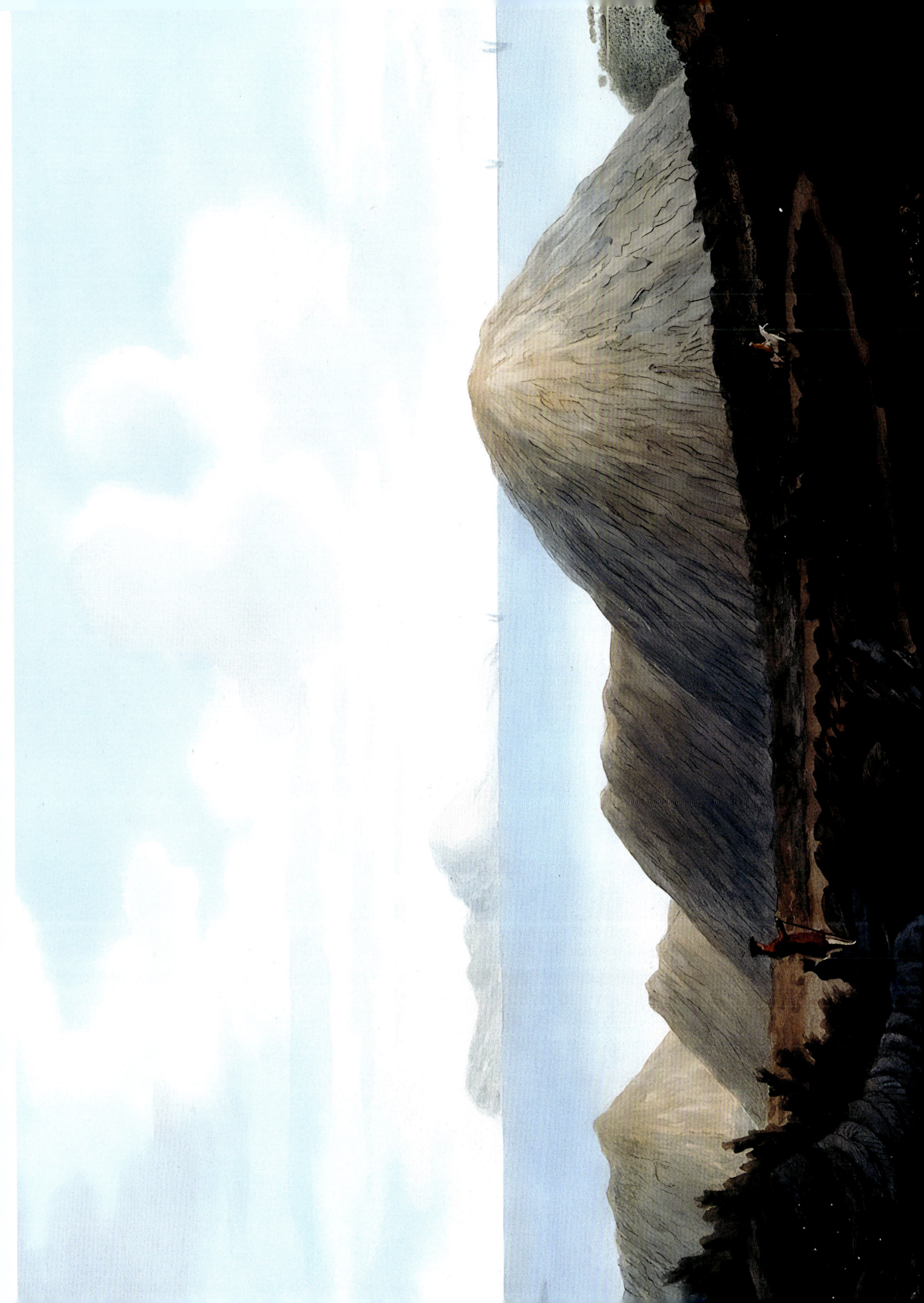

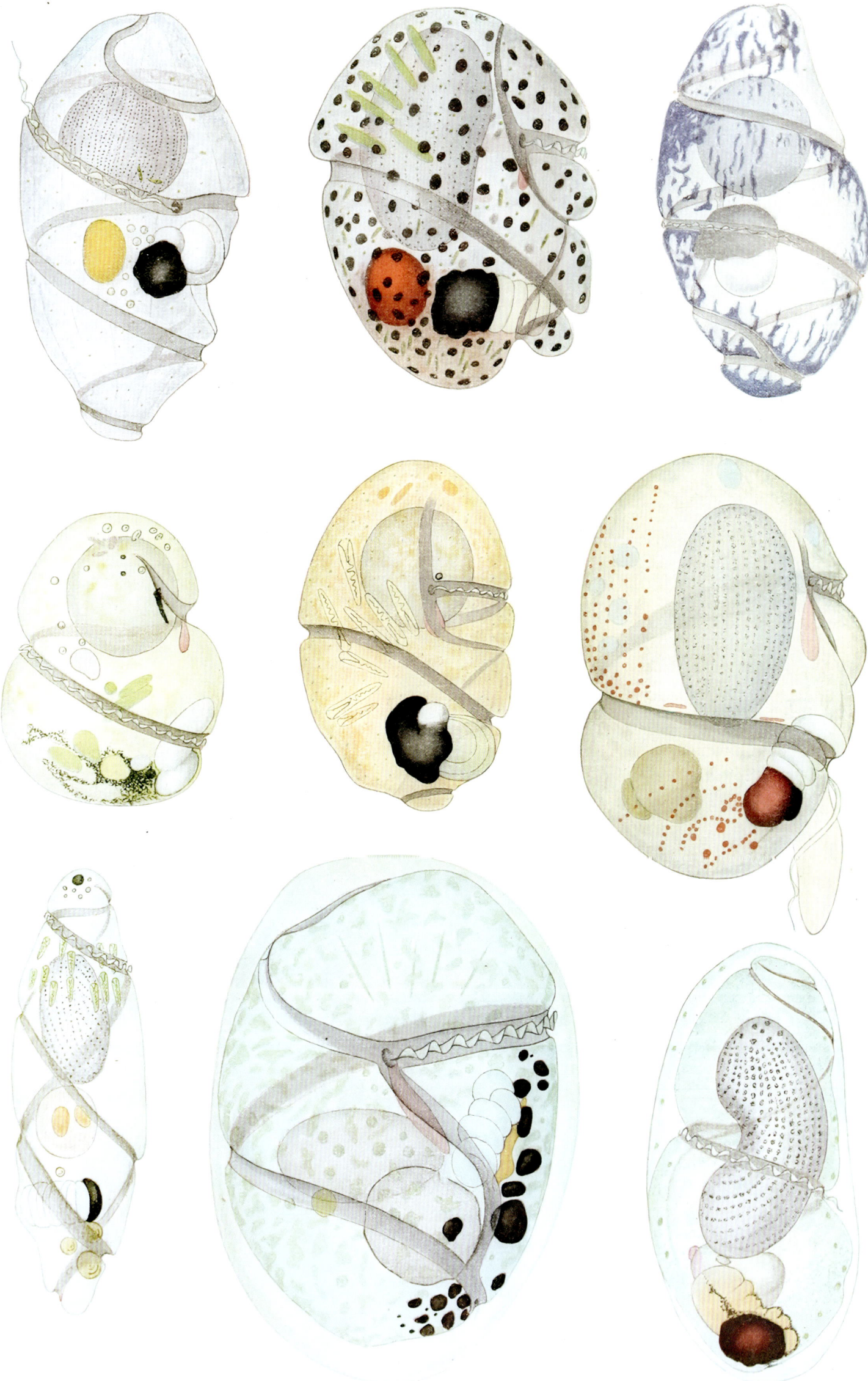

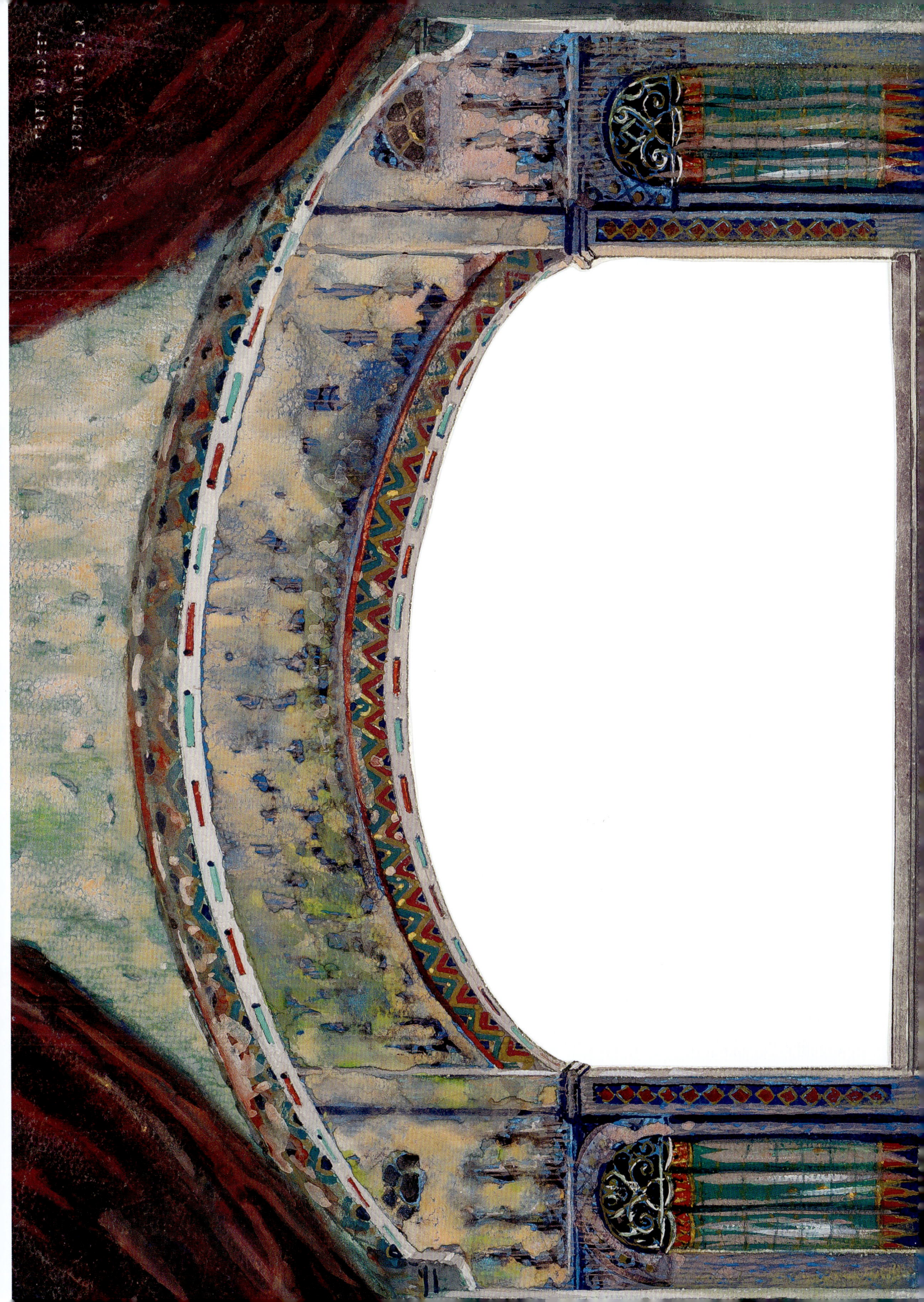

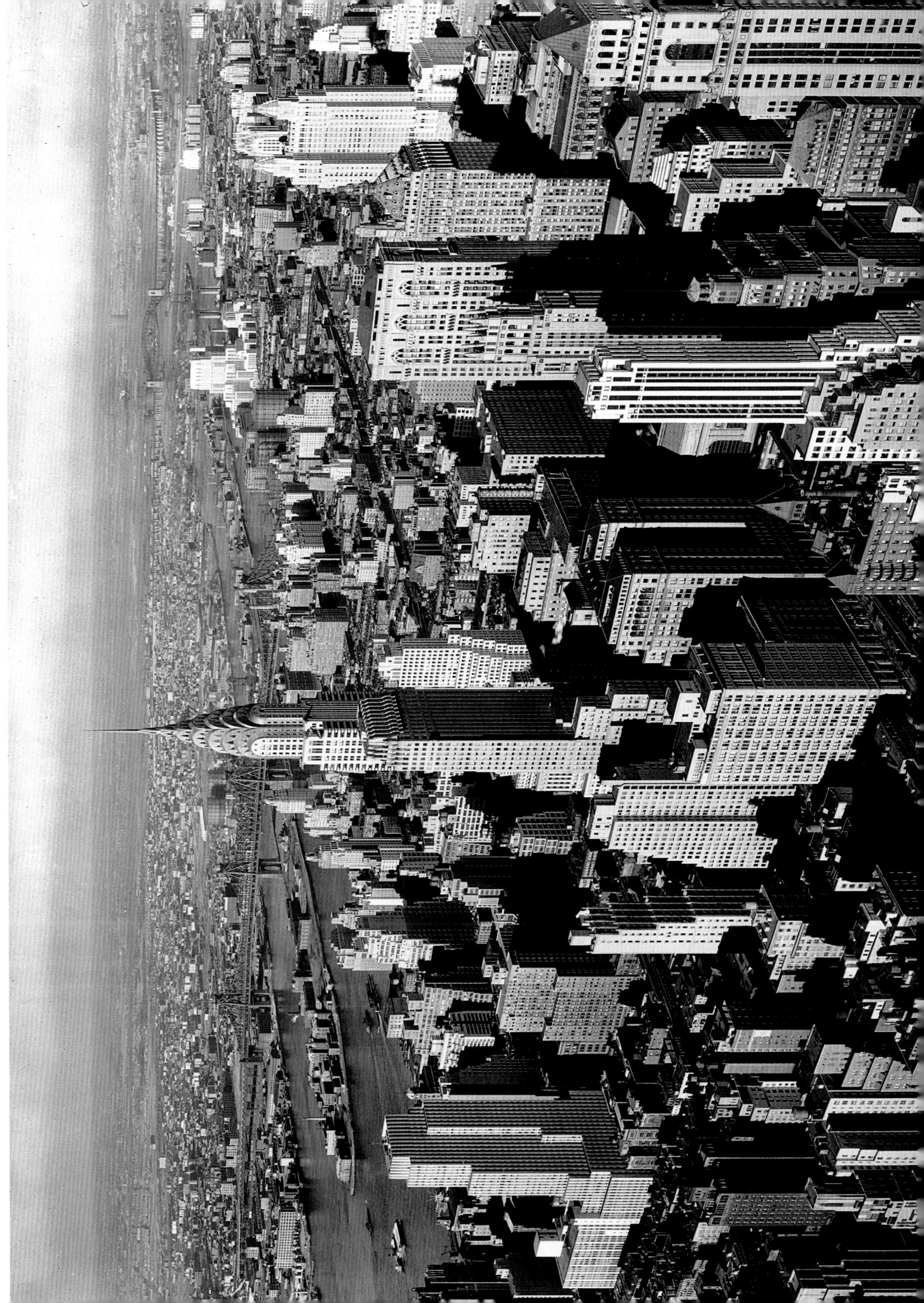

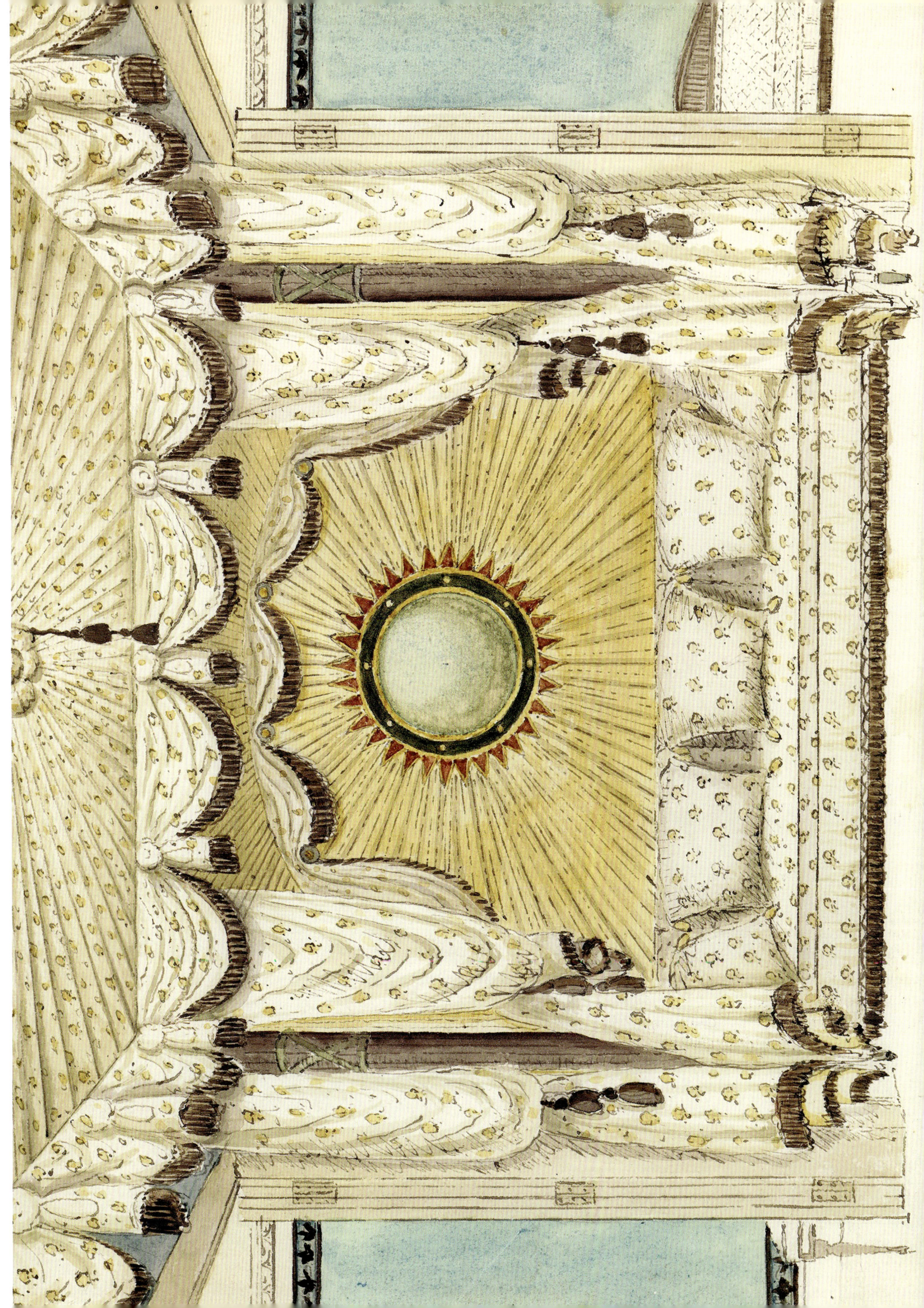

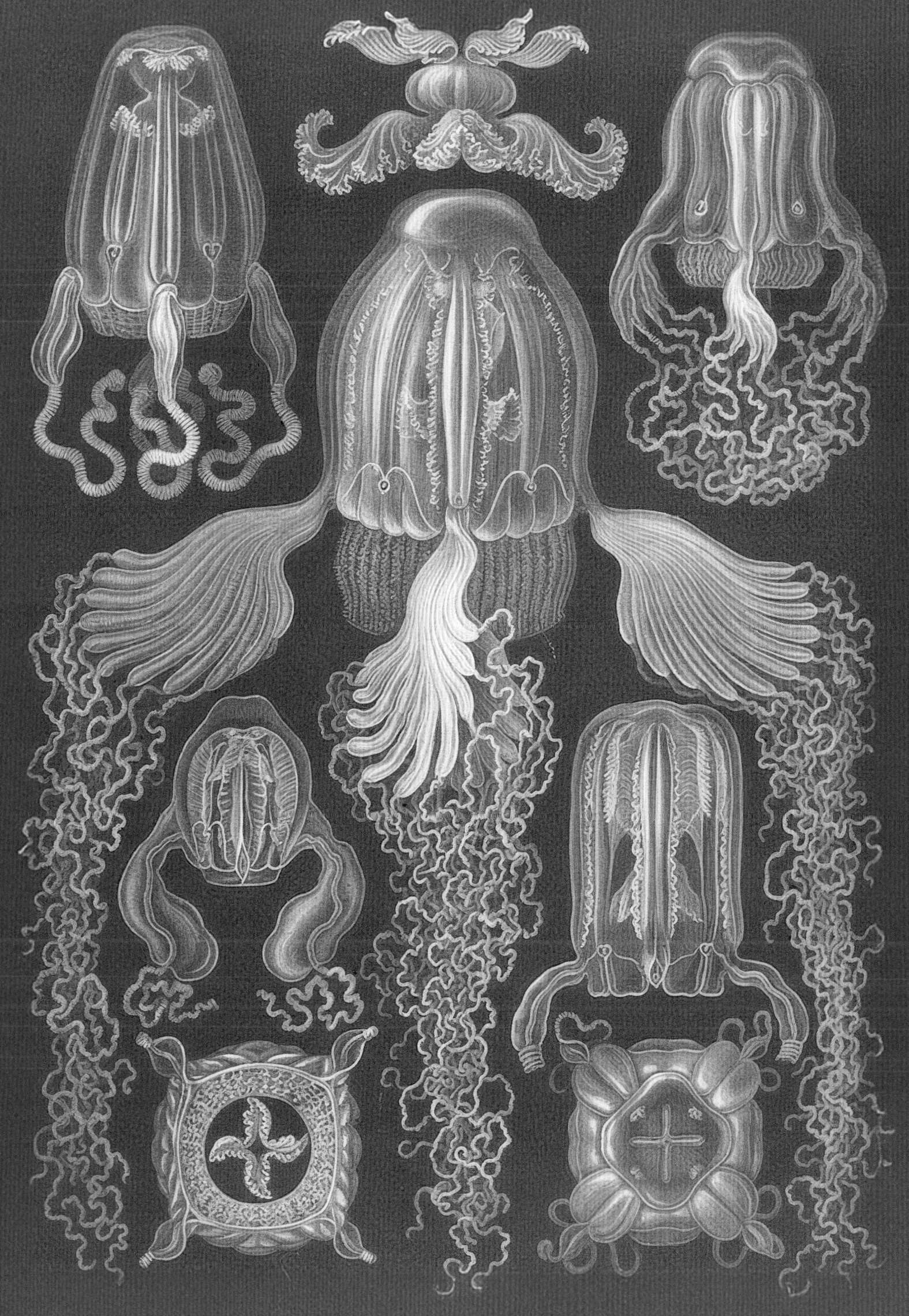

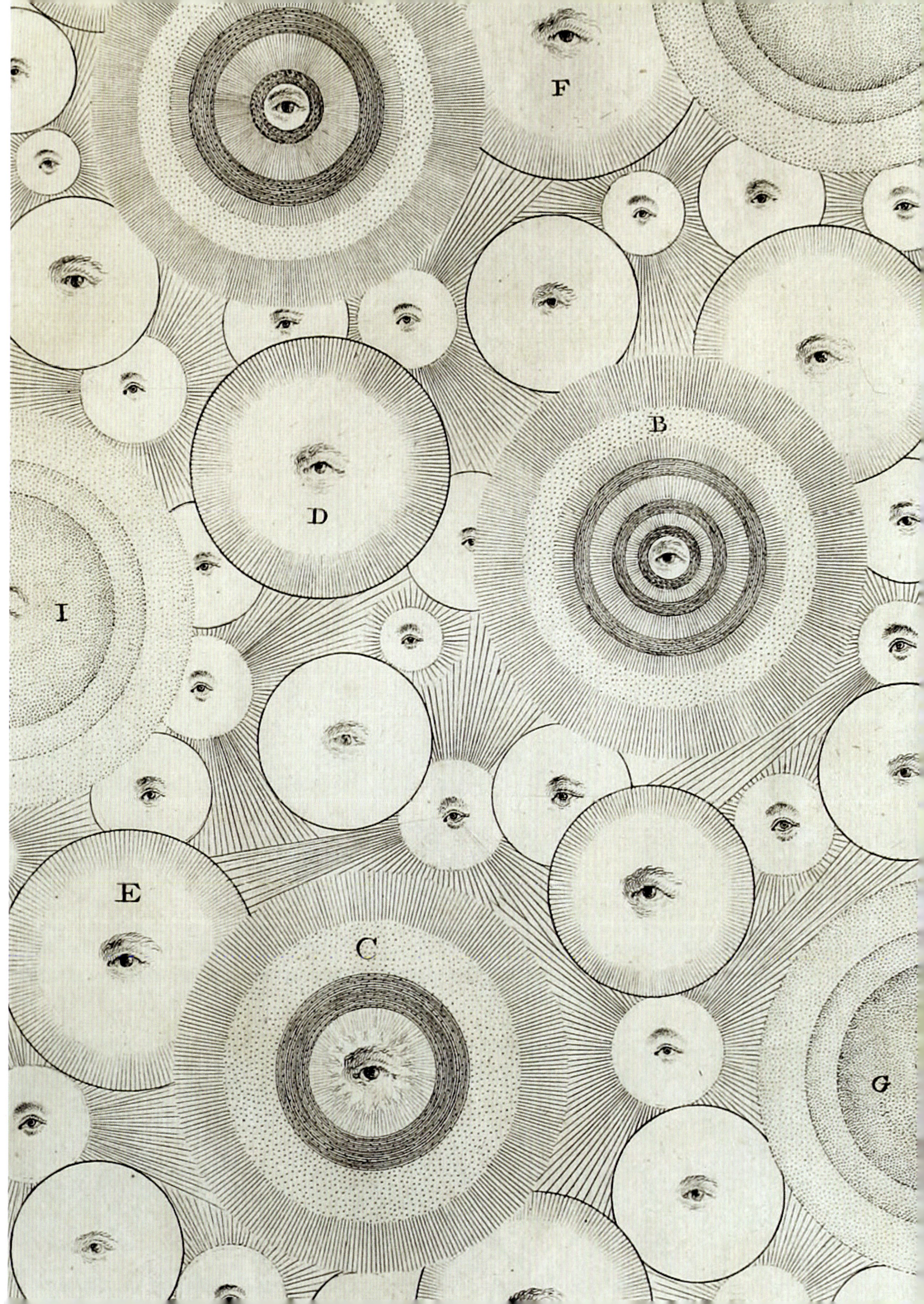

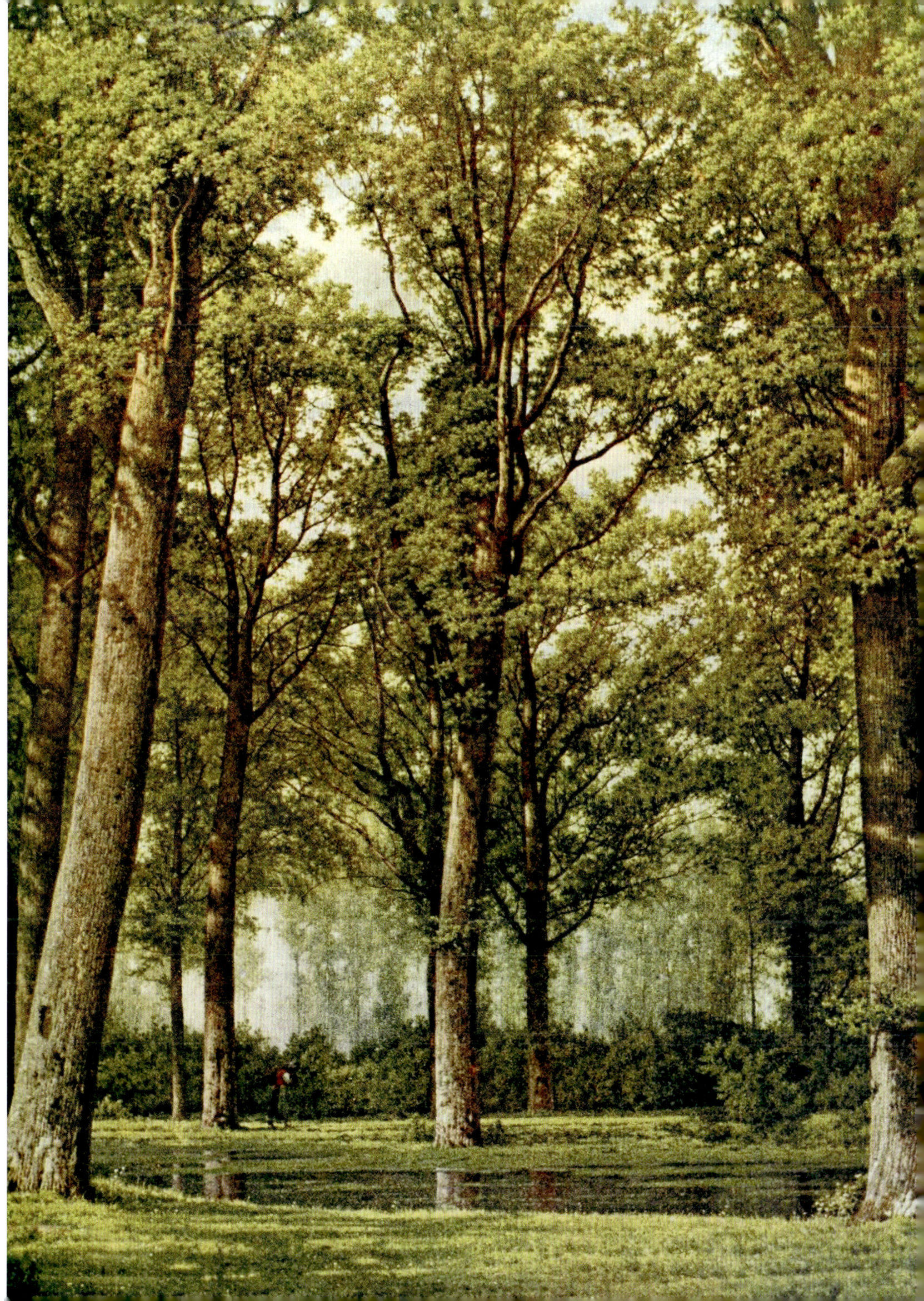

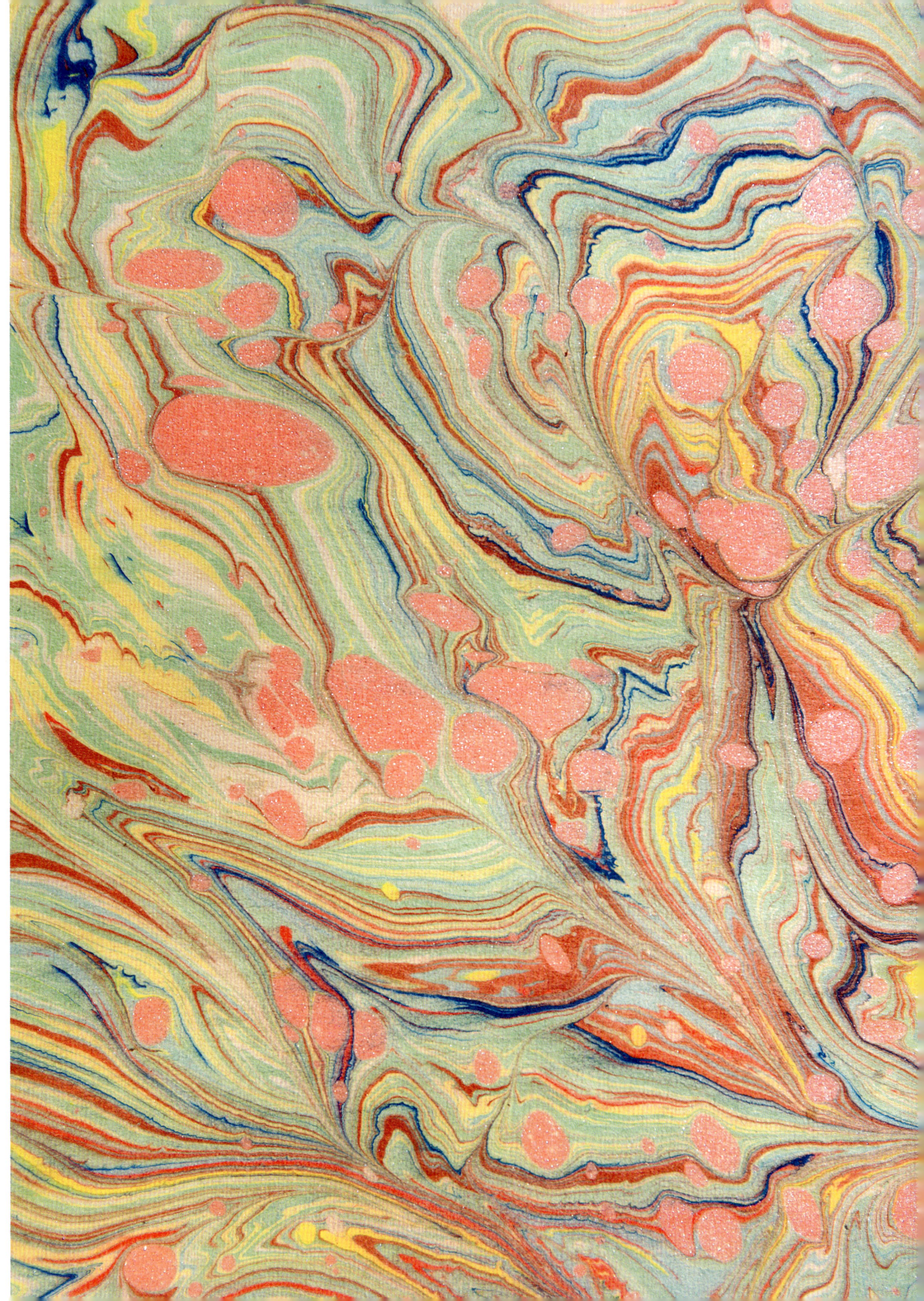

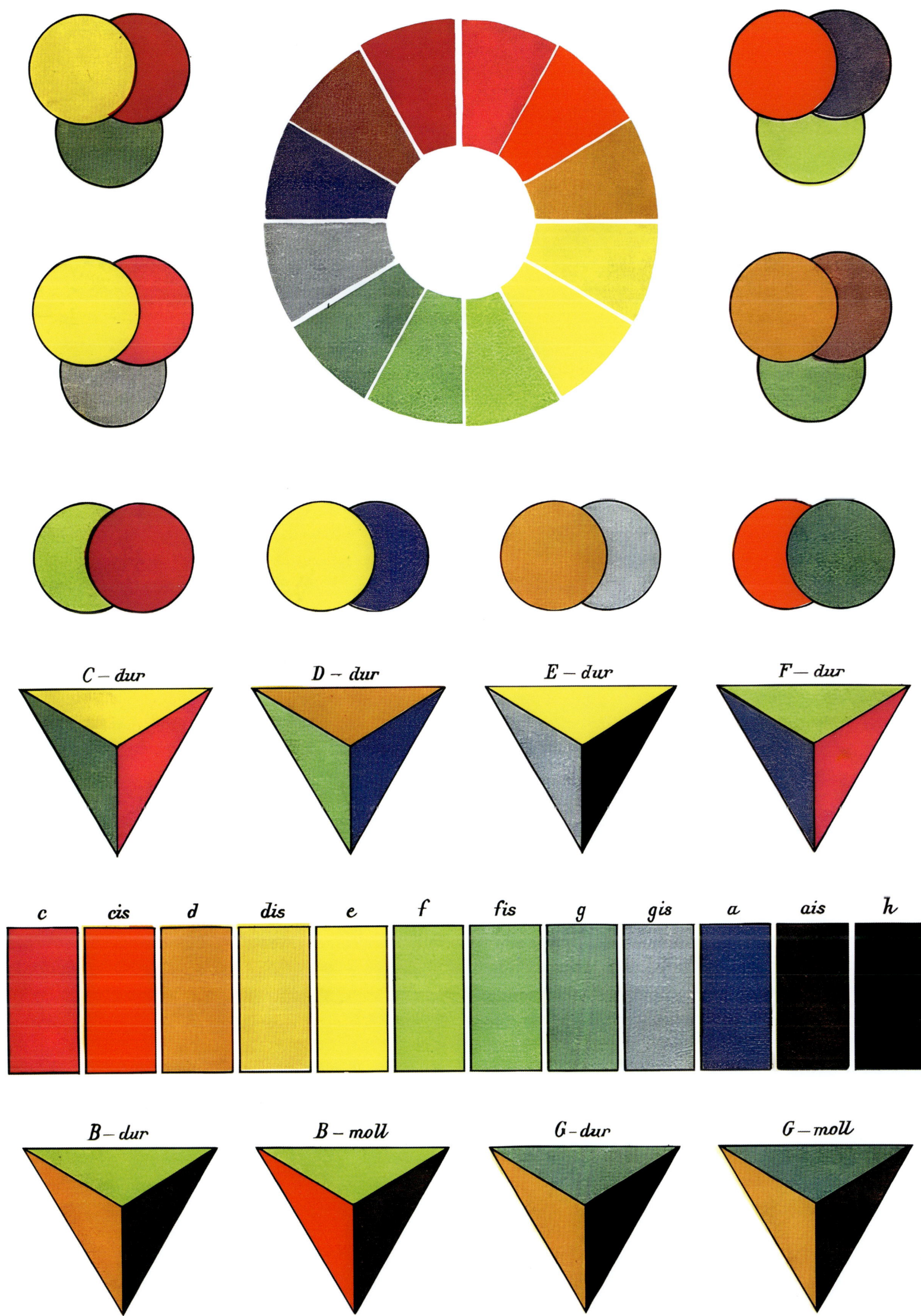

C — dur

D — dur

E — dur

F — dur

c cis d dis e f fis g gis a ais h

B — dur

B — moll

G — dur

G — moll

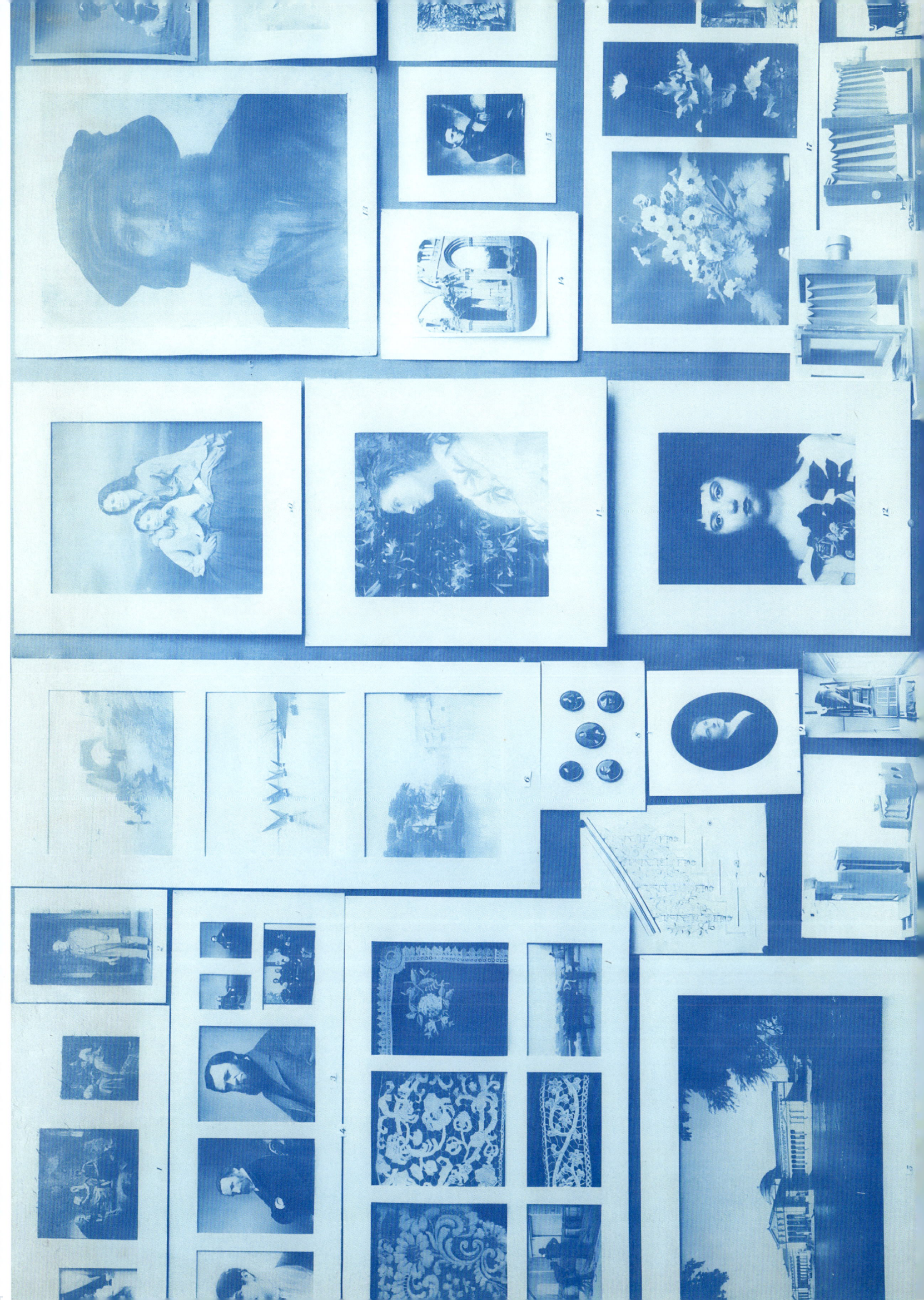

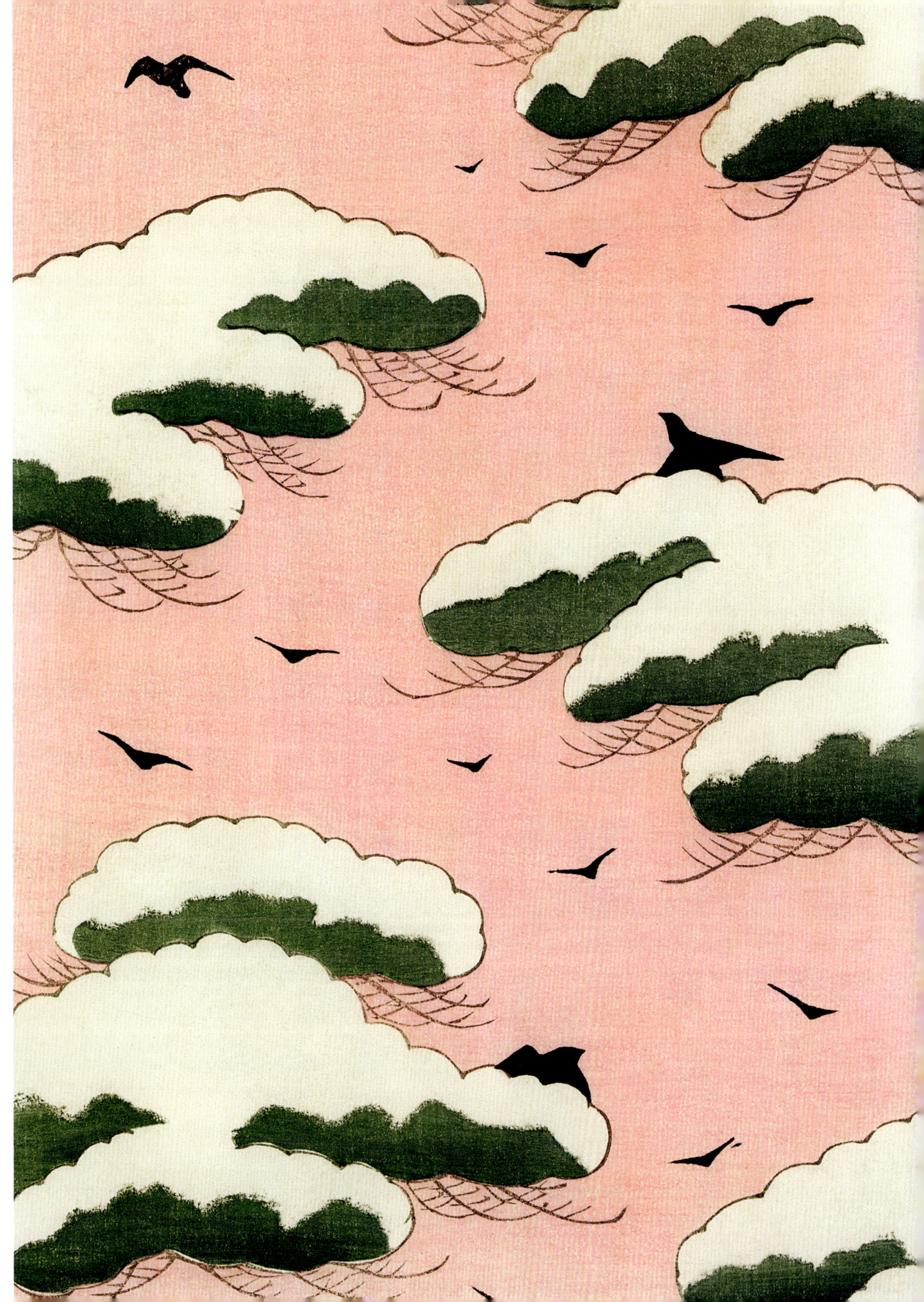

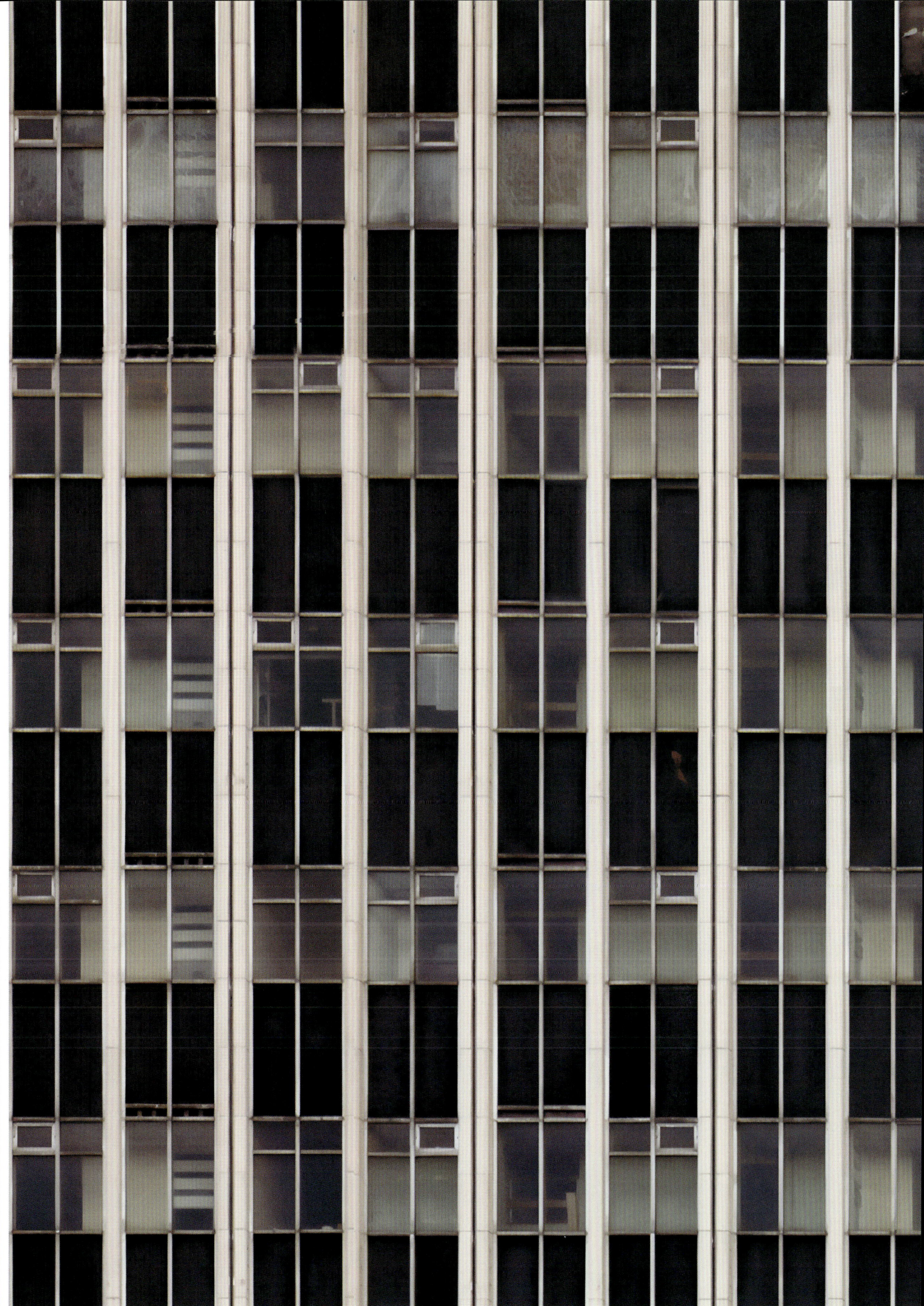

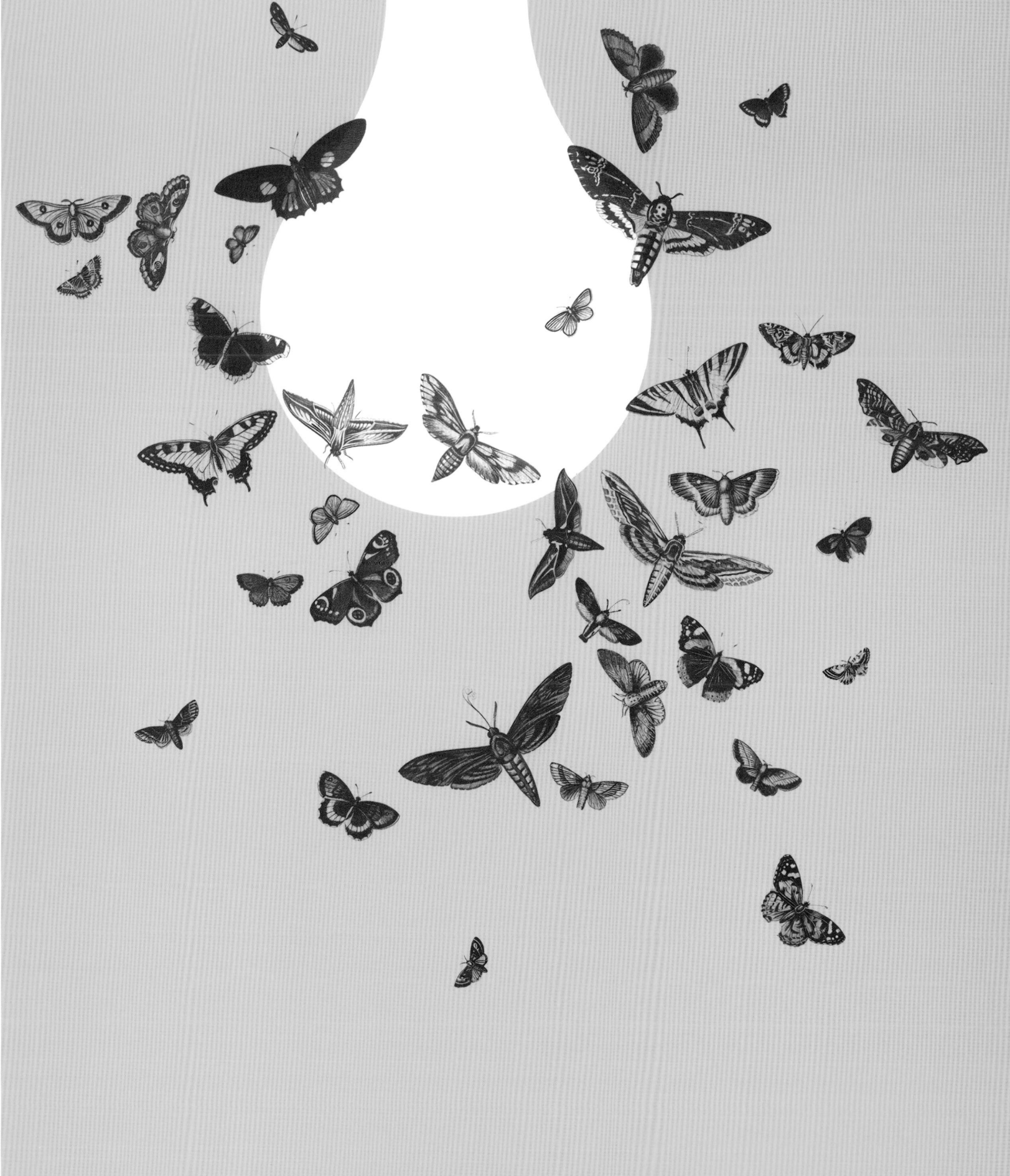

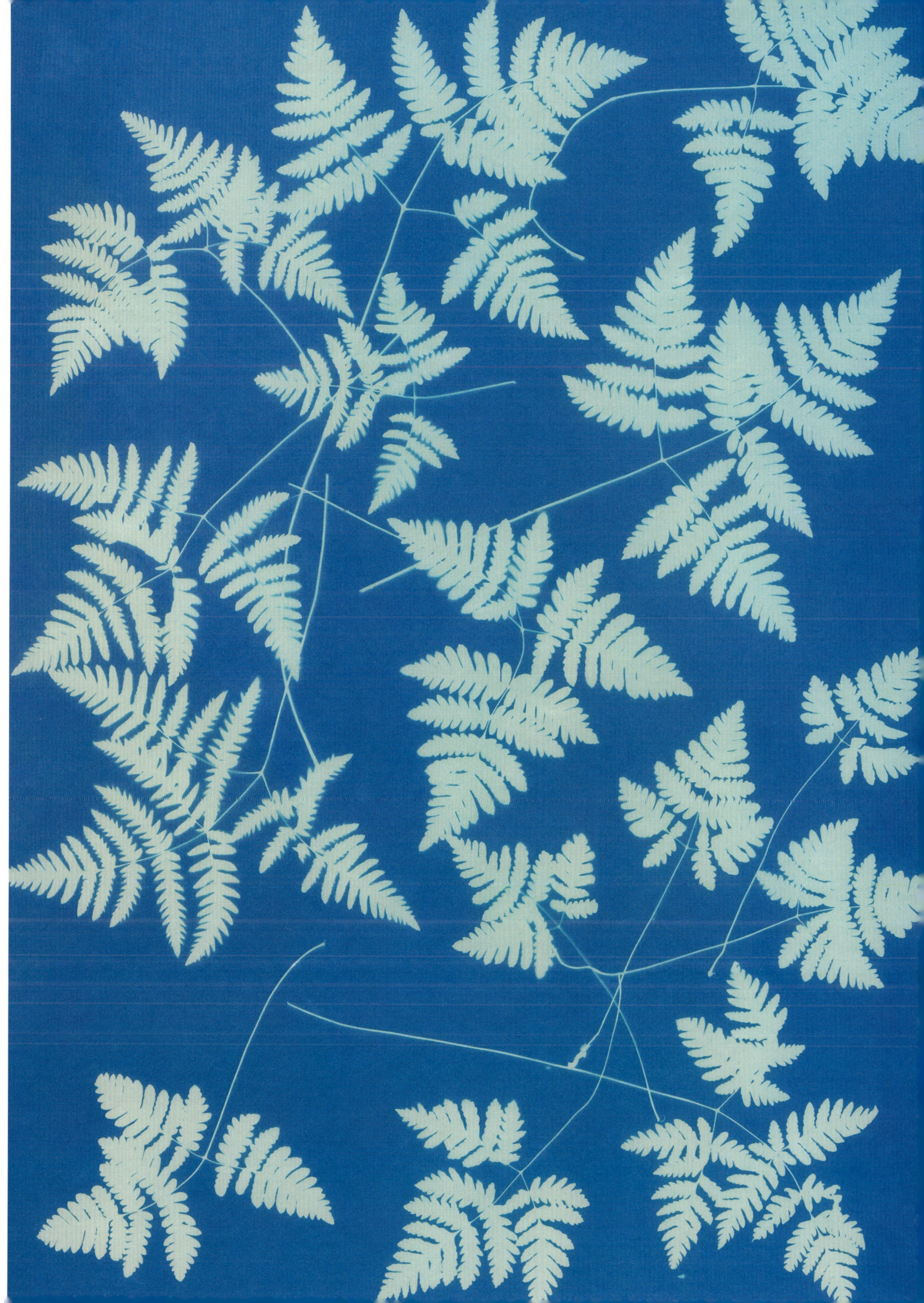

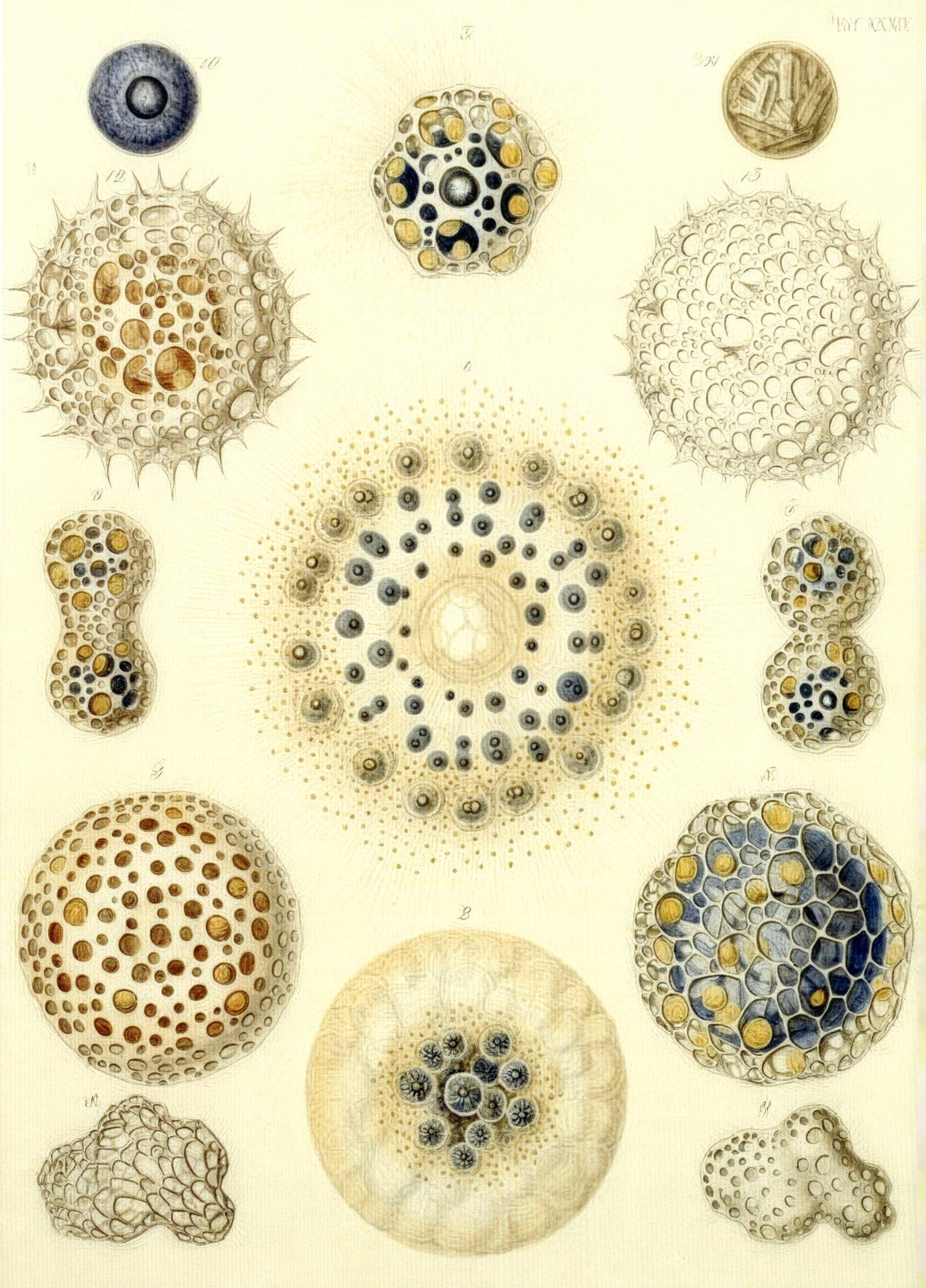

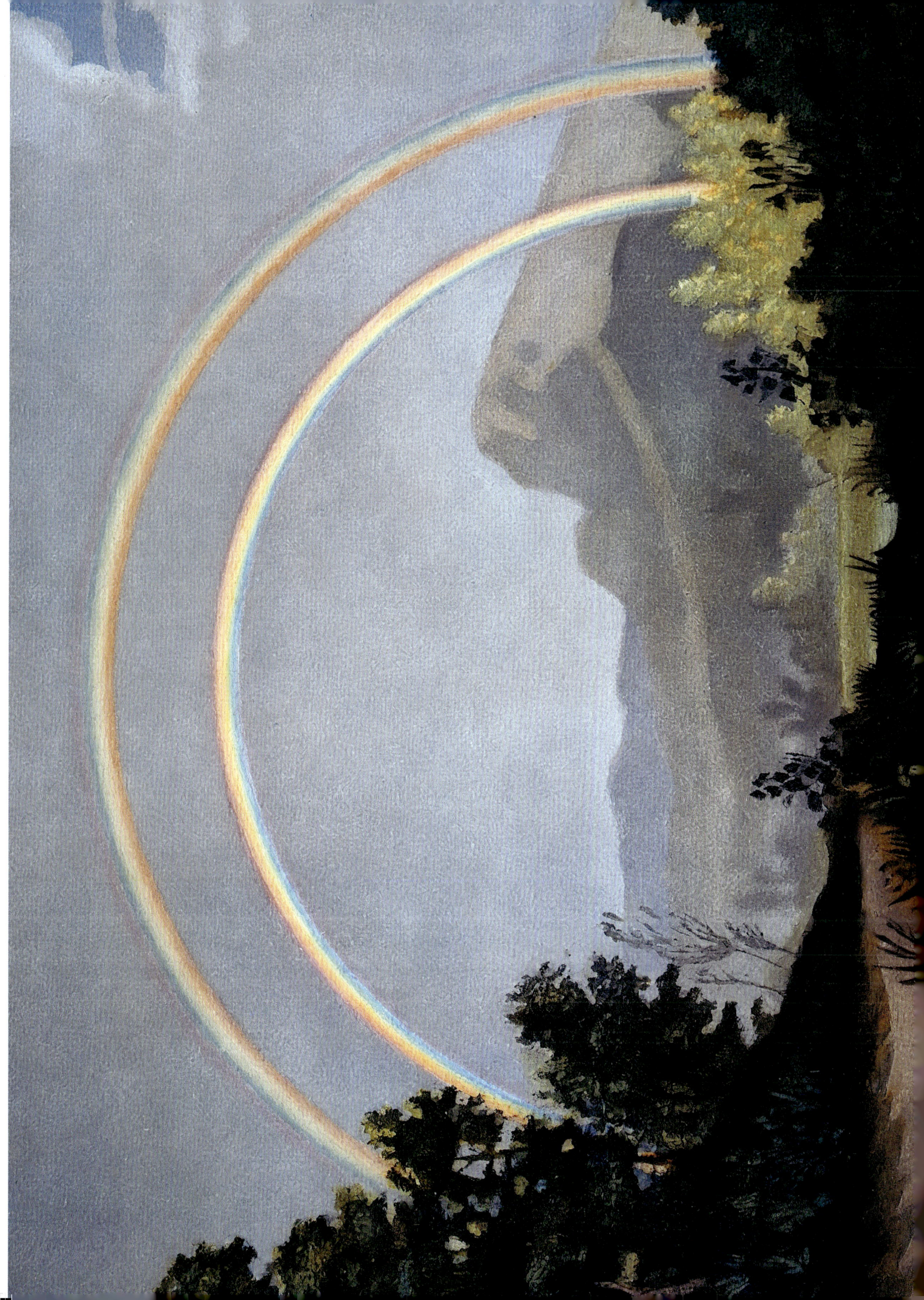

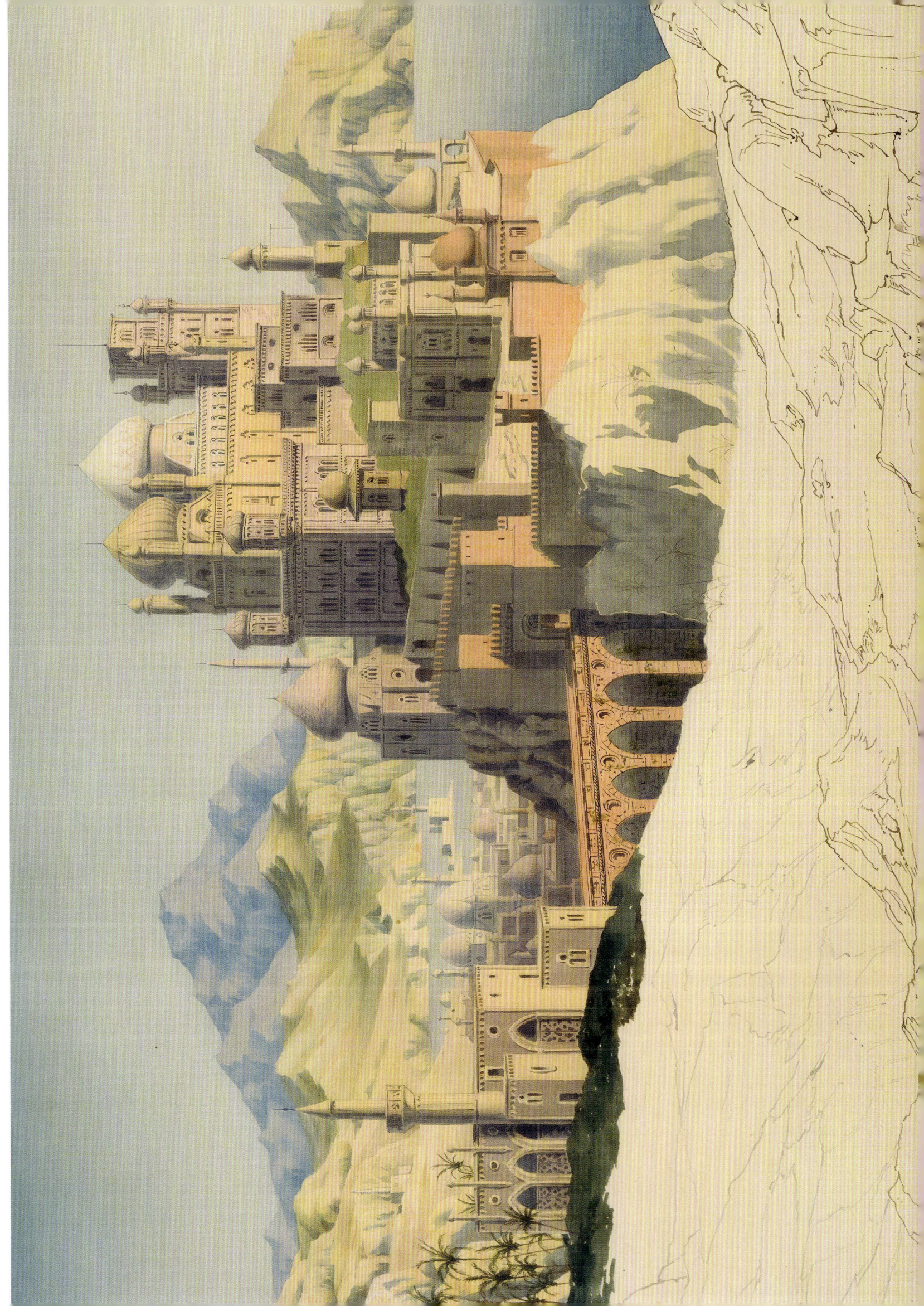

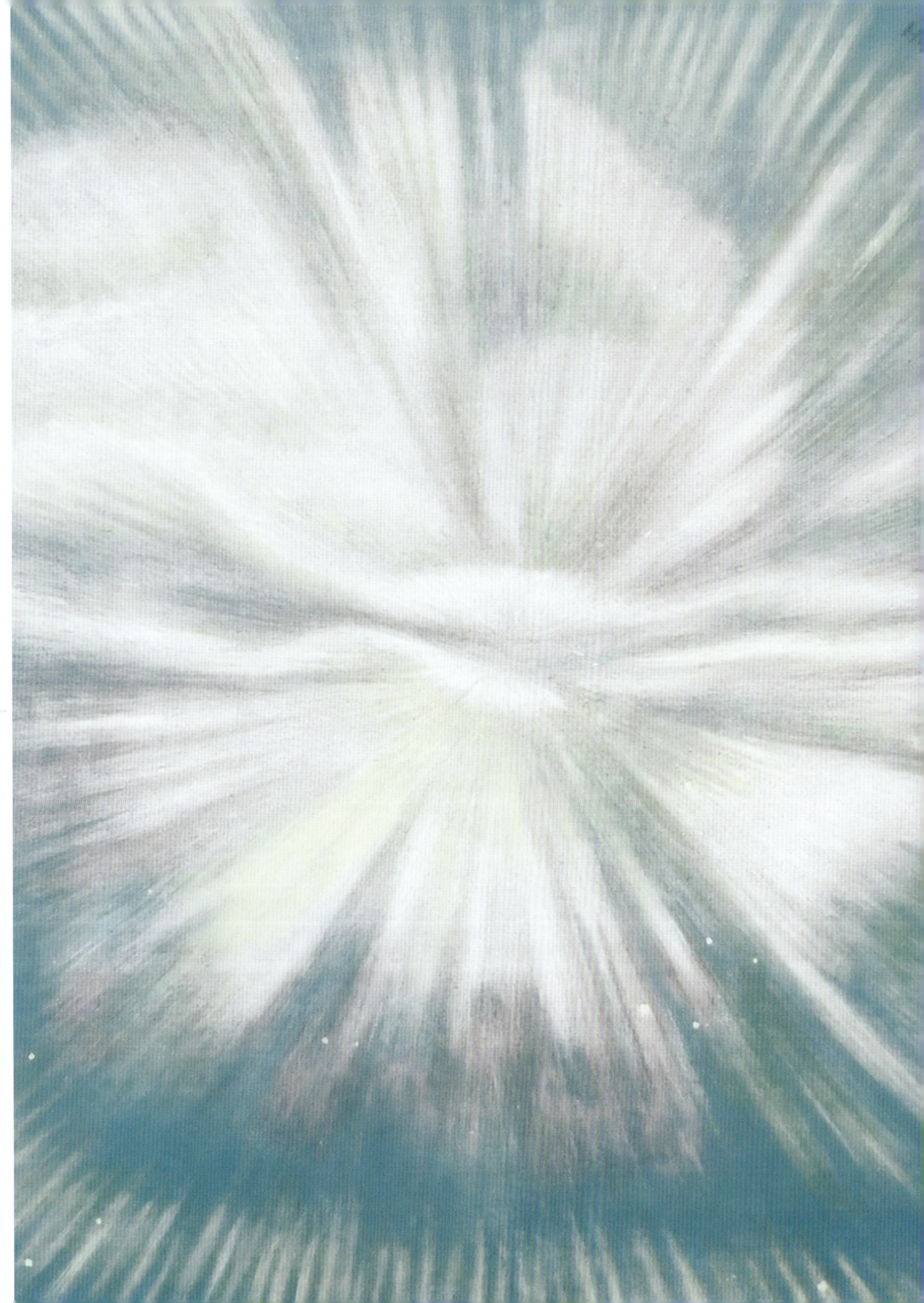

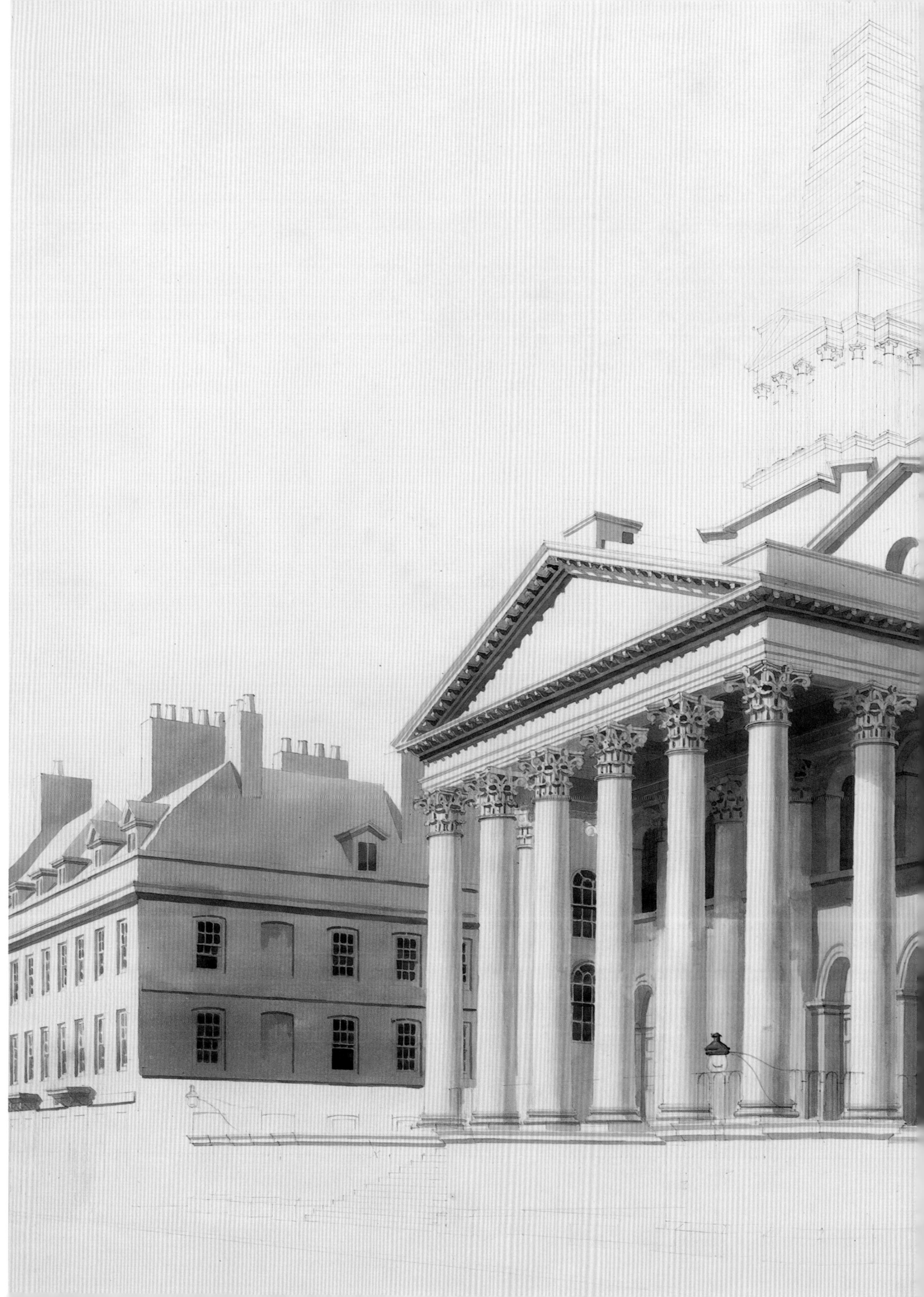

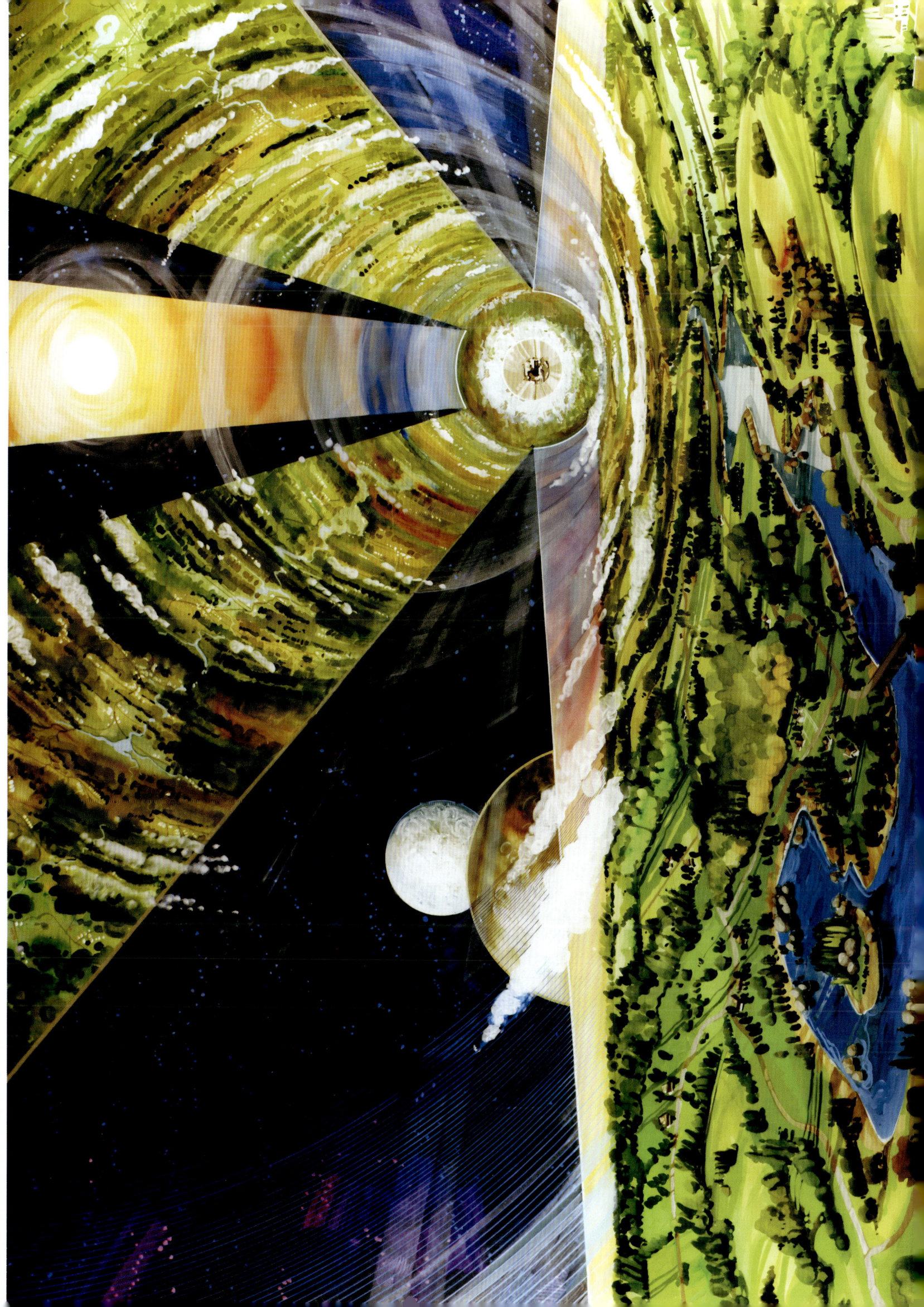

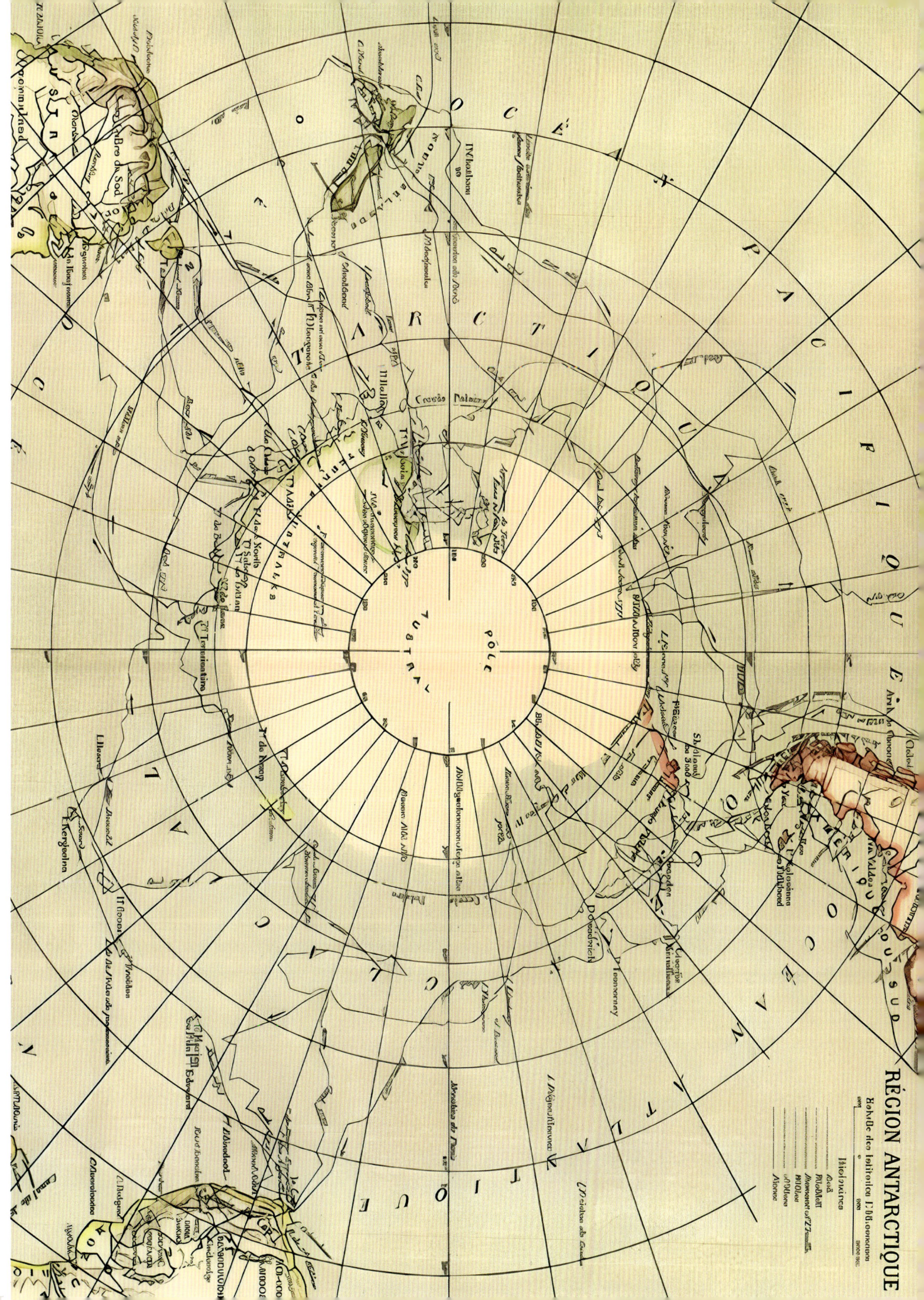

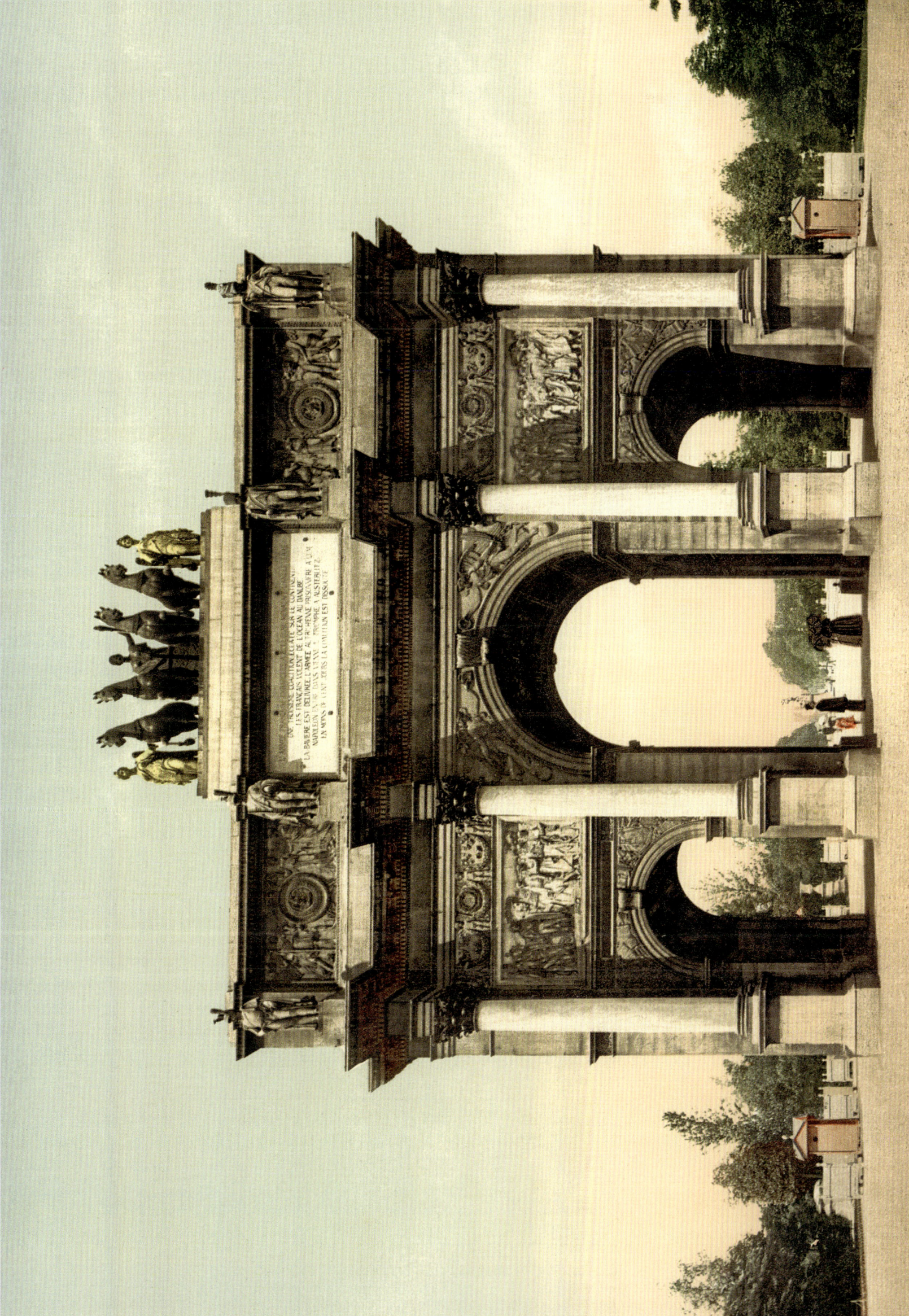

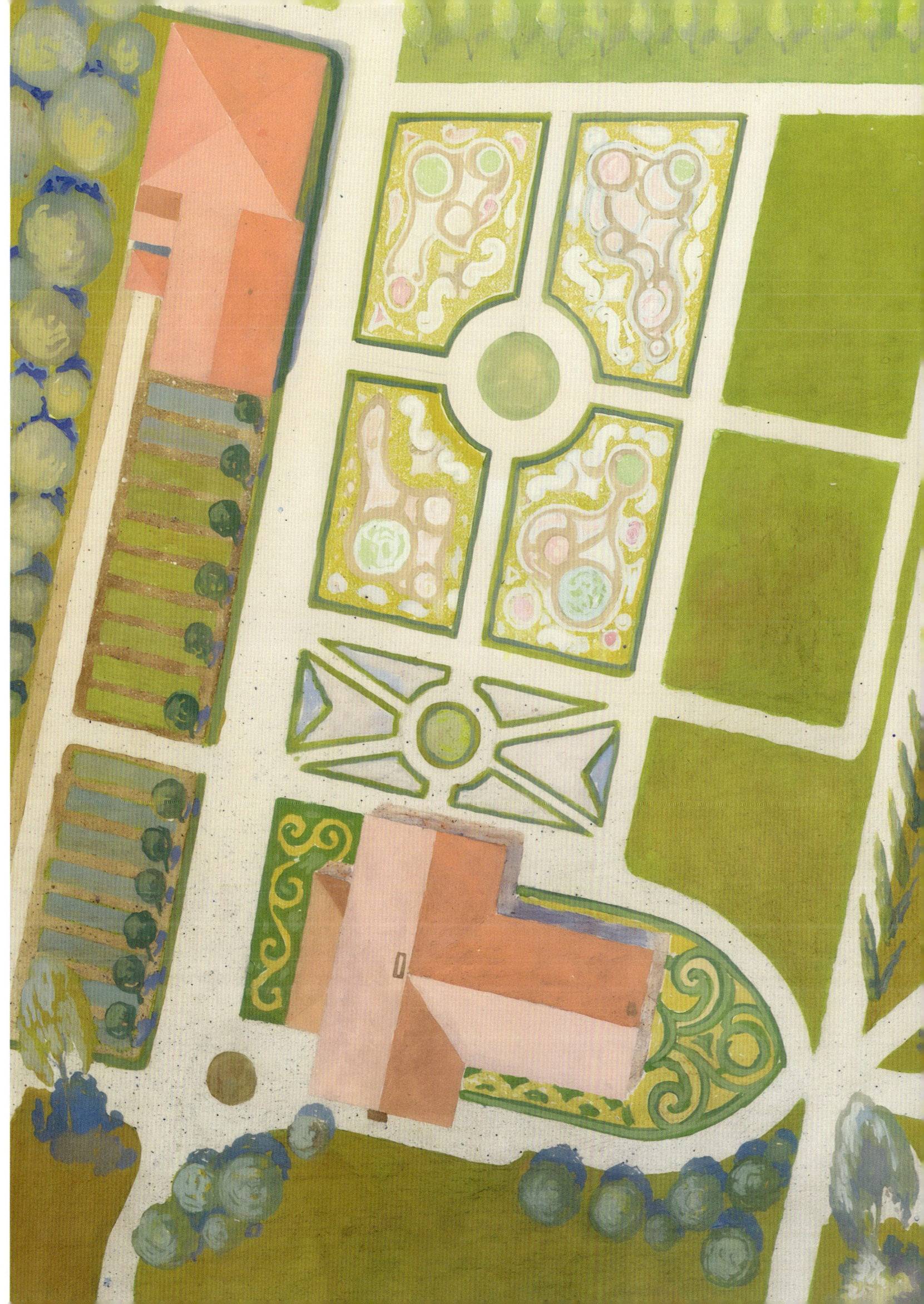

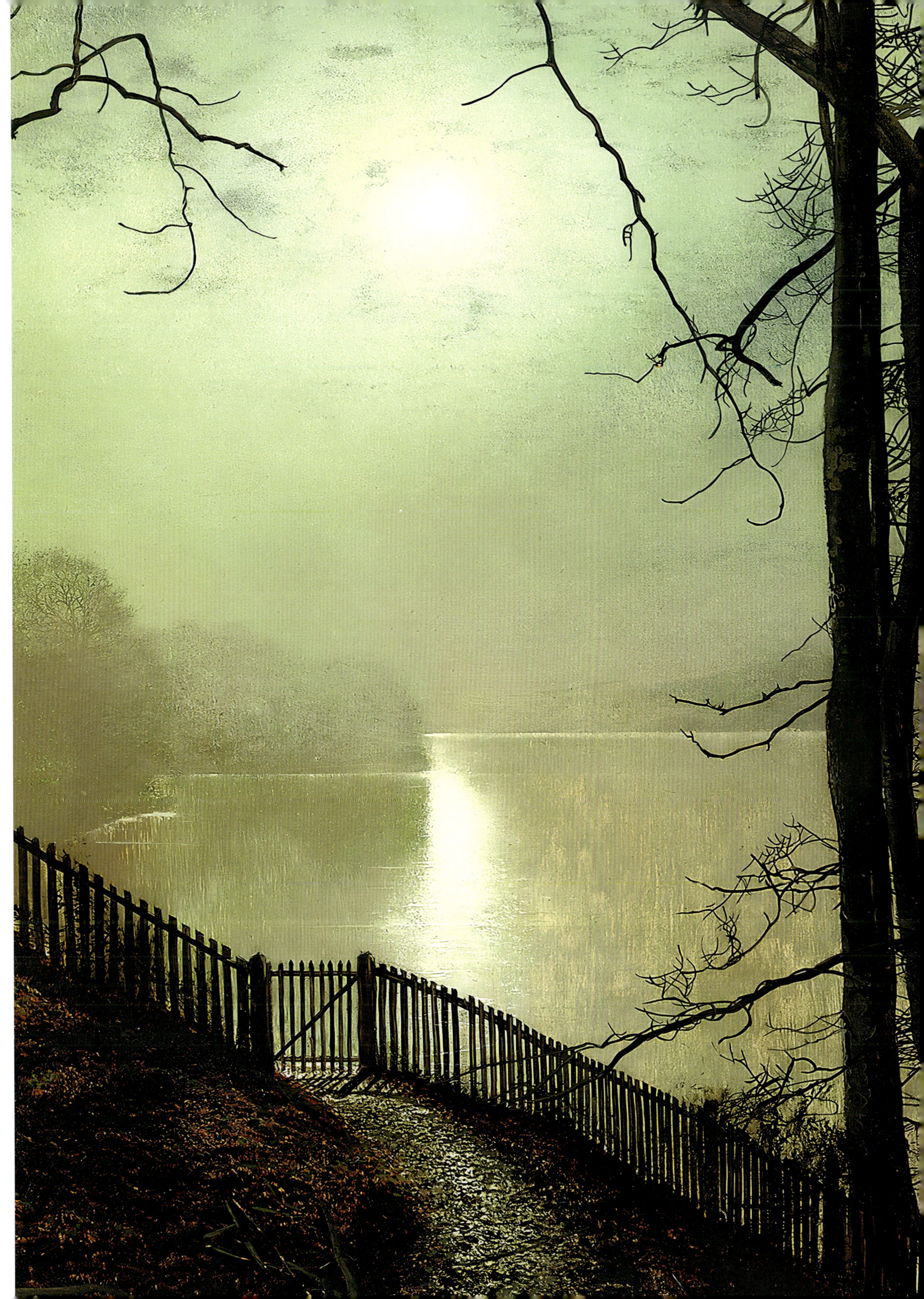

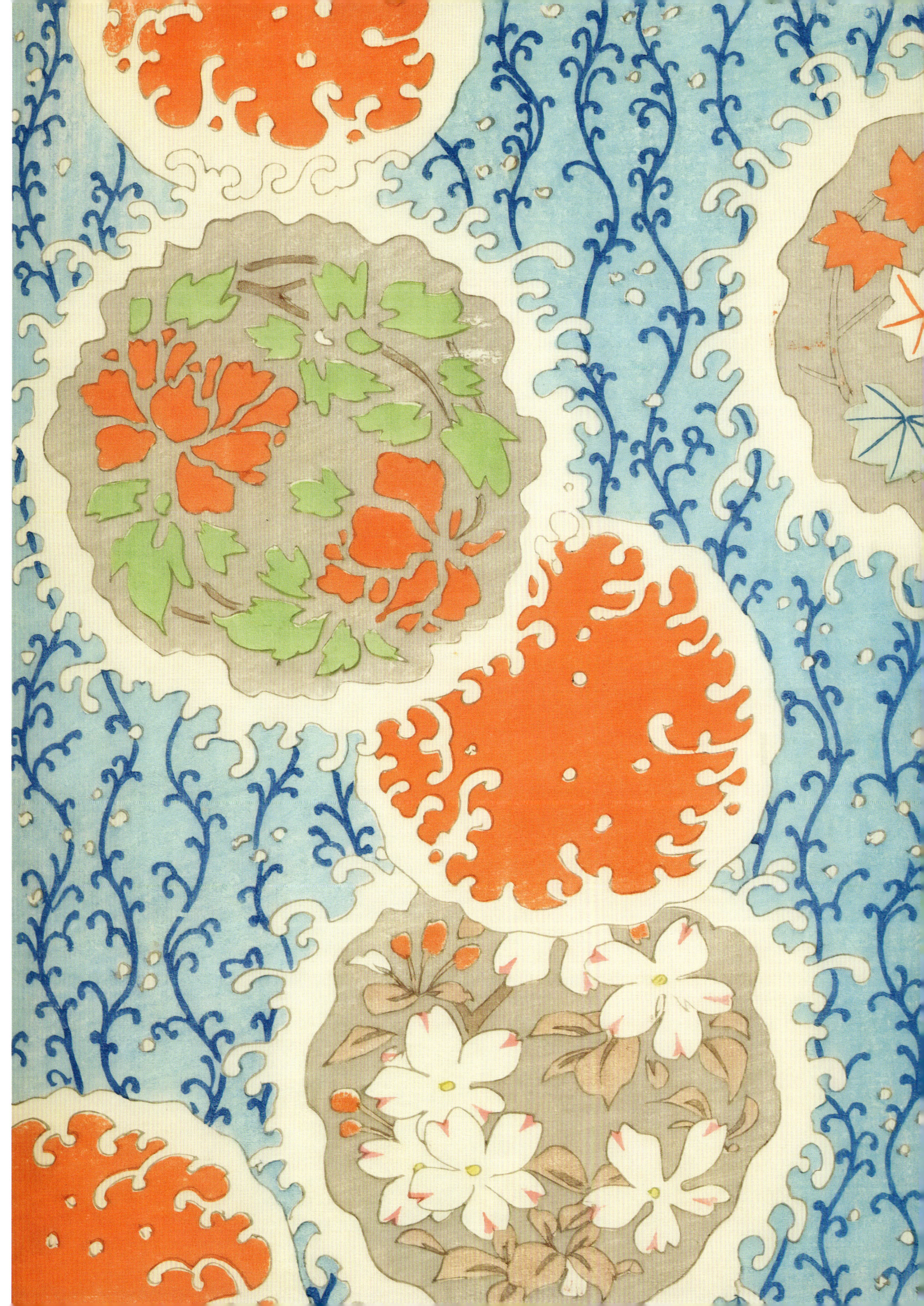

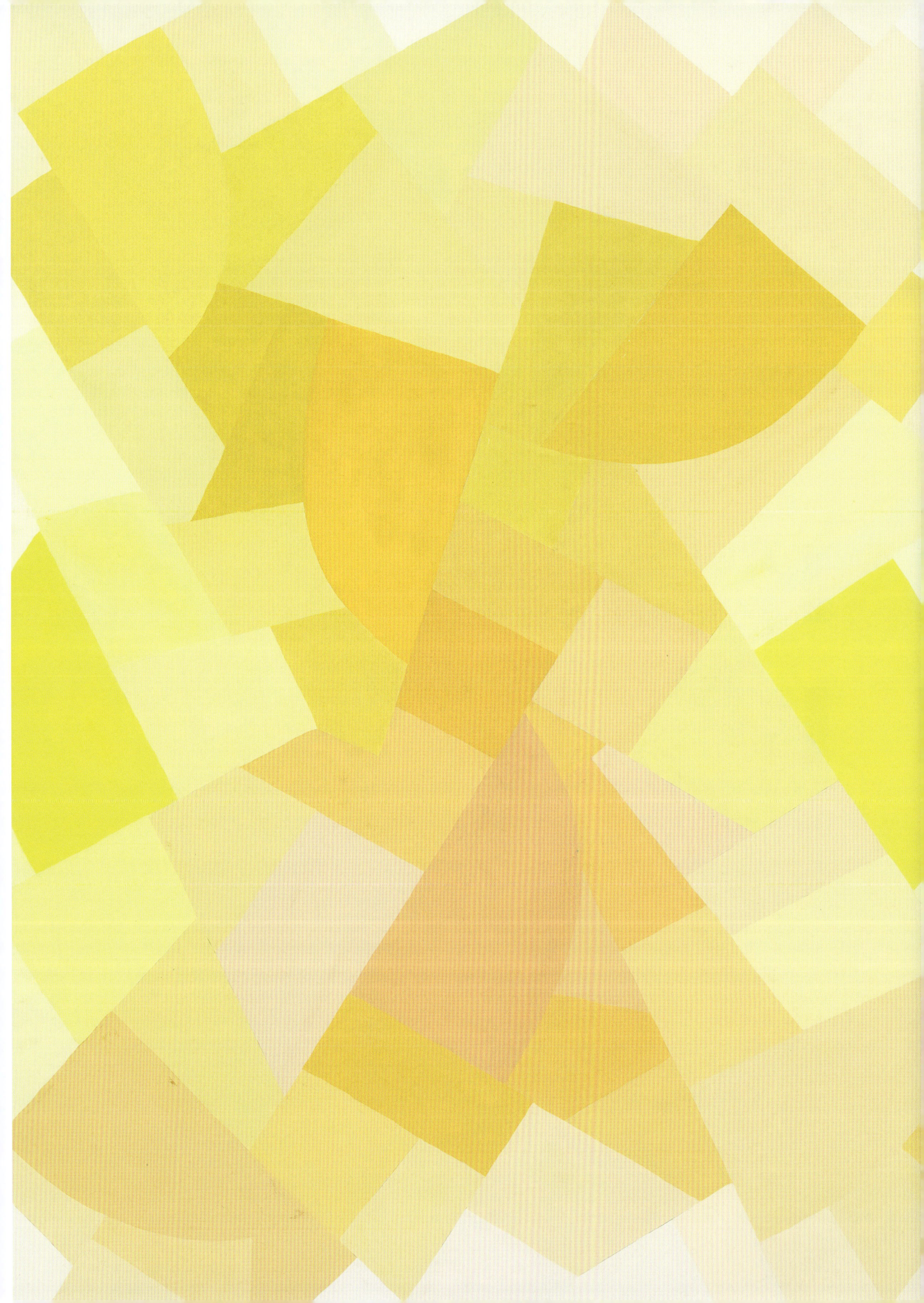

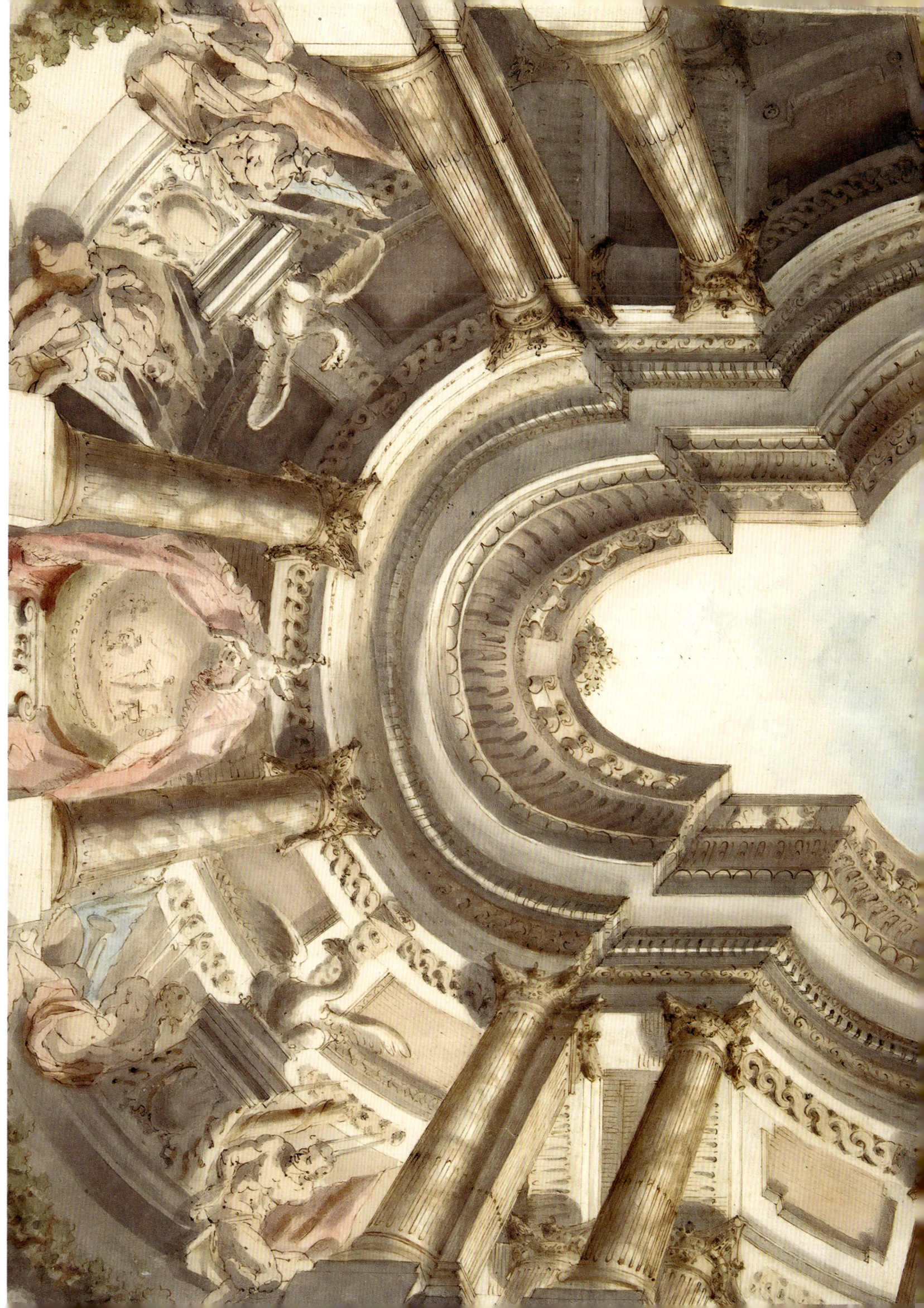

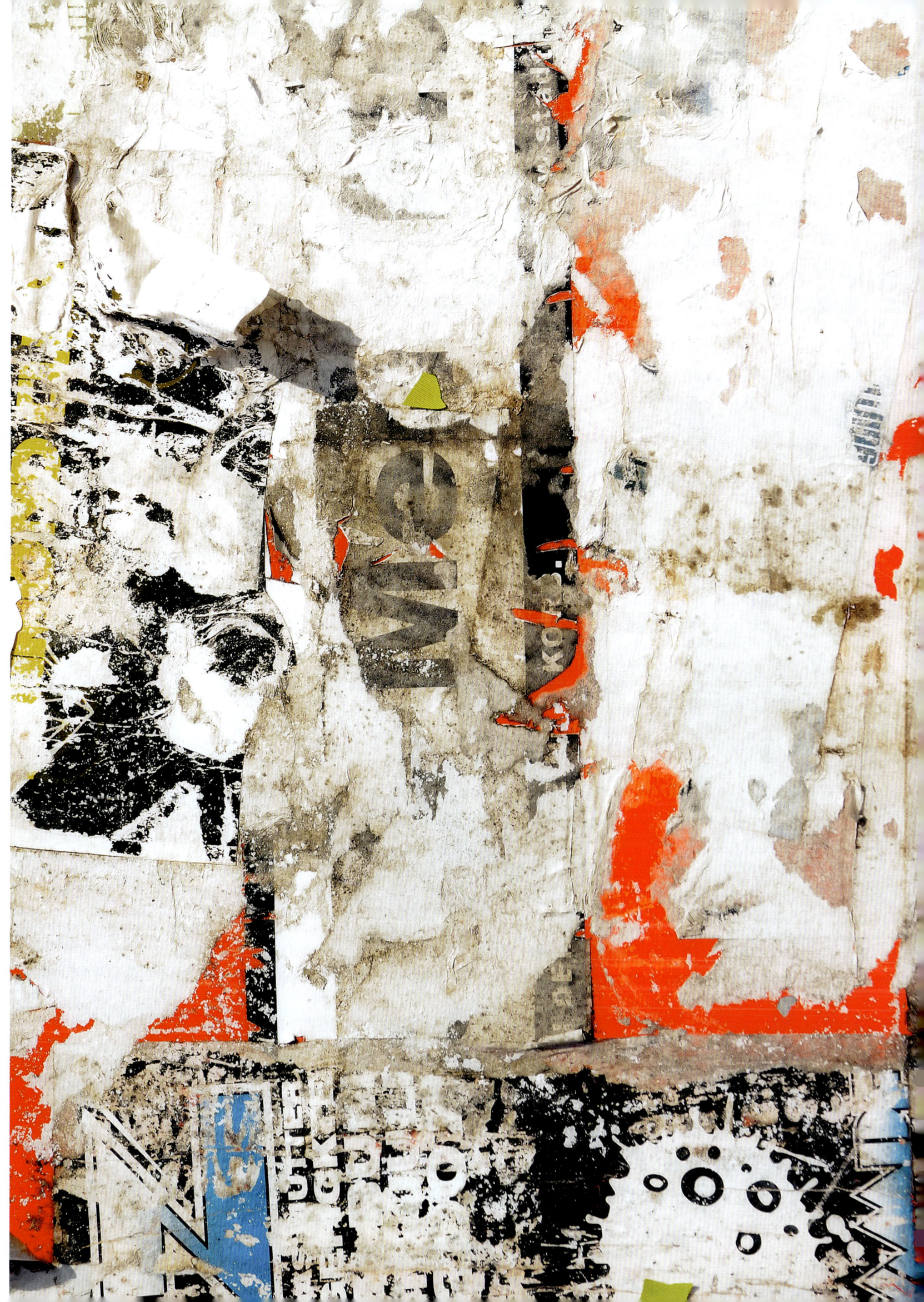

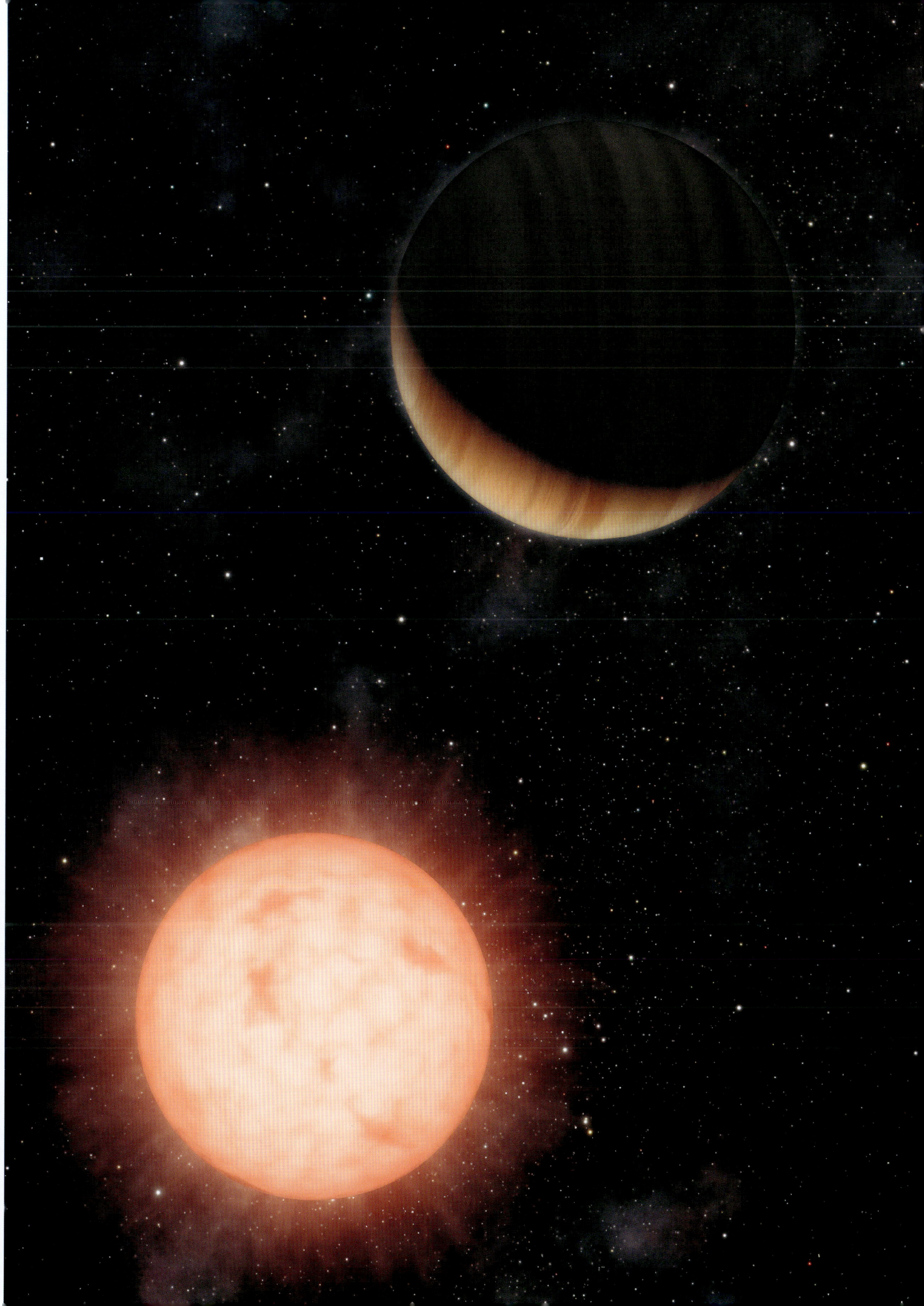

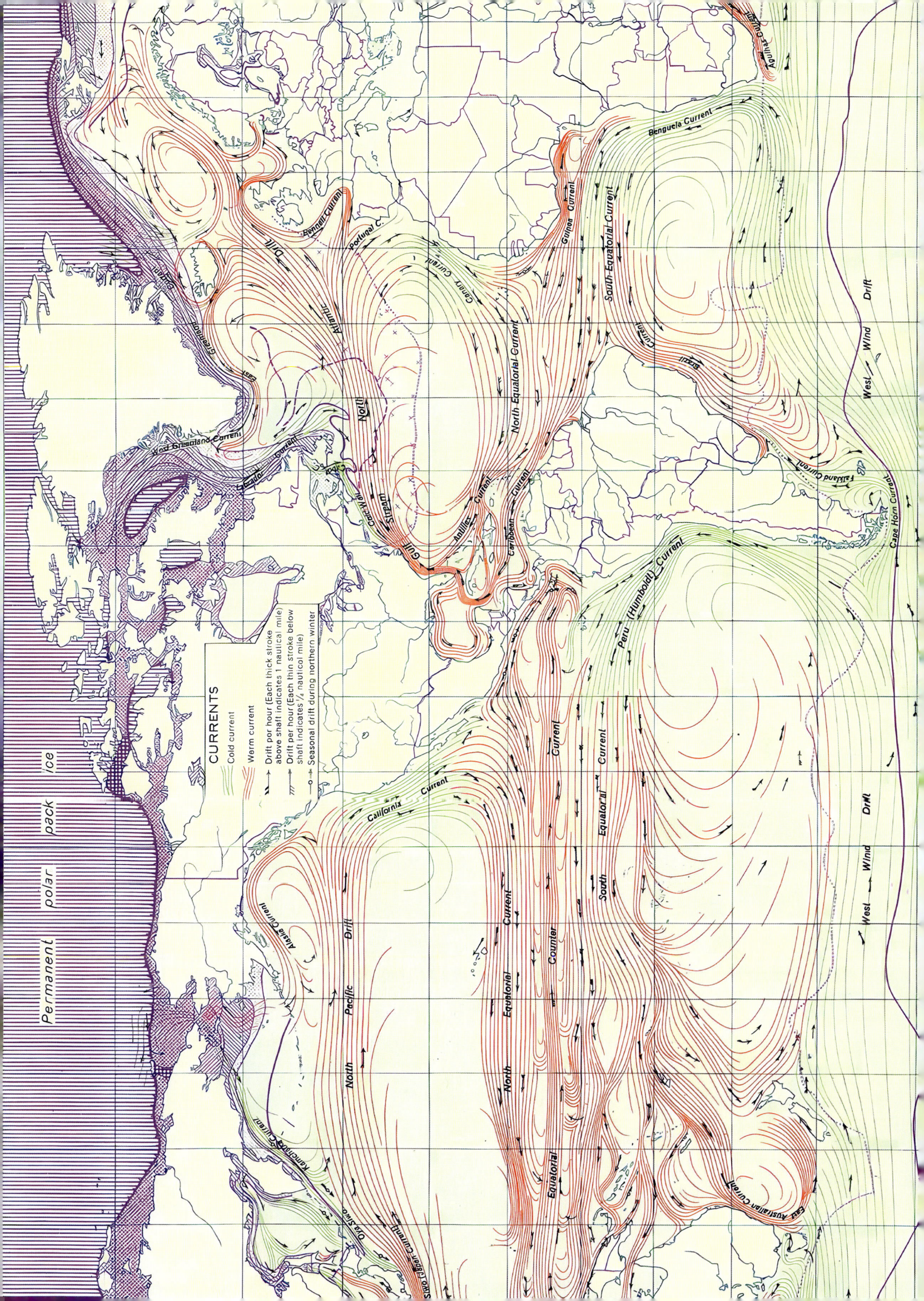

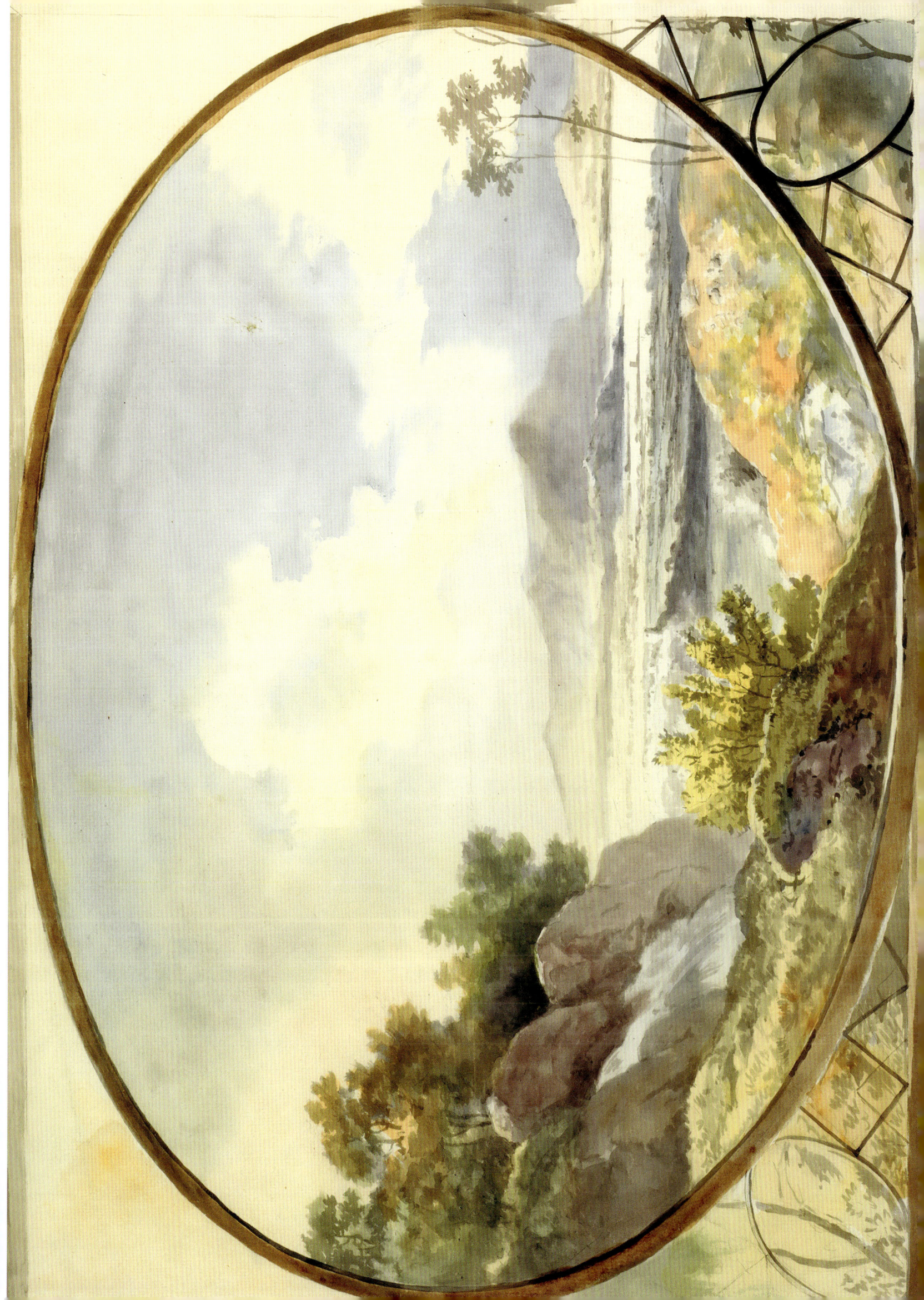

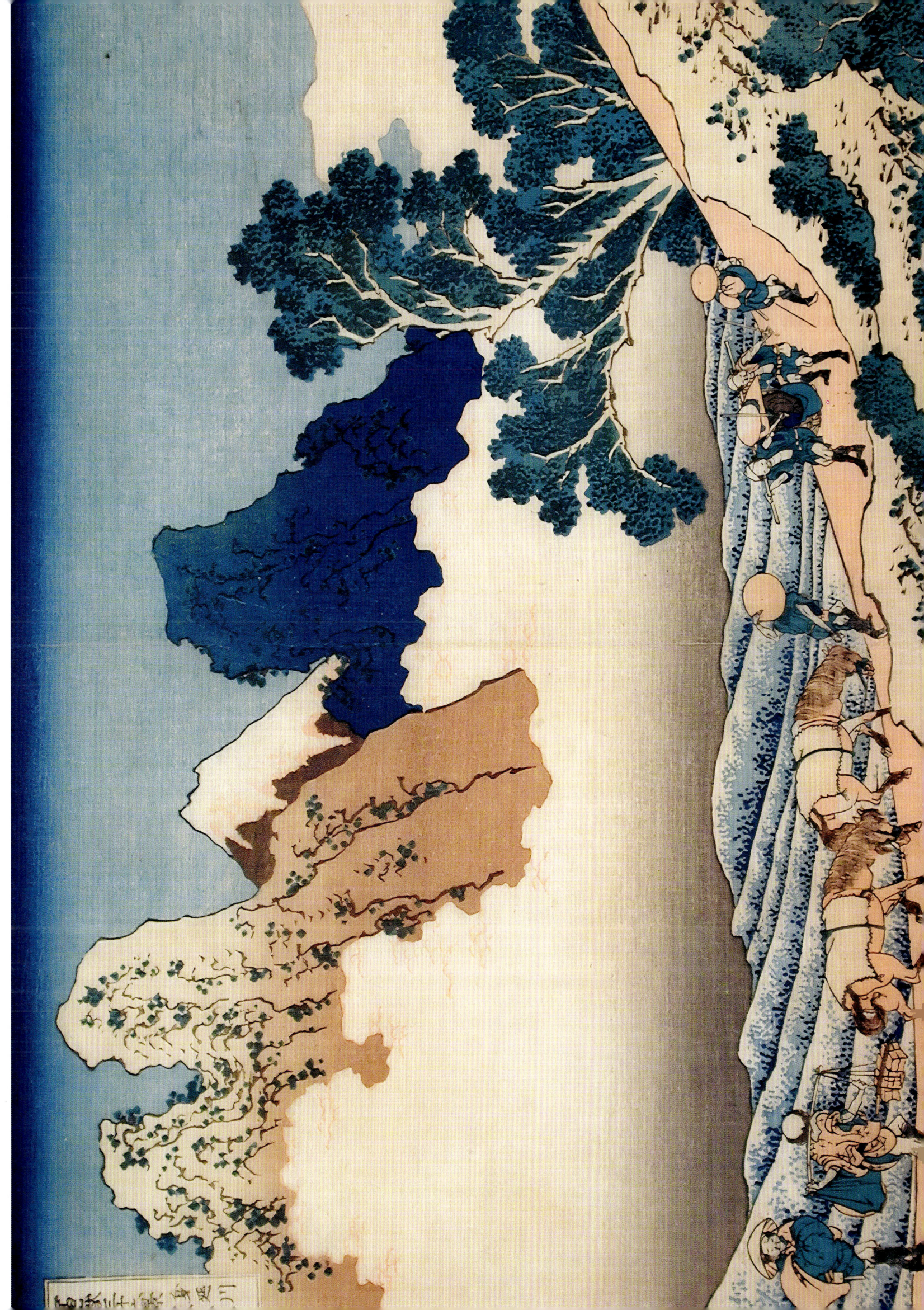

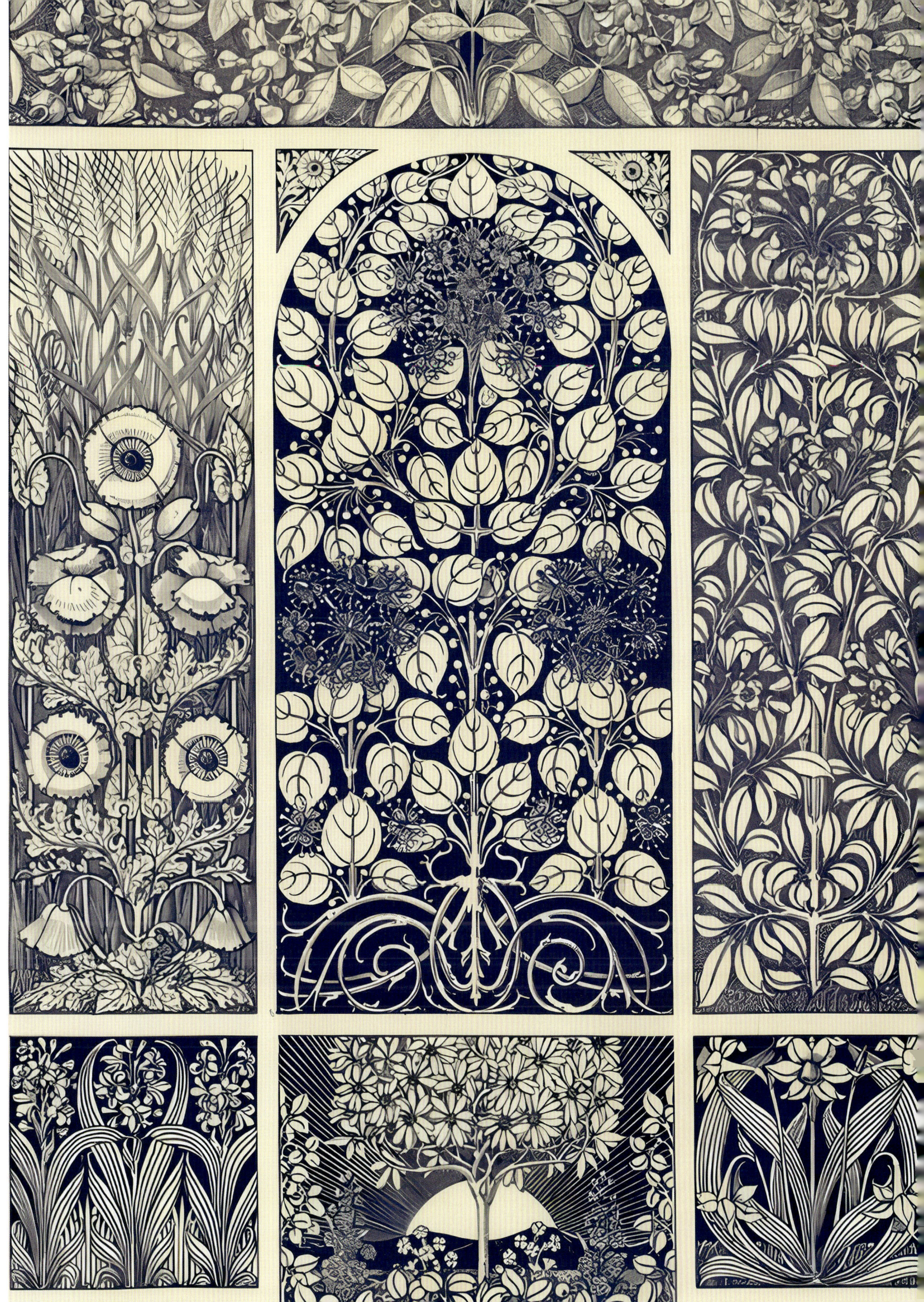

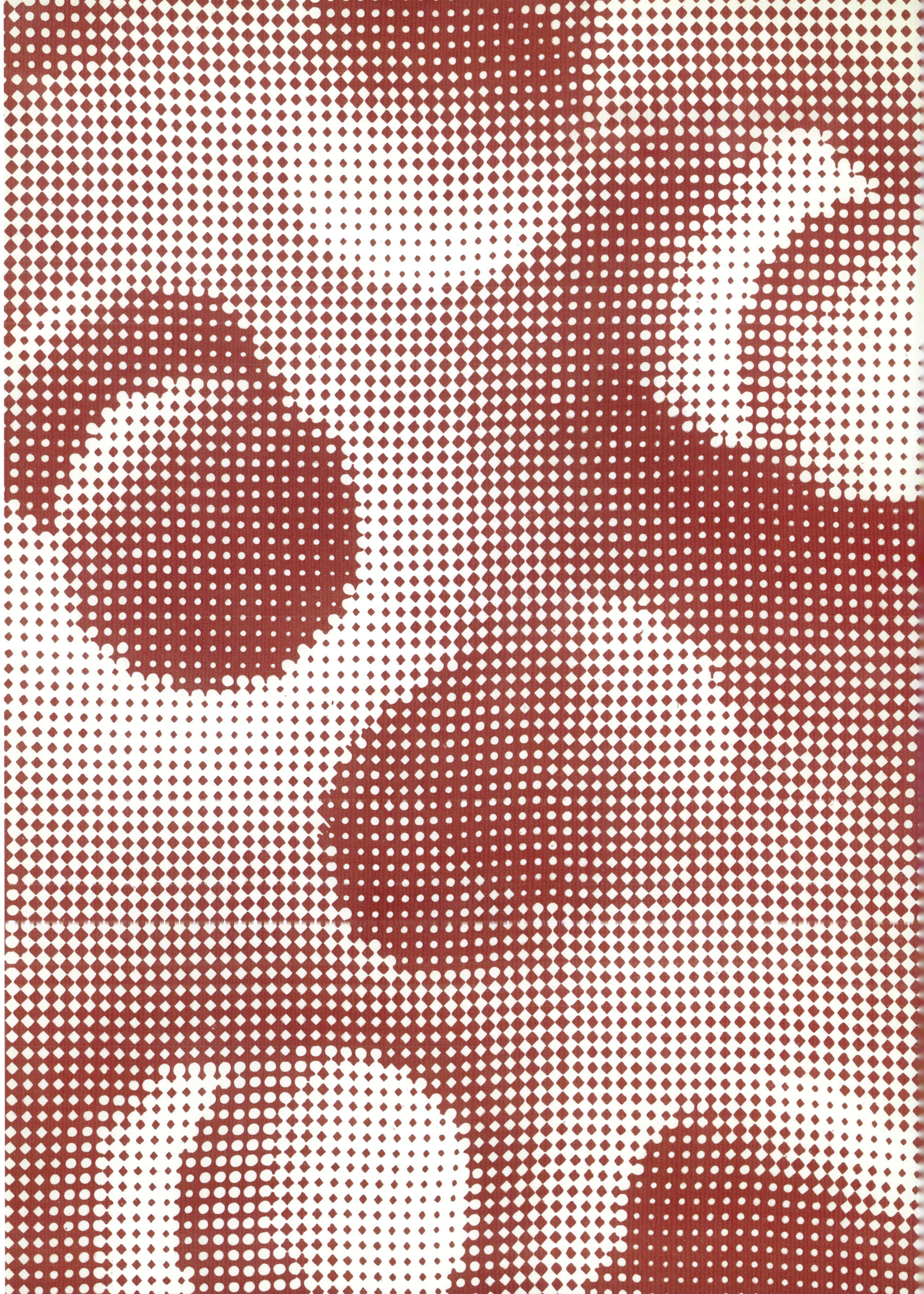

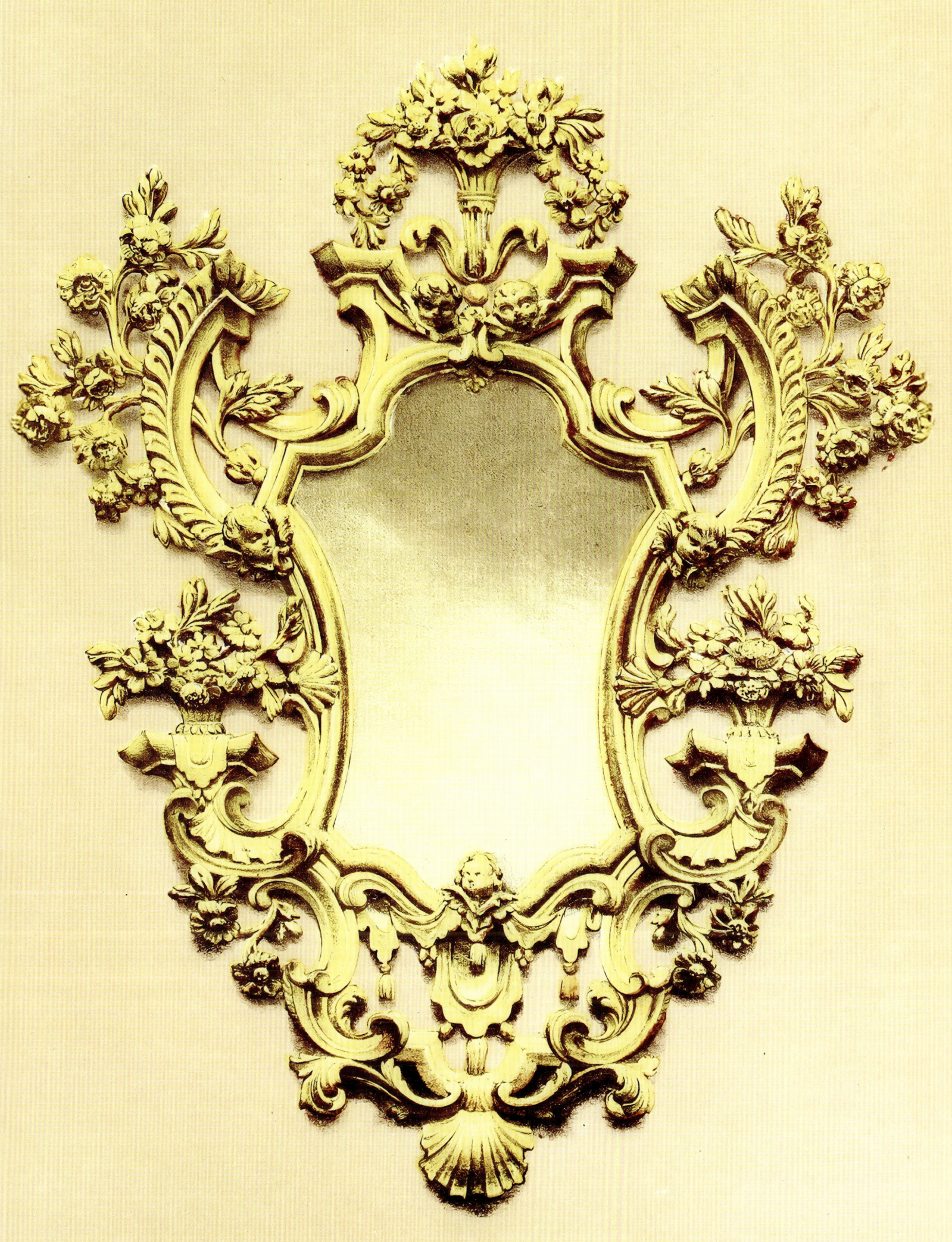

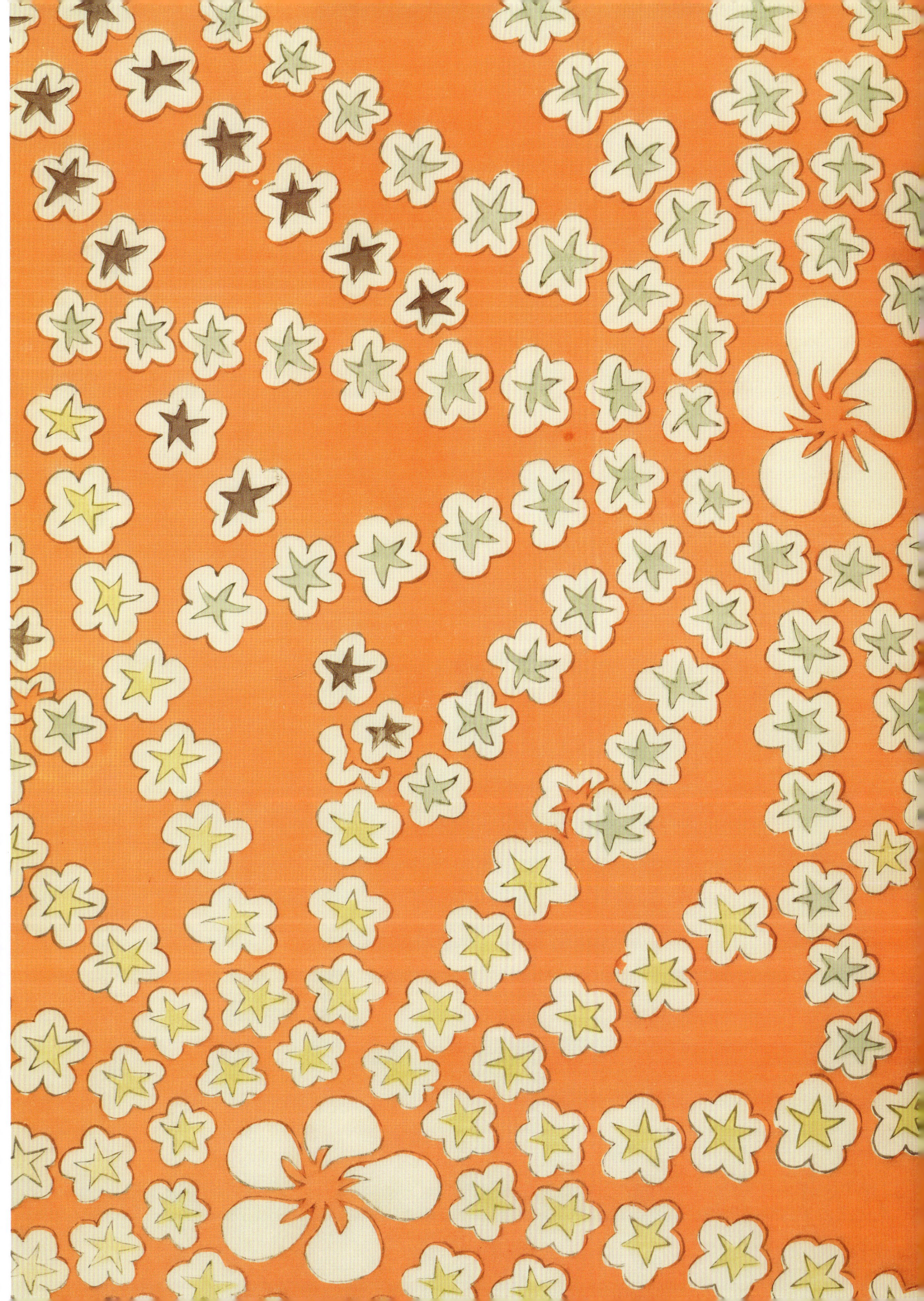

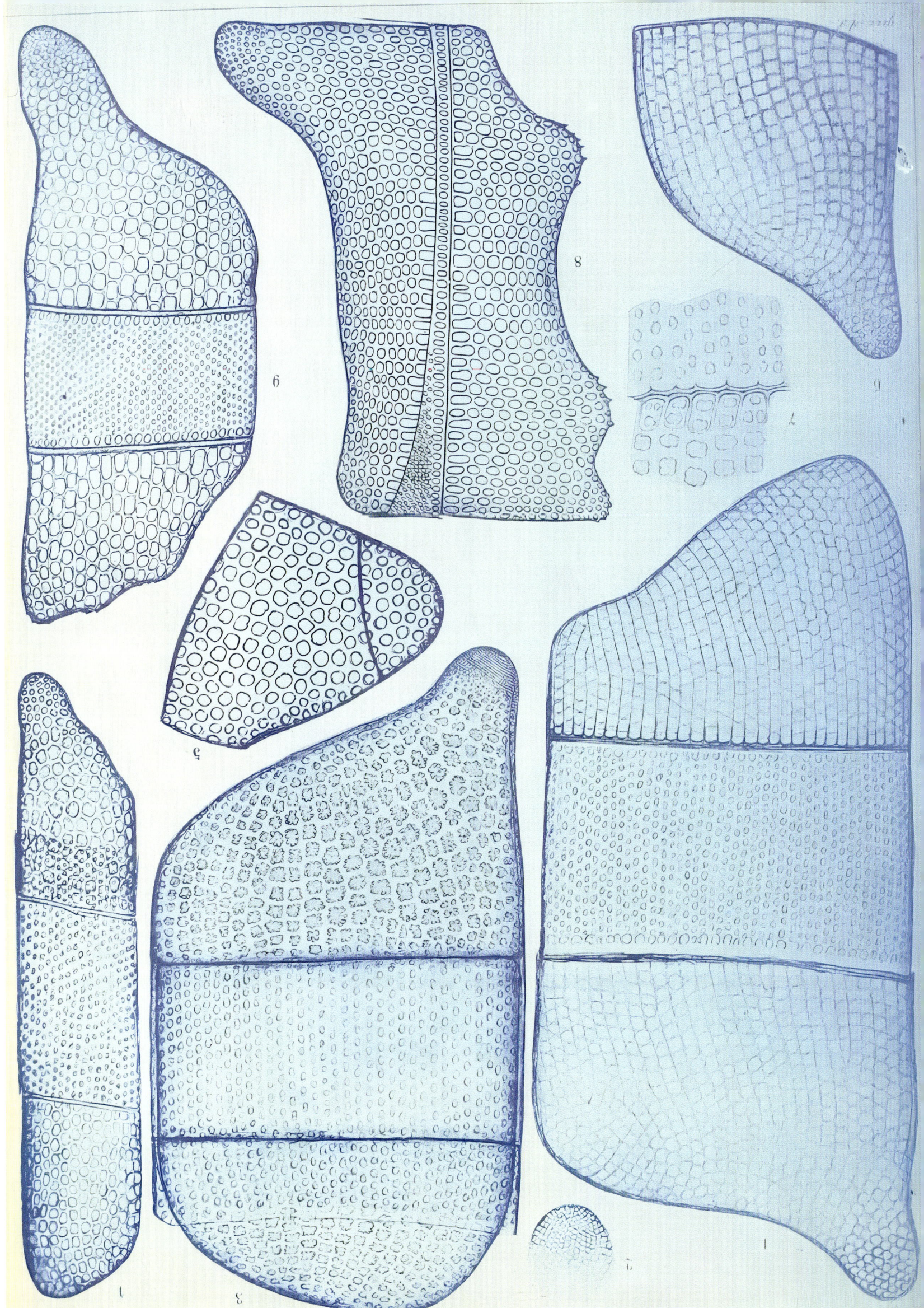

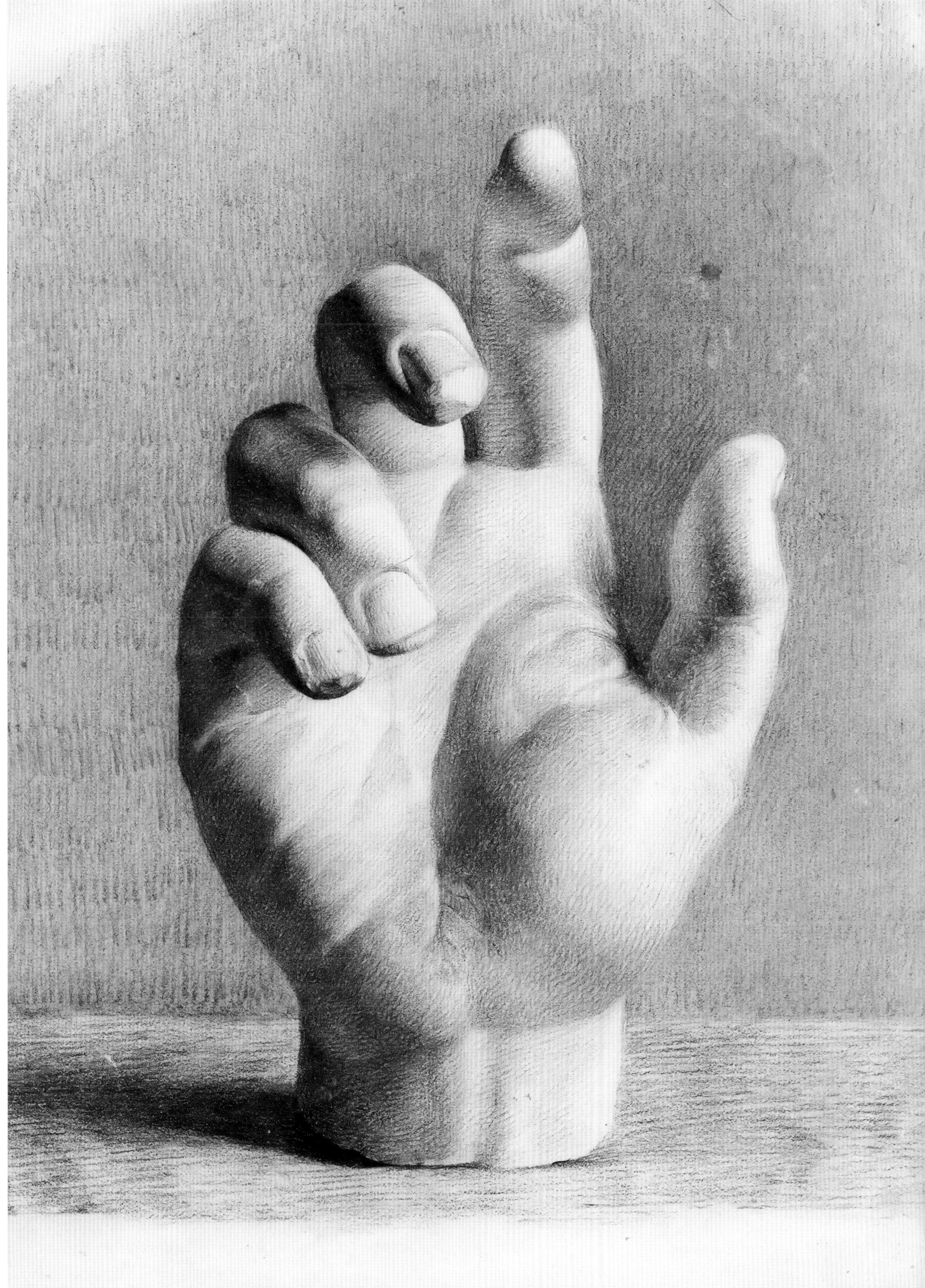

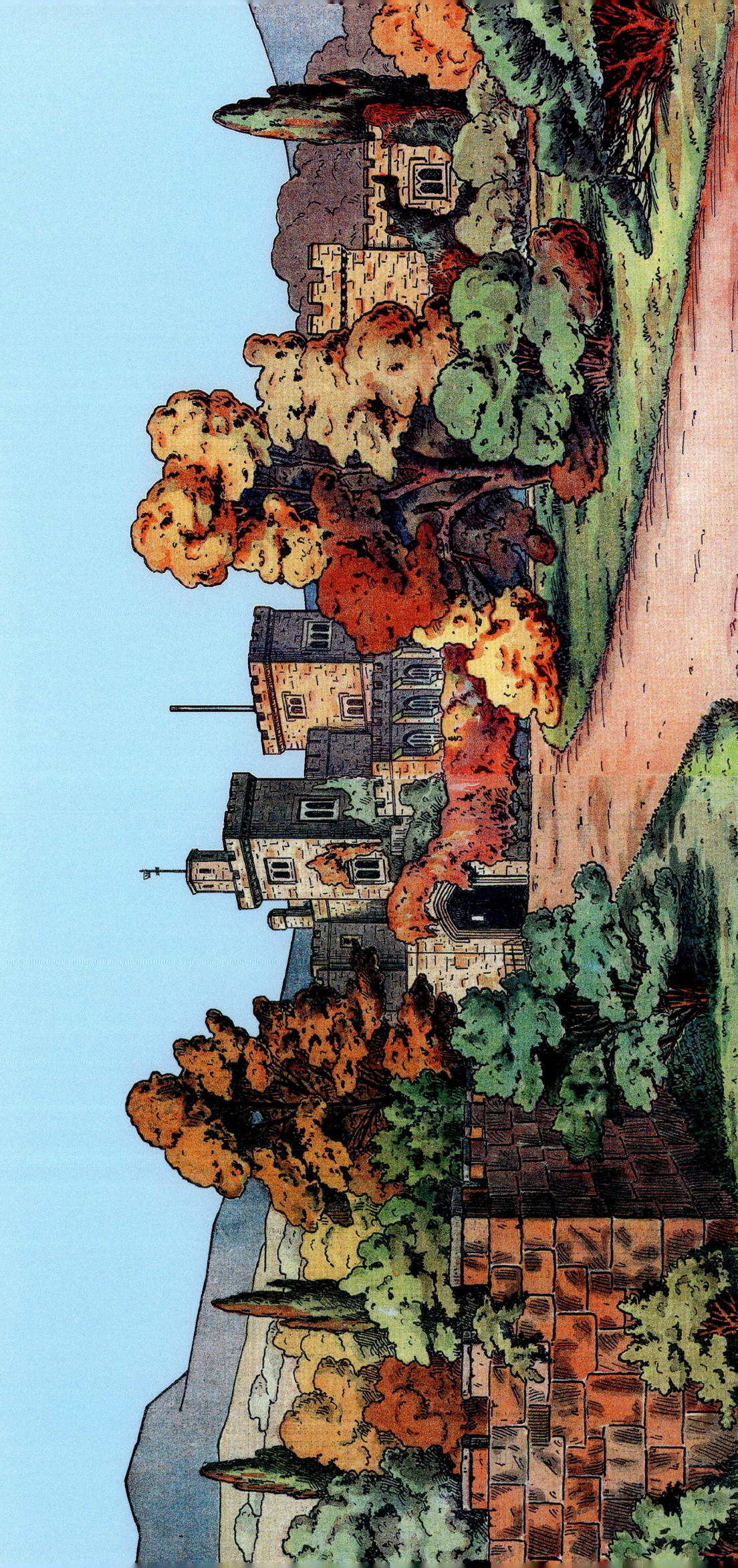

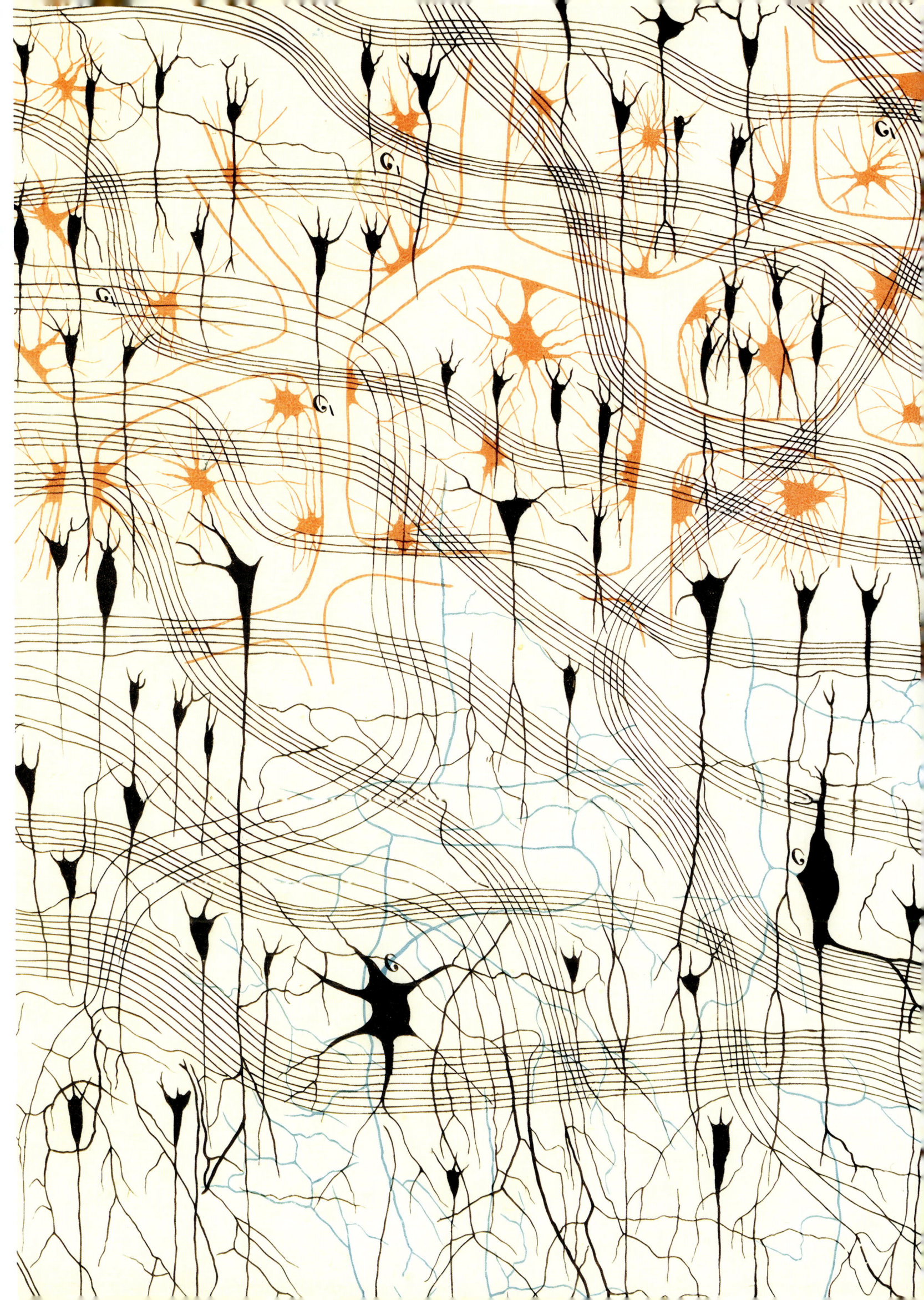

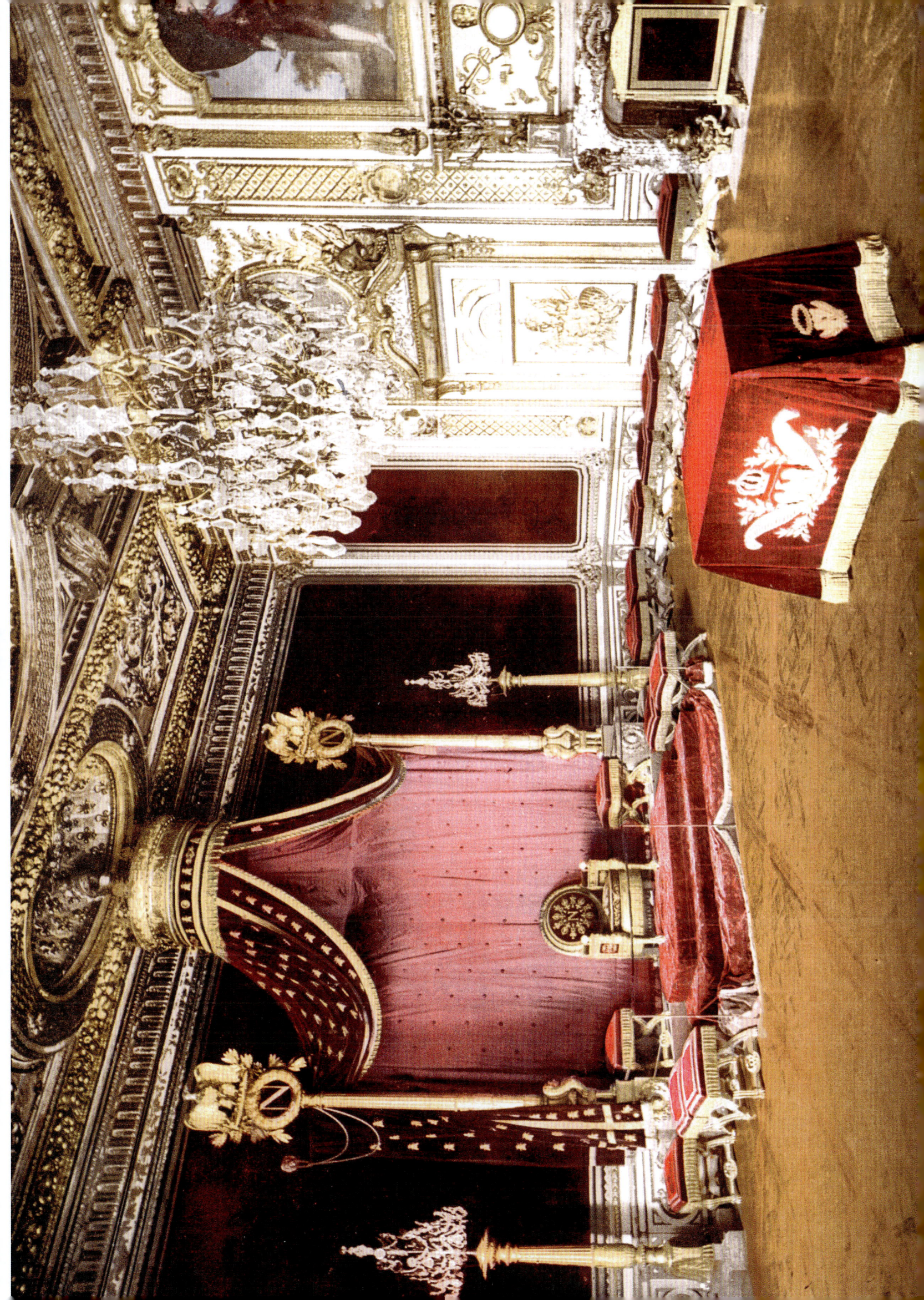

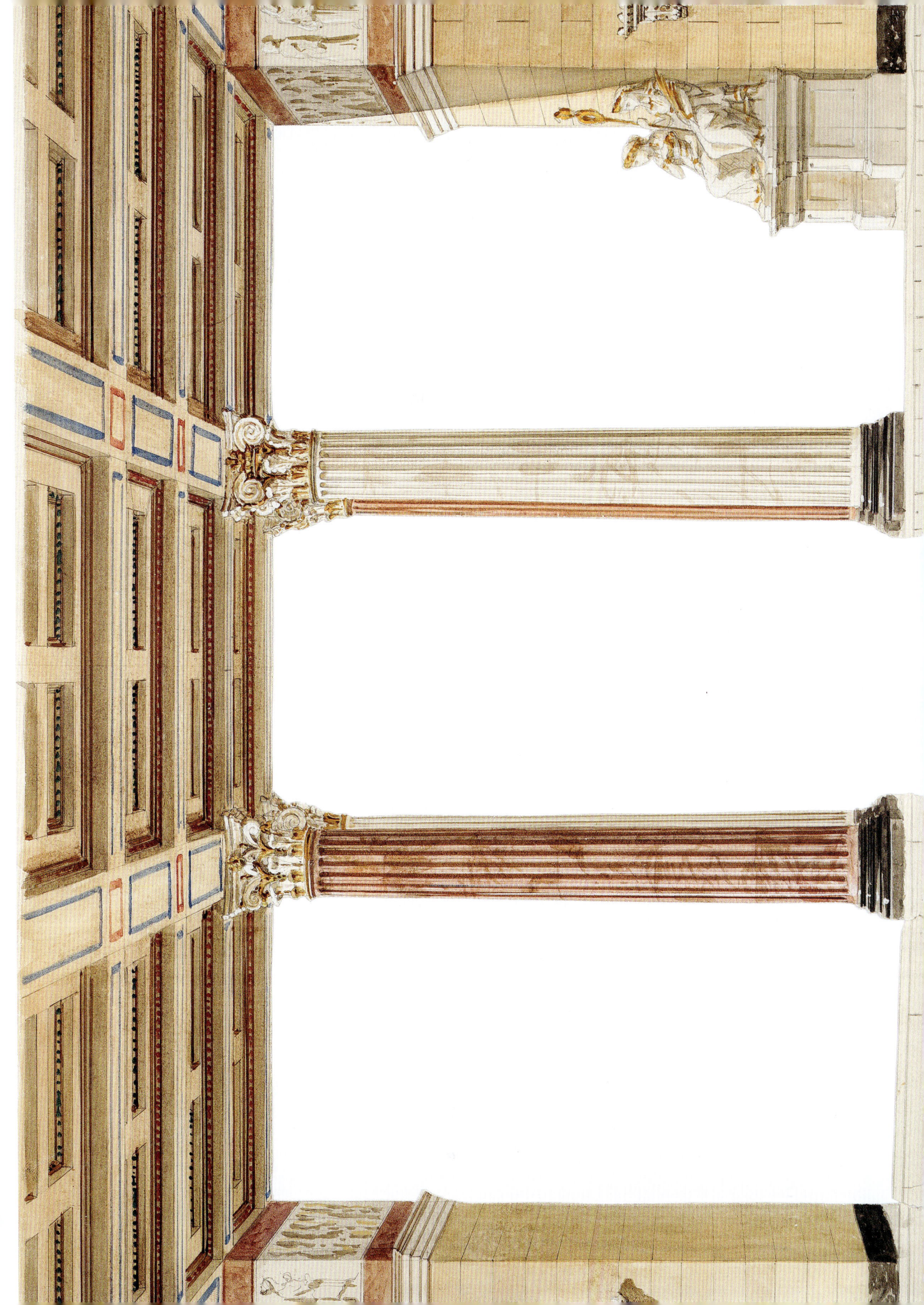

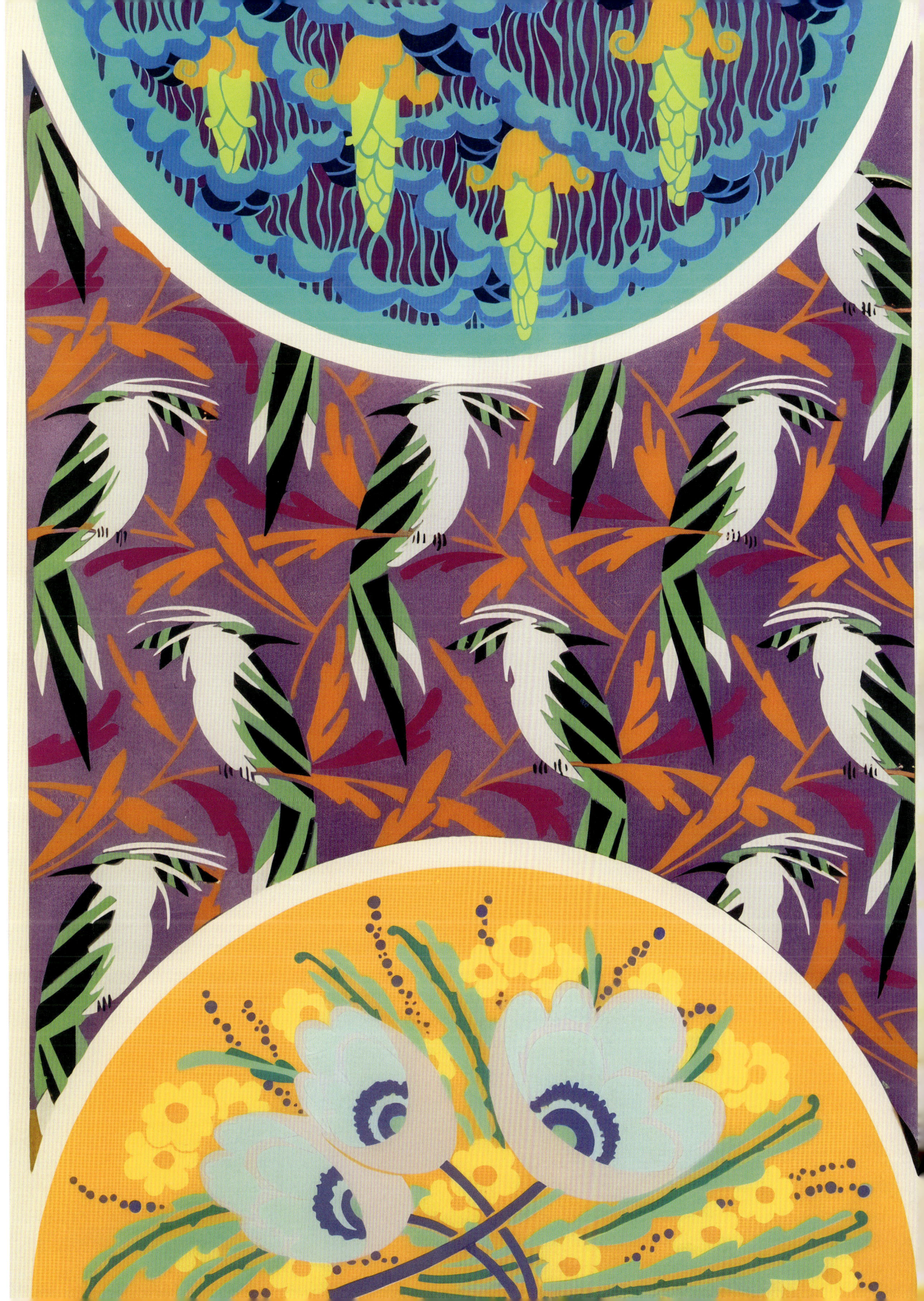

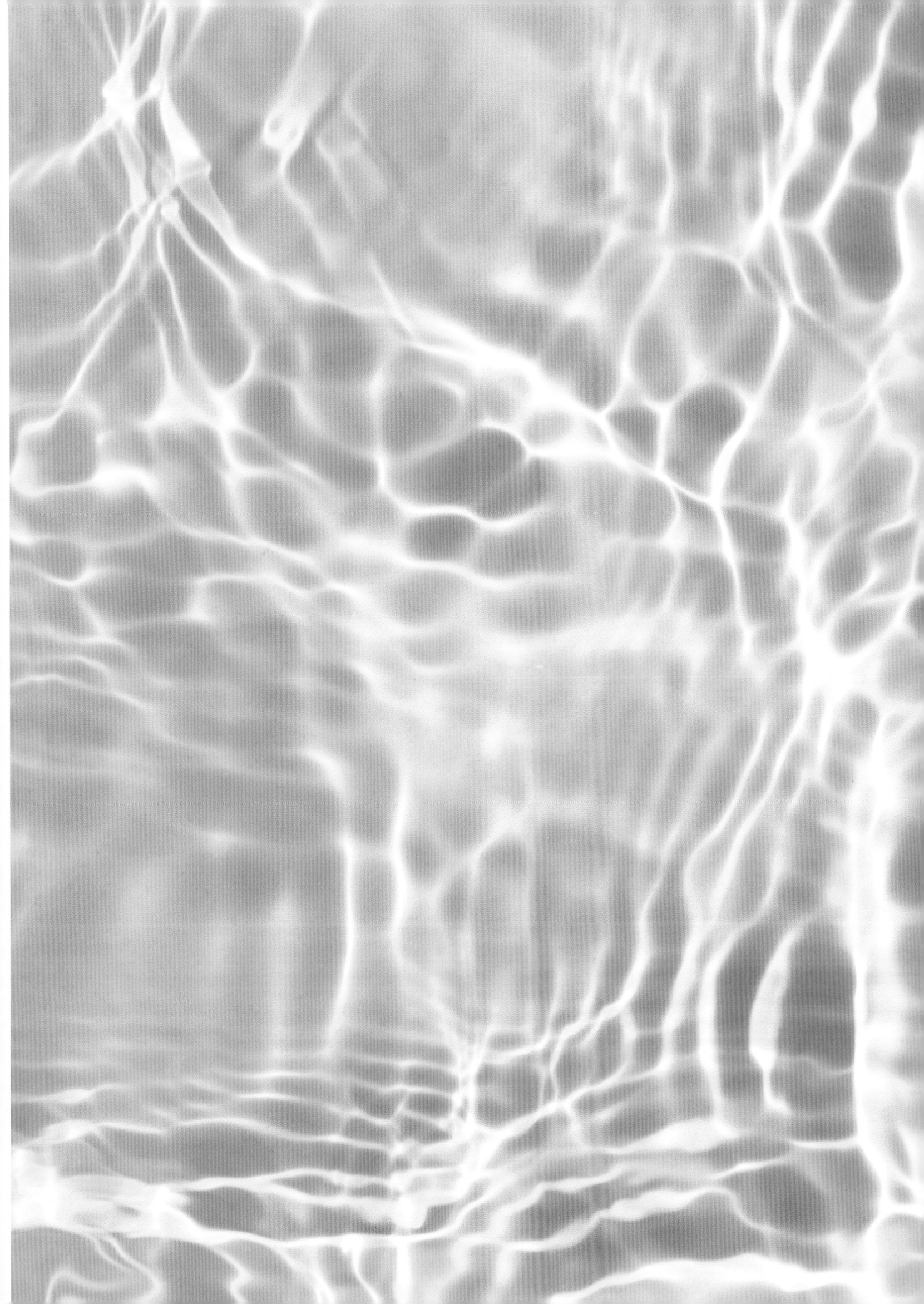

Picture Credits

1. Geological chart, chromolithograph, 1893, Levi W. Yaggy; 2. Design from *Hanafubuki* (Designs for kimonos), c.1902; 3. Lunar illustration, 1764, anonymous; 4. Advertisement from the Armstrong Cork Company, 1958; 5. *Lotus Flowers*, 1887–1897, Ogawa Kazumasa, The Rijksmuseum; 6. Movie theatre, anonymous; 7. *Kunstgewerbliche Schmuckformen für die Flacke* Pl. 13, 1920, Christian Stoll; 8. *Borghese Vase*, Johan Teyler, 18th century, The Rijksmuseum; 9. *A Colony's Interior and Human-powered Flight*, Rick Guidice, NASA; 10. Graffiti garage, unknown; 11. *Aurore boréalis, Quillet encyclopédie*, 1907; 12. Institute in Applied Health Administration, 1979, Lanny Sommese; 13. Statens musikverk, 1922, Carl Grabow, Swedish Performing Arts Agency, Photographer: Narciso Contreras; 14. Image from Japanese design magazine, *Shin-Bijutsukai*, 1902; 15. *Telaga Patengan*, 1856, Java-Album 2, Aufl.; 16. *Blue room*, Foto Miki; 17. *The World*, 1920s, Library of Congress; 18. *Prismes-20*, 1931, Emile-Allain Séguy; 19. *The Tower Bridge*, photochrom, unknown author, 1890–1905, Library of Congress; 20. *Examples of Chinese Ornament*, 1867, Owen Jones; 21. *Waikiki Beach at Sunset*, D. Howard Hitchcock, oil on canvas, 1896; 22. *Mountain and Forest*, Christopher O'Hare; 23 *Auflage Neue Gartenpflanzen, Meyers Konversations-Lexicon* 1885–90; 24 *Verschleiertes*, 1934, Paul Klee, German; 25 *Cloud Shadow with Red Diffusion Light After the Disturbance Period (Midday)*, 1884, Eduard Pechuël-Loesche; 26. *Christ*, Claude Mellan, 1649; 27. Advertisement for Miraplas Styron Wall Tiles, S & W Moulding Co., 1950s; 28. *XVIII Siecle 12*, 1880–1889, Auguste Racinet, French; 29. Ebru paper blue red, Adobe Stock; 30. *The Great Water Lily*, chromolithograph, 1854, William Sharp; 31. Villa Pliniana from *Italian Villas and their Gardens* by Edith Wharton, painted by Maxfield Parrish, 1904; 32. Brick wall, unknown; 33. Lithograph of colour palettes from *Larousse Encyclopedia*; 34. *Twilight at Sea off the Coast of Portugal*, 1872, British Library; 35. Image from Japanese design magazine, *Shin-Bijutsukai*, 1902; 36. Early photochrom of Mount Fuji, date unknown; 37. Design for Orinoka fabric advertisement, 1930, Winold Reiss; 38. *Le Corset*, x-ray photographie, 1908; 39. *The Planetary System*, Geographical study, 1887, Levi W. Yaggy; 40. *Church Street*, 1920, Charles Sheeler; 41. Garage door, unknown; 42. Baked beans, Adobe Stock; 43. *A Great Oak Tree*, c.1801, John Constable; 44. *Idea del Universo*, 1690, Vincenzo Maria Coronelli; 45. Advertisement for the Pacific Coast Trunk Store, California Historical Society; 46. Lacework, Netherlands, 1690-1699, anonymous; 47. *Hand and a Coin*, 1920, Sugiura Hisui, Japanese; 48. *Nature in Descending Regions*, chromolithograph, 1893, Levi W. Yaggy; 49. Italianate mission-style house, photograph by Frances Benjamin Johnston, Library of Congress; 50. Page from notebook, 1800s, Library of Congress; 51. *Kunstgewerbliche Schmuckformen für die Flacke* PL 03, 1920, Christian Stoll; 52 Border from addresses presented to Lord Carrington, 1888, anonymous; 53. Medical illustration, Duncan K Winter, Otis Historical Archives, National Museum of Health and Medicine; 54. *Cloud Study*, 1838, Knud Baade, Norwegian; 55. New designs and colours for wallpaper for the *Primavera* collection, 1913, Émil-Allain Séguy, French; 56. *Little Mountains Raised in 1760 by the Eruption of Mount Vesuvius*, Pietro Fabris; 57. *The Free-living, Unarmored Dinoflagellate*, 1921, Charles Atwood Kofoid; 58. Statens musikwerk, 1939, Swedish Performing Arts Agency; Photographer: Narciso Contreras; 59. *New York*, Gottscho-Schleisner, Library of Congress; 60. *Design for Bed with Tented Alcove*, Brighton Pavilion, 1801–1804, Frederick Crace; 61. *Kunstformen der natur*, Pl. 78: *Cubomedusae*, 1904, Ernst Haeckel; 62. *Art from an Original Theory or New Hypothesis of the Universe*, 1750, Thomas Wright; 63. *Chicago*, Nature Study Publishing Co, 1898–90, American Museum of Natural History Library; 64. Ebru handmade wave background, Anya Babii, Adobe Stock Images; 65. Palette from a Russian Encyclopedia; 66. Untitled image, Thomas Smillie, 1890–1913; 67. *Pink sky from Bijutsu Sekai* 1893-1896 by Watanabe Seitei; 68. Tower block, unknown; 69. IBM, 'Every man with an idea has at least two or three followers', 1974, Ken White; 70. *Ferns of Huntington*, Long Island, 1890-1900, Ella J. C. Hurd; 71. *Die Radiolarien (Rhizopoda radiaria): eine Monographie*, 1862, Ernst Haeckel; 72. *Le Monde Physique*, 1893, Amédée Guillemin; 73. *Vision of an Islamic City*, 1830–1835, Friedrich Maximillian Hessemer; 74. *Image of Aurora Borealis*, 1900, Harald Molke; 75. St George's, Bloomsbury, London, 1799, Thomas Malton, English; 76. *A Colony's Windows*, Rick Guidice, NASA; 77. *Map of the Arctic Region*, c.1890, Hachette; 78. Arc de Triomphe, du Carrousel, Paris, France, photochrom, 1890–1900; 79. *John B. Bull Garden*, 1936, Gilbert Sackerman; 80. *Moonlight on the Park*, Roundhay Park, Leeds, John Atkinson Grimshaw, English; 81. Floral Design 95, *Shin-bijutsukai*, 1902, Korin Furuya; 82. *Komposition*, 1938, Otto Freundlich, German; 83. Design for a *Trompe l'Oeil* Ceiling, c. 1750–60, Flaminio Innocenzo Minozzi, Italian, 84. Poster wall, Nazzu, Adobe Stock Images; 85. Planet VB 10b, 2009, NASA; 86. Ocean Currents and Sea Ice from Atlas World of Maps, United States Army Service Forces, 1943; 87. *Landscape Set in an Oval*, c.1775, George Barret, English; 88. Back View of Fuji from the Manobu River, 1830–1832, Katsushika Hokusai, Japanese; 89. From *Decorative Vorbilder*, 1890–1920; 90. *Art, Goût, Beauté*, endleaves, 1932, anonymous; 91. Small mirror frame in carved and gilded wood, Venetian, 1858, John Charles Robinson, English; 92. Image from Japanese design magazine, Shin-Bujitsukai, 1902; 93. *Atlas der Diatomaceenkunde*, 1890, Adolf Schmidt; 94. *En Hånd, Tegnet Efter Gips*, 1829–1833, Dankvart Dreyer, Danish; 95. Paper theatre, 1927, anonymous; 96. *Sulla fina anatomia degli organi centrali del sistema nervosa*, 1885, Camillo Golgi; 97 The Throne Room, Fontainebleau Palace, France; 98. Statens musikverk, Swedish Performing Arts Agency, Photographer: Narciso Contreras; 99. Plate 7 from *Formes et Couleurs*, 1930, Auguste H. Thomas; 100. Water, Adobe Stock Images.

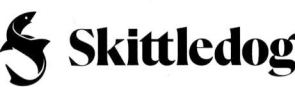

First published in the United Kingdom in 2025
by Skittledog, an imprint of Thames & Hudson Ltd,
6–24 Britannia Street, London WC1X 9JD

Creative Paper © 2025 Thames & Hudson Ltd, London

Designer: Alison Guile
Picture Researcher: Grace Wilmshurst
Production: Felicity Awdry

EU Authorized Representative: Interart S.A.R.L.
19 rue Charles Auray, 93500 Pantin, Paris, France
productsafety@thameshudson.co.uk
www.interart.fr

A CIP catalogue record for this book is available from the
British Library

ISBN 978-1-83776-089-3
01

Printed and bound in China by C&C Offset Printing Co., Ltd

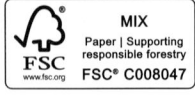

Be the first to know about our new releases, exclusive
content and author events by visiting:

skittledog.com
thamesandhudson.com
thamesandhudsonusa.com
thamesandhudson.com.au